CLOSE ENCOUNTERS

CLOSE ENCOUNTERS

A POETIC PHILOSOPHY OF POLITICAL ANALYSIS

ANDREW DAVISON

Columbia University Press   *New York*

Columbia University Press
Publishers Since 1893
New York   Chichester, West Sussex

Library of Congress Cataloging-in-Publication Data

Names: Davison, Andrew, 1962– author.
Title: Close encounters : a poetic philosophy of political
analysis / Andrew Davison.
Description: New York : Columbia University Press, [2025] |
Includes bibliographical references and index.
Identifiers: LCCN 2024038855 | ISBN 9780231218474 (hardback) |
ISBN 9780231218481 (trade paperback) | ISBN 9780231562300 (ebook)
Subjects: LCSH: Political science—Philosophy. |
Border crossing—Philosophy. | Boundaries (Philosophy)
Classification: LCC JA71 .D353 2025 | DDC 320.1/2—
dc23/eng/20241228

Cover design: Julia Kushnirsky
Cover image: Shutterstock

GPSR Authorized Representative: Easy Access System Europe,
Mustamäe tee 50, 10621 Tallinn, Estonia, gpsr.requests@easproject.com

. . . it is a question of something that has just come to pass.

—Hannah Arendt

CONTENTS

ACKNOWLEDGMENTS

The section on attuning poetically to the political speech of Donald J. Trump in chapter 2, which may be extended to any politically violent practice, emanates from a challenge issued to me in the first two seminars I taught, in 2017, on "releasing poetic attunement into serious political inquiry" at Vassar College and the Gregynog Ideas Lab Summer School in Wales. After delineating the dynamics of poetic attunement, several of my interlocutors questioned its application to the analysis of political violence. They equated poetic attunement with sympathy. I was suggesting otherwise. The core constitutive heuristic of poetic attunement—open and affective, bearing and caring for the other—yields *a range* of analytical experiences and insights unavailable in conventional empirical, interpretive, and critical approaches to social science explanation. It is not the same as sympathy, although sympathy, and for that matter, antipathy, may be one of many possible relations that occurs in the close encounters of poetic attunement.

Subsequent in-depth conversations with the participants in those seminars, in which we attuned together to the acute scenes of their research, proved especially fruitful. The topic was still evolving for me. They gave fresh conceptual expression to the very particular sensual and social empirical details and theoretical dilemmas that motivated their work. We were persuaded together, I think. I am therefore so very grateful to all the participants in these seminars, to Vassar College and the students and faculty of the Department of Political Science for providing a home for innovative political theoretical engagement, and to my Gregynog friends—Carys Coleman, Joanna Cordeiro, Martin Coward, Michael Dillon, Jenny Edkins, Tim Edkins, Anna-Karin Eriksson, Tatevik Mnatsakanyan, Himadeep Muppidi, Erzsebet Strausz, Rob Walker, and Andreja Zevnik—for welcoming me into their immensely generative summer labs.

I presented early versions of chapter 1 in forums at the University of British Columbia, Sabancı University, the North American Society for Philosophical Hermeneutics, as well as the 2018 annual meeting of the American Political Science Association. I presented early versions of chapter 2 at Sabancı and the 2019 annual meeting of the American Political Science Association. I am tremendously grateful for the insightful and encouraging feedback on those papers and presentations from Murat Akan, Bruce Baum, Walter Brogan, Arjun Chowdury, Carys Coleman, Aslı İkizoğlu Erensü, Ted George, Ayten Gündoğdu, Anton Hart, Mark Hoffman, Ersin Kalaycıoğlu, Fuat Keyman, Nojang Khatami, Faik Kurtulmuş, Minelle Mahtani, Nedim Nomer, Cem Önder, Taha Parla, Ryan Phillips, Andrew Seligsohn, Paul Soper, Alejandro Arturo Vallega, and Darren Walhof. I also want to express a debt of gratitude to Gürol Irzık, Sibel Irzık, Ayşe Kadıoğlu, and Özgür Kıbrıs for making my stay at Sabancı possible during my leave in fall 2018.

Many other steady and steadying friends and colleagues have been there to process all "things given" in the years of bringing the qualities of poetic attunement to expression. Most of them helped with the work without even knowing about it. Thank you to Cevdet Akçay, Terry Ball, Andrew Bush, Olga Bush, Alex Ciucu, Mary Deitz, Jim Farr, Lisa Gilbert, Luke Harris, David Ingersoll, Brian Johnson, Tim Koechlin, Karin Lauria, Niyanthini Kadirgamar, Craig Kannel, Candice Lowe Swift, Bill Lynn, Rick Matthews, Becky Mazur, Andrew Meade, Lila Meade, Verity Norman-Tichawangana, Sam Opondo, Joseph Perl, Quỳnh Phạm, Ed Pittman, Tricia Reidy, Katherine Restuccia, Jonathan Schultz, Kevin Shea, Patrick Swift, Fungai Tichawangana, Bill Webber, Greg White, and Mira Zaharopoulos. I thank my brothers and father—Mark, Douglas, and Maxwell Davison—for their constant support as well.

After preparing the first draft of the manuscript in late 2019, I asked a former student, Justin Saret, to work with me on polishing the work. At Vassar, Justin took more courses than could fit on his transcript, and, having finished his master's degree, was just starting his career as a writing consultant. As we began to read and discuss *Close Encounters* together, I quickly found old teaching roles reversed in the best way imaginable. Justin carefully led me in weekly conversations about each and every aspect of the work at a level of depth that I can only hope I was once able to offer him. I'm so grateful for his bearing and caring for the book with me. Many of the ideas I was trying to convey in earlier drafts are better expressed because of his "eye for the genuine" and utmost care. Wendy Lochner, Alyssa Napier, and Leslie Kriesel of Columbia University Press, Ben Kolstad, Mary Ann Blair, and several peer reviewers, picked up later where Justin left off. I am tremendously grateful to them for their time and valuable suggestions. Wendy saw the publication process through the extremely difficult circumstances of the pandemic. I can't thank her enough for her support, expertise, and tireless efforts.

The idea that political analysis may be modeled on poetic encounter was sparked while teaching poetry in the course

Diasporas with Andrew Bush while I was also teaching Interpreting Politics, a course on the philosophy of social and political inquiry that I have been teaching since the earliest days of my academic career. As a cross-listed course in Vassar's curriculum, Diasporas conjured relations between three academic disciplinary and multidisciplinary zones of exposure: Jewish Studies, Political Science, and International Studies. Social science students in the class welcomed but sometimes struggled with the place of poetry in their formal studies. I learned so much listening to Andy work and respond from the site of the poetic.

When Gürol Irzık and Sibel Irzık visited Vassar during their sabbatical in 2017, they sat in on the advanced undergraduate political theory seminar in which I first took up the topic of this work. Our conversations between busy hours on the nuances of social scientific and literary analysis challenged me to consider and address fundamental social theoretical issues at stake in proposing an analogy between the interpretation of poetry and the interpretation of political life. Built upon years of friendship, these explorations were like constantly going to familiar places unknowingly. They even included several delightful attempts to translate Behçet Necatigil's poems "Nilüfer" and "Zar," although it would be more accurate to say "attune" and "find care" in them. "*Çıkarır bakardım kimseler yokken.*" "*Bakardım*: I looked, *looked after*. Ah, Andy, care. Bakmak. He was not just looking at it, he *cared* for it." Comma, *almışlar.*

Our conversations continued the next year in Istanbul, and Gürol and I drank *çay* with Ercan Kesal. I had jumped at the chance to meet Ercan Bey at one of his book signings after my friend and former student Igal Ers told me about the event. As I waited in line, I could see that Ercan Bey was sitting at a table and conversing with everyone before signing the books they had brought with them. When it was my turn, I introduced myself and told him about this book, and that I was writing about the confounding final scene of *Once Upon a Time in Anatolia*. He listened intensely as I quoted something he had written about the scene that I hoped I might have the chance to discuss at more length with him. "It was *just* like that," he said, referring to the scene, and he was already writing his email and cell phone number on the cover page of *Aslında* . . . before I could finish my next sentence. This led to a remarkable conversation a few weeks later in a café near his home. Gürol and I posed questions and listened intently as he shared crystalizing clarity and piercing insight about the film and the uncoercive teachings of its final scene. It was an overwhelmingly important exchange. *Bir kapı sessizlik işte bütün hepsi* that was there all along. I thank Ercan Bey for his attunement in this conversation, and Gürol, Sibel, Taha Bey, and Sahara Pradhan for being there right away to dwell, always so dependably and constructively, within it.

Sahara has been thinking, feeling, and circling through all this with me, in its fullness, from even before it became something to *write*. A few phrases from our poetry archive come to mind, some from Adrienne Rich. "I wanted to show her one poem, which is the poem of my life." We agreed it could be something else. Not what will happen, but how it will be *lived*. We began to map routes together and, seasons later, with Shaiyan Lal, too! Worthy. Gift. Rose. "So common, nothing/like it."

CLOSE ENCOUNTERS

INTRODUCTION

Poetic Attunement

"**A**ll her parameters are now set up."[1] Asya al-Ulama begins to classify and code her "data set of 1750 Minimal Metaphor Units (MMUs)" that she has compiled from 160 poems.[2] She is working on her doctoral dissertation and analyzing the semantic relationships between the Primary Syntactic Units ("PSUs")[3] in the verses of the following extended metaphor:

> A little flower of love
>> Is ours without a root
>> Without the end of fruit
> But take the scent thereof.[4]

The tenor, or subject of the metaphor, is "love." Its vehicles are "flower," "root," "fruit," and "scent." Asya carefully describes the syntactic units—"(love is a flower), (love has roots), (love produces fruit) and (love has scent)"—and characterizes their relation. "The three last units reinforce the first semantic transfer (love:flower) by expressing statements implied by it, e.g., (x:flower) implies (x has roots) etc." As Asya formally codes the interpretive "rules of implicature" between each poetic unit, other meaningful associations between "love" and "roots" suddenly occur to her:

> The rules of implicature determine how we interpret the metaphor
> e.g., since Semantic Transfer 1 d (love:flower)
> which implies (love has roots)
> we interpret Semantic Transfer 2 d (love:ø <ø.HAVE.roots>)
> as (love:flower<which has roots>
> rather than (love:anything else<which has roots>)—like a pumpkin
> or a cabbage—[5]

At this moment, Asya pauses and thinks, "which isn't so ridiculous anyway," and a verse from another poem comes to mind: "'My vegetable love would grow/vaster than empires and more slow.'"[6]

"Asya puts down her pencil" and reflects, "Well—what this will do is teach machines to interpret metaphor. That's about it."[7]

Something is amiss. Asya is realizing that her doctoral dissertation on poetic metaphor will teach machines to piece together meanings between coded poetic units to find that "love," like a "flower," has "roots"—that's about it.

But what about "a pumpkin or a cabbage"? It *isn't* "so ridiculous."

Asya is the protagonist in Ahdaf Soueif's postcolonial and autobiographical novel, *In the Eye of the Sun*. The novel chronicles Asya's life from her high school exams in Cairo during the war of June 1967 and her doctoral studies in linguistics in England to her return to Cairo as a professor of literature.

In the scene above, Aysa's invocation of "a pumpkin or a cabbage" exemplifies what I describe in this study as a *poetically attuned* relationship to data and data analysis. She encounters and makes sense of data in terms that are semiotically open, affective, and profoundly and ethically responsive to the silent, subaltern otherness of the data. Asya's data analytical disposition represents an alternative to dominant empiricist and interpretive approaches to social scientific explanation that shape her dissertation.[8]

Asya's study uncovers and analyzes statistical and semantic patterns between the linguistic units of poetic metaphor. If successful, it will enable machines to "read" poems as data and to discern generalizable patterns of poetic metaphor in the data. It may be tempting to view Asya's pause and invocation of "a pumpkin or a cabbage" as consistent with these goals. The coded rules of implicature about "rooted love," for example, may be formulated in more general terms that account for "vegetable love." But something else is happening in Asya's poetic pause, here and elsewhere in the novel, something that exceeds dominant social scientific understandings of the data analytical relation. Asya is *poetically attuning* to her data. As she does, the data withdraw from her immediate conceptual grasp, palpitate with new meaningful possibilities, and affectively move her into a relationship of profound responsibility. It's not ridiculous.

In attunement, Asya's responsiveness may be viewed more like what Gerald Bruns describes as "an instance of *attentiveness*, as if to another human being."[9] Such attentiveness is "not scrutiny, mere attention to details."[10] It is "an attentiveness of the ear and of memory."[11] Drawing on the poet Paul Celan, Bruns characterizes this attentiveness as "a condition of attunement in which one is turned toward the other in an event of listening."[12] Jacques Derrida further elaborates the specifically ethical dimensions of this event, suggesting that the poem, as other, "entrusts" itself to the "bearing" and "caring" responsibility of its other, to "our care"; as it does, it "secretly" brings *all others* (and otherness) into this relationship as well.[13] Secretly implies subtly, imperceptibly, without consciously choosing or willing it to happen.

In the scene above, "vegetable love" comes to mind from another poem for Asya partly because, as I shall further elaborate in this work, she often thinks of the world in poetic verse. But its interpoetic textual status, which a database can identify as well, is not what matters. What matters is that Asya is affectively *moved* by the poem to receive, bear, and care for loves and roots other than <"love:flower"> in her relation to the data: "A little flower of love/Is ours without a root." "Loves" other than those stated in the poem "secretly" reach Asya in the trusting and caring relationship established by the verse.

A few moments later, the poetic signs "love" and "ours" continue to palpitate for Asya. She pauses and again silently recites, "Is ours without a root." This time, in attunement to "love" and "ours," she is moved to bear and care for another "otherness" within her own life—her deeply disappointing and troubled marriage. Her unsatisfying relationship with her husband—her "ours"—is so painfully strange relative to what she had wanted, wished, or dreamed married life to be. It is the otherness of this "ours," within her own life, to which she now capaciously attunes and bears. She receives the poetic signs "ours" and "love" in a space of open indeterminacy, where "other" meanings occur, and she feels and bears "ours" *without* "love." "It isn't love," she reflects, sitting before her dataset at the kitchen table. "Remember that. *Know* that."[14] Her poetically attuned thought, "*know that*," underscores that there are other, sometimes profoundly difficult, ways of *knowing* what data, given in poetic attunement, may yield.[15]

Asya's dissertation will teach machines to "interpret" patterns in metaphors, but it will not teach what she *knows* in her attunement, namely that poetry "entrusts" the other and otherness—in the verses above, *all* loves, flowers, non-loves, once loves, never loves, pumpkins and cabbages and vegetables loves, all or *anything* with or without roots in ear and memory—to the responsible bearing care of another, to Asya's, to our, care.

Close Encounters proposes a new philosophy of data and data analysis for the social sciences. As a radical alternative to dominant empirical and interpretive approaches, its central thesis is that the analytical relationship between social scientists and their data should be modeled on poetic encounter, compelling the same open, intimate, and ethical attentiveness that is elicited by, and granted to, poetic texts and expression. Reconceptualizing data as poetic phenomena involves attuning to what Gayatri Chakravorty Spivak characterizes as the silent "teachings" of the subaltern. Like poetic signs, subaltern dimensions of data rearrange thought and desire with original and transformative insight.[16] Data conceived on the model of poetic encounter *yield* more than what is knowable in conventional empiricist, interpretive, or, as I shall explain, any form of *empiricalist* social scientific analysis. A poetically attuned data analytical disposition enables the palpitating subaltern teachings of social scientific data to enter into the analysis of social and political life.

In *Close Encounters*, I explicate the qualities of poetic attunement in a variety of literary, philosophical, and political theoretical sites and in relation to a range of pressing social and political issues, such as immigration and border politics, torture, occupation, violent political speech, medical care, criminal justice, gendered legislative practices, algorithmic and datafied governance, environmental drought, and the coronavirus pandemic.

Chapter 1 traces the underlying hermeneutical and subaltern philosophical foundations of poetic attunement and demonstrates their significance in relation to the politics of borders and immigration. This analysis introduces the concept of *living on* as a key constitutive element of poetically attuned analysis, itself an encounter at the borders of unfamiliarity. Chapter 2 offers a reading of poetry and philosophical accounts of poetic encounter to elaborate and illustrate in detail the semiotic, affective, and ethical qualities of poetic attunement as a mode of social and political inquiry. I argue that "poetic possibility" resides in every data analytical encounter. Chapter 3 returns to the concept of *living on* to disclose and elaborate the "knowledge constitutive" purposes of poetically attuned social scientific explanation,[17] and chapter 4 revisits foundational texts in the history of the concept of data to clarify the meaning of a poetically attuned understanding of "data."

In the conclusion, I emphasize possibilities for poetic attunement in the social sciences by identifying its qualities in contemporary social science scholarship that employs "natural language processing" in computer programs to interpret patterns of political speech—precisely the kinds of mechanized tools that Asya al-Ulama anticipated as she coded her metaphorical units. Throughout, I suggest that qualities of poetic attunement are always immanent in data analytical encounters, and when unveiled and manifested fully, they deepen and intensify the empirical, interpretive, and critical aspirations of data analysis in social and political explanation.

An alternative, poetically attuned understanding of data and data analysis offers fresh perspective on explanatory encounters, like Asya's, within an increasingly datafied and algorithmically governed world and academy. In the latter, *Close Encounters* aims to contribute to a relatively stagnant, long-term debate over the meaning of data in the social sciences. A recent iteration of this debate in political science, in which I have participated, is the intense dispute between empiricists and postempiricists (mainly interpretivists and critical theorists) over data access and research transparency (DART) publication standards. Scholars with deeply held commitments to different modes of inquiry—and different understandings of the meaning of "data"—have clashed over requirements to make the "evidence base" of their published knowledge claims accessible to other scholars for independent review, evaluation, testing, and replication.[18] A brief review of the debate discloses the most resolutely held understandings of the concept of data in the social sciences today, as well as the place of *Close Encounters* as a poetically attuned intervention that transcends the reified empiricist/postempiricist divide.

DART's advocates constitute "data" in classic empiricist terms as "sense-data," "information," or "evidence" that is "observed," "extracted," and "collected," either directly or with instruments, like computers, to enhance the senses. "Our prescriptive methodologies," assert Arthur Lupia and Colin Elman, "all involve extracting information from the social world, analyzing the resulting data, and reaching a conclusion based on a combination of the evidence and its analysis."[19]

DART's critics oppose its empiricist underpinnings and their imposition on the rest of the discipline.[20] They reiterate postempiricism's philosophical view that there is absolutely nothing "raw" or "given" about "data," or that its representation, evaluation, or replication is not uncomplicated. Data are not, as Dvora Yanow and Peregrine Schwartz-Shea put it, "objectified, free-standing entities available ('given')" for extraction or collection.[21] Data are *constituted* within particular conceptual, theoretical, sociohistorical, etiological, methodological, biographical, paradigmatic, technological, and power (e.g., race, class, gender, colonial) contexts. And these contexts vary, such that differently situated analysts observing the "same" "data" may offer different basic descriptions of them.[22] This postempiricist view of data in the social sciences has gained increasing recognition in the philosophy of the natural sciences as well,[23] but it is especially significant in interpretive social science, wherein basic observations are "coproduced in and through field-based interactions" with social actors.[24] Katherine Cramer, a prominent interpretivist scholar, writes that her "conversational data" are so deeply constituted by her "presence" that "another scholar would not have all the relevant data needed for replication unless he or she is me."[25]

From the perspective of *Close Encounters*, the fundamental dispute between advocates and critics of DART lies in their different positions on the "givenness" of data. DART advocates reiterate the empiricist view that data are "given" in the sense that they are extracted or collected through sensory-based observation. Critics explicitly reject that idea and argue that data are constituted and coproduced in highly contextualized ways. Postempiricists insist on the need to abandon "the belief that the unmediated apprehension of the 'given' by a passive or receptive observer is possible," as Timothy Luke, Antonio Vázquez-Arroyo, and Mary Hawkesworth assert.[26]

The postempiricist perspective on the contingent and constituted meaningfulness of data has several implications in broader political theoretical debates about datafied life in the era of algorithmic governance and big data domination.[27] The philosopher Sabina Leonelli, for example, argues that a postempiricist, relational, and historical perspective enables theorists to ask critical questions about what counts as data, and for whom, how, why, and under what conditions data "travel" and mutate in their collection, processing, dissemination, and evidentiary usages.[28] Attentiveness to what is available and unavailable, accessible and inaccessible, analyzed and overlooked, and present and absent contributes to ensuring practices of openness, accountability, reliability, accessibility, inclusivity, and transparency in data-centric knowledge creation.[29] It therefore *also* supports confronting illegitimate practices of closed, unaccountable, manipulative, unequal, discriminatory, marginalizing, harmful, and unjust data usage in both algorithmic policy making and the big data corporate economy.[30] Leonelli argues that "ethical reasoning" must be institutionalized "at every step" of data scientific processing so that "*all* individuals"—researchers, computer engineers, data providers, and data users—"take some responsibility in relation to their specific roles."[31] Rob Kitchin further emphasizes that a future of individual and collective "data sovereignty" must be informed by an ethics of "reciprocal and non-reciprocal care with respect to digital life, including data practices." Such an ethics requires that "we care for ourselves and others in ways that we expect to be treated, and are supportive and promote well-being, and are not exploitative. This means acting in moral ways with respect to the generation and use of data."[32]

From a philosophical perspective, it is important to see that efforts to cultivate responsibility, emancipate individuals and collectivities from unjust forms of technocratic data domination, and inspire agency among algorithmically reduced subjects are not just shaped by normative ethical and democratic theoretical commitments.[33] They are shaped as well by the idea that data are not "givens prior to the study of what those data can be evidence for."[34] As data "travel," Leonelli avers, there is nothing "stable" in their "format and content."[35] "This impression of fixity, often associated to the idea of data as 'given,' is highly misleading. . . . Data are everything but stable objects ready for use."[36] Data are, profoundly, what they are contingently purposed to be in the dynamic and interrelated conceptual, technical, material, etiological, structural, and discursive assemblages of their usage. Today, big and small data are constituted not only as objects of knowledge but also as tools to mobilize people to confront the injustices of their data-governed existence.

Close Encounters endorses forms of care and responsibility toward data as well, but it does so by rethinking the very meaning of data prior to their use, travels, and democratization. And it does so not by abandoning the idea of the given but by revising it in poetically attuned terms. In what follows, I offer a philosophical account of data and the "data analytical" relation that dispenses with empiricism's conflation of data with sense-data without abandoning the givenness of data. In a poetically attuned relation to data, something *other than* extraction and *more than* relational coconstitution occurs. Poetic attunement occurs because data are received, like poetic verse, as given for the open, affective, and ethical bearing and caring of their subaltern others. This relation is a form of justice as well, one founded not only on principles of emancipated, responsible, and caring democratic life but also on bearing and caring for the other, including the otherness *of* data, as central to their immediate coconstitution. A poetically attuned philosophy of data therefore complements and extends current thinking about the meaning of data and possibilities intrinsic to the data analytical relation in both the philosophy of science and in contemporary political theory. Another relation to data in scientific inquiry and life—a relation that transcends the empiricist/postempiricist divide—is possible.

This possibility does not arrive through a simple change in perspective. It requires a paradigm shift—supported by a thorough philosophical account of "data" and its conceptual history—that understands Asya's poetically attuned relation to her dataset as a legitimate way of knowing what data may yield.

A level of poetic attunement may always already be occurring in social science data analysis. Like Asya, individual social scientists routinely, if imperceptibly, *bear* their data. They care for their datasets and are open to viewing them in multiple ways. *Close Encounters* highlights and amplifies the analytical significance of these and other poetic dimensions of data analysis so that they may flourish as explicit and fully developed features of social scientific inquiry.

1

LIVING ON AT THE BORDER

It was in a dream. I'm in Istanbul in a wooden house, and there I see a friend, a Communist, he doesn't laugh. I tell him about someone who tells stories out of the corner of his mouth, only half believing them. My Communist friend says, "Everyone talks like that." I say, "What does one have to do in order to talk about deep, meaningful things?" He says, "Kaza gecirmek." Experience accidents of life.

—Emine Sevgi Özdamar[1]

Reports of hundreds dying in shipwrecks in the Mediterranean; thousands of refugees climbing over newly erected barbed-wire fences . . . thousands more living in camps . . . 14 million . . . displaced by war in 2014, the largest number in a single year since World War II. . . . 59.2 million displaced people globally . . . the largest number ever.

—Reece Jones[2]

VIOLENCE AND VIOLATION

In the contemporary immigration debate in the United States, many opponents and supporters of immigration have something in common. Significantly, both understand border encounters as constituted by violence, where *crossing over* borders is almost always discursively associated with one form of harm or another.[3] For those who oppose immigration, border violence occurs as migrants "invade" or "cross"[4] illegally with an intent to destroy and cause harm—steal jobs or property, murder, violate, corrode, terrorize, and, in Donald Trump's terms, "so much else," including "poison."[5] For those who are sympathetic toward immigration, migrants crossing over the border are understood as "fleeing" conditions of violence—the primary "root cause" among other "circumstances in-country," as Joseph Biden describes them.[6] Once at the border, immigrants meet further violence in state practices of interrogation, arrest, detention, deprivation, and deportation, administered in varying dosages by advocates of both dominant positions. In his aptly titled work *Violent Borders*, the political scientist Reece Jones criticizes such worldwide practices as imposing illegitimate restrictions on the movement of "mobile people." With a "desire for freedom" and searching for "a better life for themselves and their family," he argues, their movement is itself a "refusal" of "unjust" practices of border "exclusion."[7]

These dominant categories of the immigration discourse capture important and indispensable elements of contemporary border experience but fall painfully short in addressing others. I am interested here in illustrating the value of hermeneutics and subaltern inquiry—two related and foundational components of poetic attunement—in rethinking basic practices of border life, especially "migration" and "border crossing," as modes of *living on*. This rethinking, in turn, reveals *living on* to be a key constitutive element of poetic attunement, within which the fundamental aims of social scientific inquiry may also be rethought, as I elaborate in later chapters. Here, in order to offer a more compelling analytical relationship with issues of borders and migration, I argue that inquirers, while attending to questions of violence, must *also* attune to other facets of encounter at the limits of personal, political, or discursive familiarity. The following story, from Emine Sevgi Özdamar's *Mother Tongue*, is set in the context of those limits.

SURVIVING ACCIDENTS

In the 1920s, the "Westernizing" language reforms of the Republic of Turkey changed the script of the Ottoman language from Arabic to Latin. The reforms also "purified" the language in "national" terms by purging words derived from Arabic and Persian, replacing them with either their "original" Turkish words or neologisms based on Turkish grammatical rules.[8] In *Mother Tongue*, a young woman from Turkey sets out to learn Arabic so that she may reconnect with part of her linguistic history. Atatürk—the "founder" of modern Turkey and leader of the cultural reforms—"should not have forbidden Arabic writing," she says. "This ban, it's as though half of my head had been cut off. All the names in my family are Arabic: Fatma, Mustafa, Ali, Samra."[9] If she "had been unable to speak" with her grandfather and they "could only tell each other things in writing," they would "have been unable to tell each other stories."[10] She recalls how her father listened to Arabic singers on the radio at night, enraptured. "In my sleep, these voices entered me. I loved my father, my father loved these voices. I thought at that time, these Arabic singers are my father's best friends."[11]

In the story, the woman studies with Ibni Abdullah, an Arabic writing master—both of them are migrants living in Berlin. They each face difficulties; she is ridiculed on the street,[12] and he says he has had no joy in the nine years he has been in Germany.[13]

Together, they dream of a better world—with "no brothers born to kill each other," no workers "whose fatigue doesn't vanish even in their death," and "no more immigrants moving from country to country looking for death."[14] In the course of her studies, the narrator and her teacher come to realize they have many words in common between Turkish and Arabic. An archive of words that are the same or similar in both languages begins to emerge: words like *ikbal*—goodwill, *hasret*—longing, and *sabir*—patience.

> When those words rose and travelled from your country to my country they were somewhat changed on the way."[15] . . .
> "How do you say patience?" says Ibni Abdullah.
> "*Sabir*."
> "We say *Sabr*," said Ibni Abdullah.[16]

A love emerges between them, but it becomes impossible. Ibni Abdullah is poor, and his concentration on his work is slipping.[17] He beseeches her to leave him: "You that I love, soul of my soul (*die Seele in meiner Seele*). . . . Leave me. . . . I will become a ruin."[18] He asks her for "sacred love" with a "silent body."[19] She tries to love him this way, but she cannot. He tries to keep her from leaving, but, after "precisely forty days in the study," she departs with "Ibni Abdullah in my body."[20]

While staying at a mission hostel in the city, the narrator's mind travels back to her grandfather and her journey through her mother tongues, from experiencing "life's accidents"—words of advice she remembers from a dream—through the Arabic she has learned from Ibni Abdullah.[21] "I had fallen in love with my grandfather," she reflects. "The words, whose love I tried to grasp, all had their childhood."[22] One by one, she then recalls all the words in common between Turkish and Arabic that she has learned—twenty-seven words in total.

The woman leaves the hostel. "Taking the words with me. I said to myself, If you see a person who looks like someone who's survived an accident, speak to him."[23]

The first person the woman sees is "a girl, sitting on a park bench, she was eating some carrot salad with mustard, she was crying."

"Why are you crying?" the narrator asks the girl.

"Thomas," the girl responds, and she tells a story of tragedy, when her Thomas unexpectedly took his own life.[24]

After sharing the details of Thomas's death, the girl asks the woman, "What are you doing in Germany?"

> I said: "I'm a word collector." And Ibni Abdullah, the soul of my soul, I thought. And remembered another word in my mother tongue.
>
> *Ruh* in Turkish, like *Ruhe*, "peace and quiet" in German—"*Ruh* means soul," I said to the girl.
>
> "Soul means *Ruh*," said the girl.[25]

The story ends there.

Mother Tongue challenges the idea that languages are somehow hermetically sealed and singular. Purifying language reforms have not cut off all traces of connection between languages and, therefore, between the lives of people who speak them. The original German text uses the word *Seele* for soul. The word appears to carry the narrator to the Turkish word for soul, *ruh*. And this to the German *ruhe*. In sounds and resemblances, our narrator hears the *likeness* of several languages at once. *Ruh*, in Turkish, like *ruhe*, "peace and quiet" in German—"*Ruh* means *soul/Seele*." "Soul/Seele means *ruh*." German and Turkish, Turkish and German. Similar sounds, close meanings. Close meanings and similar sounds with an Arabic word for soul/*Seele*—*rūḥ*. Arabic and

Turkish and German. *Seele, ruh, Ruhe, rūḥ* . . . many souls. German and Turkish and Arabic (and, here, English). All on the bench.

This exchange has hermeneutical and subaltern significance in relation to attuning to borders and what it might mean to be on, at, near, or move across them. The narrator is not only an immigrant. She is a "word collector." If she is moving, she is moving through languages as a collector and sharer of words, making the sharing and collecting possible. She has not *crossed* a single *border*, not even into Berlin.

LETTING, LOSING, AND TEACHING

Hermeneutics is a mode of social inquiry that views the relationship between life and the meanings that people give to their lives as *constitutive*: meanings *make* their lives *what they are.* They mark the identity of their lives and practices, such that without those meanings, or with different meanings, their lives and practices would also be different. Hermeneutical inquiry involves actual or text-based conversational study, in which inquirers seek to explain people's lives and practices by listening or reading in ways that are closely attentive to their interlocutors' constitutive meanings. Conversation is viewed as an essentially transformative practice: It requires that inquirers place their preconversational classifications and "prejudgments" about the lives they seek to explain at play and at risk as they receive the various meanings that constitute the lives of others. Any compelling hermeneutical explanation consciously attempts to *let* and to *lose*, that is, to *let* the meanings constitutive of the lives of others come to presence in conversation and to *lose* or jettison preconversational categories or prejudgments that, in the course of conversation, are found to hinder understanding.

For example, a preconversational category and prejudgment that readers may have about the narrator in *Mother Tongue* is that "she is an immigrant in Germany." "Immigrant" is an analytical category in and through which one may, prior to conversation, understand the narrator's identity. In hermeneutical practice, "immigrant" must be put at play and *at risk* in conversation that is receptive to the meanings the narrator gives to her life and practice. As we have seen, the narrator may indeed understand herself to be an immigrant, but that description does not exhaust her meaningful understanding of herself. When she is asked what she "is doing" in Germany, she constitutes herself, meaningfully, as a "word collector." Understanding the narrator simply as an immigrant precludes a deeper and more complex understanding of her identity. That word fails to attend to the primary meaningfulness that she gives to her life and experience precisely when she is identified by someone "from" Germany as coming from elsewhere. Immigrant, as an explanatory category, fails to give the woman's own understanding of her life a chance in interpretive claims made about her life. Conversational receptivity entails losing or modifying the place of "immigrant" and letting "word collector" have a chance, a place, in understanding who she is and what she is doing in Germany.

There are significant limits to hermeneutical interpretation. Sometimes the transformation that occurs in conversation is radical, as in losing "immigrant" for "word collector." Often, it is more nuanced, as in understanding that the word "immigrant" has different meanings for different people. Sometimes losing involves resolving perplexities. Often it entails encountering new ones. The meanings the narrator may subjectively give to "word collector," for example, or the meanings that it may have in the intersubjective landscape of the narrator's languages, remain questions of ongoing curiosity. Whatever the character of the losing, hermeneutics maintains that some measure of understanding "differently"—some transformation in the content of the inquirer's prior understanding—is always possible.[26] One may even come to understand "conversation" and "understanding" very differently. Rather than disappoint, however, these qualifications of hermeneutical practice buttress the aspiration to let the constitutive meanings of others have a chance in explanations formed about their lives. Imagine if one only ever described the narrator simply as an immigrant and systematically ignored or dismissed her understanding of herself as a word collector. Descriptions of the narrator that are inattentive to her constitutive meanings would be simple projections—descriptions that are meaningful for her observers but not for her. Such projections fail to offer the narrator a place, a voice, in analytical claims about her. Despite its limits, therefore, hermeneutical letting and losing becomes a permanent disposition of conversational receptivity to otherness—necessarily open-ended and yet indispensable to any compelling effort to explain other people's lives and, as we shall see, a central element of poetic attunement.

A subaltern teaching, by contrast, is what Gayatri Chakravorty Spivak describes as the "uncoercive rearrangement of desire" and "nurturing of a public intuition" that occurs when inquirers contemplate the meaningfulness and significance of silenced or erased voices that are unavailable for hermeneutical conversation.[27] For Spivak, the model of subaltern teaching was set by the suicide of her great aunt, Bhubaneswari Bhaduri, in 1926 in India, at the age of seventeen. Spivak explains that, at first, Bhubaneswari's death was a mystery because she had waited for the onset of her menstrual cycle before hanging herself. Her suicide, that is, was impossible to explain in conventional terms as the result of a pregnancy from a premarital affair. Years later, a note she had left to a family member indicated that she had been a member of a group involved in the armed struggle for India's independence and was entrusted to carry out an assassination. "Unable to confront the task and yet aware of the practical need for trust," she killed herself.[28]

Spivak's description of Bhubaneswari as a subaltern was a response to how, decades after her death, family members spoke about her in ways that continued to silence and erase the constitutive purposes of her suicide. They called her "hapless" and said she had killed herself because of "illicit love"—precisely the interpretations that Bhubaneswari had tried to foreclose by waiting to menstruate.[29] In the broader terms of Spivak's classic essay, "Can the Subaltern Speak?" Bhubaneswari "could not speak." By characterizing subalternity as such, Spivak did not mean that the subaltern lacks a capacity for speech. Rather, she meant that the constitutive purposes of subaltern experience cannot be acknowledged or heard in the terms of dominant discourses that purport to represent them. The code of gendered expectations erased the meaningfulness of Bhubaneswari's death, assimilating her purposes to dominant patriarchal understandings of why a young woman would commit suicide—as if the constitutive significance of her act could only be understood in relation to a man. Her purposes were otherwise.

In the silence of her erasure, the subaltern nevertheless *teaches*. Spivak reads Bhubaneswari's "displacing gesture—waiting for menstruation"—as an effort to rearrange the desires of women who participate in culturally sanctioned practices of "legitimate" female suicide.[30] Spivak focuses on the practice of *sati*, in which "the Hindu widow ascends the pyre of the dead husband and immolates herself upon it."[31] By waiting to menstruate, Bhubaneswari not only displaced anticipatable, gendered, and patriarchal interpretations of her suicide but also reversed interdictions against "a menstruating widow's right to immolate herself." "The unclean widow," Spivak writes, "must wait, publicly" for her cycle to end.[32] For Spivak, Bhubaneswari's waiting to menstruate was thus a revolutionary intervention in the practices of *sati* suicide. In the text of her body, she undermined and displaced common interpretations and governing rules. "Displace" is crucial here because it implies taking conventional interpretations (of why a young woman would kill herself) and rules (concerning *sati* suicide) to another place of thought and consideration, making the meaningful contemplation of another world possible. Bhubaneswari "spoke," as it were, for women subjected to life-negating and self-debasing, patriarchal traditions like *sati*. She opened up the possibility of rearranging their desires and of nurturing a different public intuition about the practices of *sati*.

Attunement to silent subaltern teachings requires attentiveness to more than constitutive meanings. It also entails deep affective and reflective contemplation of the meaningfulness and significance of subaltern silence for those receiving it. Spivak exemplifies this attentiveness in a remarkable passage about her aunt's death.

[Bhubaneswari Bhaduri] taught me yet another lesson: death as text. She made me read situations where no response happens. If the peace process carries no credibility, if a whole country is turned into a gated community, young people who do not yet know how to value life—and Bhubaneswari was seventeen years old—may feel it is possible to write a response when you die with me for the same cause. Suicide bombers form a collectivity whose desires have been rearranged. The decision to die was something like that in Bhubaneswari as well. It was the gendering of the second decision, to postpone death, that made her exclusive. The idea that when you die with me for the same cause since you will not listen to me, since I cannot speak to you, we do memorialize in accord—is action in extremis. How much do the Scriptures arbitrate desire? The question of the Koran, of the *Dharmaśāstra*.[33]

Subaltern teachings are uncoercive because they occur in an encounter with a silent or silenced subject. Hermeneutical conversation is unavailable, and any "response" from the silenced subaltern—any affirmation, denial, or further suggestion—*could* be experienced as an attempt to "coerce" a *particular* teaching. As Spivak attunes to the silenced meaningfulness of her great aunt's suicide, her affective and reflective sentiments about Bhubaneswari's death surface for rearrangement. Spivak unexpectedly contemplates the conditions of suicide bombing: a flagging peace process, a shuttered country, a youthful perspective on life. These dimensions of significance lie outside what we have come to understand as Bhubaneswari's constitutive purposes, but they speak to Spivak's desire to make meaning from her aunt's "death as text," on the basis of what she has come to understand about those purposes and their subsequent silencing. Spivak's intense thoughtfulness and receptivity within this silence culminates in the form of a fundamental question about the relationship between revered scriptures and human desire: "How much do the Scriptures arbitrate desire?" This profound question arises out of Spivak's extensive study of the *sati* women and the conditions of their deaths. It is a question that Bhubaneswari's death raises to challenge the desires and intuitions of an attuned public. Questions are teachings from the silent space of subaltern life that intervene uncoercively where desire may be rearranged. And Bhubaneswari's teaching could not have been more uncoercive: she took her life rather than kill another; "made" Spivak and others read her bodily intervention without asking; and neither affirmed nor denied the teaching.

What, then, may be the hermeneutics and subaltern teachings of *Mother Tongue* in relation to the violent discourse of border crossing and its constitutive desires?

THE HERMENEUTICS AND SUBALTERN TEACHINGS OF SURVIVING ACCIDENTS

The concept of "experiencing accidents" arrives in a dream in the narrator's mother tongue. In the dream, she asks her communist friend, "What does one have to do in order to talk about deep, meaningful things?" He replies, "Kaza gecirmek."[34] The Turkish is rendered in the original story in German as *Lebensunfälle erleben*; it is translated first as "experience accidents" and later, in a different conjugation (*Lebensunfall-erlebt*), as "has survived accidents."[35]

Among its meanings in both English and Turkish, accident/*kaza* has the meaning of an *untoward*, unforeseen happening—an accident as a wreck, crash, or misfortune.[36] In translating *Lebensunfall-erlebt* as "survive" at the end of the story, therefore, the translator of *Mother Tongue* puts an apt hermeneutical touch on the meaning of all of these concepts, especially since the German, *erleben*, with its root in *leben* (to live), connotes (among its many meanings) experience as enduring, bearing, and going through life's difficulties and misfortunes. This meaning resembles a cluster of meanings related to another German concept, *fortleben*, or "continuing life" (or "continuing living") described in Walter Benjamin's account of translation and explored in several places by Jacques Derrida under the heading of its French equivalent, *survivre*, translated into English as "living on."[37]

In Derrida's "last interview" before his death, "Learning to Live Finally," he underscored the distinction between two different

German words for "survive". Derrida asserts that Benjamin "took pains to distinguish between *überleben* on the one hand, to live after death, as a book can survive the death of its author, or a child the death of parents, and on the other hand, *fortleben*, living on [*survivre*], to keep on living"—as in the ongoing living of a text in its repetition or translation with difference through time and space. Asya al-Ulama's recitation of Digby Mackworth Dolben's verse, "A little flower of love/Is ours without a root," for example, may be seen as the poem's "continuing living" or "living on." For Derrida, "living on" is an "original concept," referring to something other than either the binary coupling of "to live or to die."[38] "[Living on] does not derive from either to live or to die. . . . It is something that does not wait for so-called 'actual' death."[39] As Derrida underscores in the essay "Living On," the *sur* or "on" is operative here: living *on* is a kind of "super, hyper, 'over,' *über*, and even above and beyond" life.[40] Living on proceeds from an affirmation of "the most intense life possible," "an unconditional affirmation of life . . . life more than life."[41]

Neither of the German terms for survival—*überleben* or *fortleben*—appears in our story above. The latter is quite rare, in any event.[42] But the nuances in different meanings of "survive" are valuable both to explore the constitutive meaningfulness of "surviving life's accidents" and to understand central qualities of poetically attuned "data analysis," as I evolve those qualities in the discussion ahead.

"Surviving unforeseen accidental happenings in one's life" appears to mean something like "*survivre*/living on after life's accidents." The difference between "living on" and "life after death" is most important: Surviving life's accidents is a survival "after" but not "after death" (*überleben*). It is survival after 'life'— *Lebensunfälle*, which are *life's* accidents. "Surviving" them is, then, about continuing living life after the experiences of life. Insofar as "continuing living" is primary, the "after" in "living on after life" further connotes a kind of continuity of the accident, its own living on, in the survivor's survival. The accident remains constitutive (to varying degrees) and available for reflection, conversation, and reconsideration in one's living on.

The idea of "life after life" runs counter to common understandings of the "after life" as "after death." Because here, in "surviving life's accidents," life does not exclude death. Death, suicide, murder, war, political oppression, economic exploitation, social vulnerability, environmental catastrophe, and pandemic—the many posited "causes" of migration—all of these are among life's unforeseen happenings *in the constitutive horizon of the survivor of life's accidents.* Life's accidents may be more or less accidental (some may be seen as parts of explicable larger patterns); they can also be "happy," as in meeting a friend by accident (one of life's unforeseen, unplanned happenings).[43] Nevertheless, *Lebensunfälle* include the misfortunate *kazalar* that happen *in Leben.* Life's most painful and traumatic accidents are included, not excluded. So "after life," in the meaning of survival in our story, is not "after death"; "after life" is "(life) after life." Surviving is about living on after (the unforeseen accidents and happenings of) life.

Word collecting in this context of life after life takes on even greater importance. The word collector is also a survivor of accidents. Her word collecting is centrally constitutive of her life after life, insofar as word collecting is a mode of life after life that begets more life. In this way, the word collector epitomizes what Derrida describes as a "commitment" to "the language of the other" that overruns all borders between languages.[44] The exchanges between our narrator and both Ibni Abdullah and her interlocutor on the bench are "procession[s] of one language into another, massive movement[s] . . . over the border [*rive*]

of another language,[45] into the language[s] of the other[s]."[46]
For Derrida, this procession exemplifies living on, the affirmation of the most intense life possible always already occurring
in language, in our repetition and recitation, with difference, of
every mark of language. *Ruh, Ruhe, soul, Seele* . . . *hasret, sabir,
sabr* . . . words rising from country to country, and changing—
living on—along the way. This movement from one language to
another is comparable as well to Benjamin's notion of a translation as the *fortleben* of the original, its transformation and "continuing living."

In the story, the narrator describes her Arabic teacher as "*Seele*
of my *Seele*." This sets off a living memory in her other tongue
of *ruh*, "soul" in Turkish, a term that is related to both Arabic
and Persian words (among others) for soul as well but has *survived* the identitarian, nationalist Turkish language reforms. *Ruh*
is "living on" in the living language that is Turkish's constitutive
Ottoman-Arabic-Persian Other.[47] The narrator's tearful interlocutor on the bench recites *ruh* in another living on, elsewhere.
In *ruh*, our storyteller and her fellow survivor of accidents, her
body crying for Thomas, live on together in the living on of the
language of their others. This continuing living introduces more
"change" in everything in the scene, including its readers, also
collectors of (these) words, living on after life's accidents, now
including *our* narrator's separation from her teacher and lover, as
well as the death of Thomas.

Collecting entails giving more life to that which is already living on (after life's accidents). It further exemplifies what Derrida
refers to as "a sort of overrun [*débordement*]" that "spoils" "boundaries and divisions." Each word gathered is "a fabric of traces
referring endlessly to something other than itself."[48] All selves
now entwined, no longer themselves (even as they may claim to
be), always already living on even *more* in the languages of the

other. So it is with language: each statement made "survives [all parties] *a priori*, lives on after them. No one inflection enjoys any absolute privilege; no meaning can be fixed or decided upon [even as decisions are made]. No border is guaranteed, inside or out," even as borders may be established.[49] At the very beginning of both stories, the narrator observes, "In my language, 'tongue' means 'language.'" Her unstated reference is to Turkish, where the same word (*dil*) is used for both tongue and language. "A tongue has no bones: twist it in any direction and it will turn that way."[50] Tongues and languages twist and may turn and move, like the bodies that speak them, in any direction.

In the simultaneity of her twisting-and-turning word collecting, while anticipating someone who has survived an accident, the woman in our story lives on most intensely after life's accidents—after the Republic of Turkey's erasure of her family's Arabic, the silencing of the voices of her father's best friends, the exploitative migration of the *Gastarbeiter* to Germany, and her departure from the man, the survivor of wars, whose love and soul she had become. The narrator has experienced life's accidents so intensely that she now cannot but *see* and *speak* meaningfully in these terms as well. When she spots another woman on the park bench, she sees not only the carrot salad and tears but also someone who has survived life's accidents, who is living on after some wreck in her life. When she opens a conversation, her speaking is a receptive and hospitable reaching out by a word-collecting survivor, an establishing of a relation from one who is living on to another.

This relation is already a *continuing living* of her other relations—Ibni Abdullah (whose "*Seele* of my *Seele*" carried her into conversation on the bench), her parents, her communist friend, and her grandfather.[51] Recall that the narrator entered the study of Arabic after realizing that if she and her grandfather "had been unable to speak and could only tell each other things in writing, we'd have been unable to tell each other stories."[52] The narrator has imagined what it would be like *not* to be able to speak to loved ones, so speaking *with others* has special value: speaking creates and sustains a relation in which stories between people living at a distance may be shared. As Walter Brogan has observed, "the desire to speak is intrinsically a reaching out *for*."[53] If our narrator were to tell her grandfather a story, what story would she tell? One imagines a story about surviving life's accidents. She will not be "talking out of the corner of her mouth" because living on meaningfully constitutes her basic disposition toward life and others in it.[54]

The relation between the word-collecting survivor of life's accidents and the other is an affirmation of life that overruns life with more life, a lively living on in language and spoken conversation that is living for more living. It shows that surviving is not life after death. It is life after life. It is a living from living on, for life, that gives more life to life.

ATTUNED BORDER OPENINGS

Our narrator is living and relating in a(nother) constituted world where crossing over borders appears not to occur at all. As subaltern teacher, she turns the desires and imagination of a subject produced by the violent discourses of border crossing toward life and living. The "migrant" is not "fleeing violence," as dominant accounts of the causes of "migration" posit.[55] She is surviving life's happenings, collecting words and living on and pursuing more life.[56] Alive, "the migrant" is *committed to life*, to continuing living life on, and on, and on. Seeing and speaking with other survivors of accidents, she is actively collecting more words—the words of her many others—in ways that not only affirm life but affirm life *together*, in difference and "likeness," as more than possible.

Mother Tongue rewrites the social texts of "the migrant" and "movement across borders" in an interventionist way, displacing discursively violent representations of those moving through spaces deemed politically distinct, and it offers a chance for a radical reconstitution of what is currently coded as the "movement" of "immigration." The teaching of the subaltern in our story lies in her uncoercive rearrangement of desires toward, and her nurturing of a different public intuition about, the figure of "immigrant." Pervasive anti- and pro-immigration discourses today project "violation" onto the body and purposes of immigrants. One constitutes the immigrant as "suspicious illegal invader" seeking to do harm (violation as crime) and the other as "freedom seeker" challenging unjust exclusions (violation as legitimate resistance). Both constitute the immigrant as *crossing over* at borders.

Emine Sevgi Özdamar teaches otherwise, without teaching: at borders, the immigrant does not *cross*. The immigrant lives on. If the narrator is violating anything, it is the perverse desire to produce her as illegal, alien, violator, criminal, invader, undocumented, seeker, and fleer—as coming from anywhere other than living on and loving over border relations. *How much do borders arbitrate desire?*

To be sure, the immigrant prepares for and encounters the violence of the dominant discursive projection, especially the incessant assault of anti-immigrant prejudices and governing administrative techniques (the militarized encounter, suspicion, frisk, arrest, handcuffs, detention, surveillance, separation, management, deportation/"sending/turning back," etc.).[57]

But, at the border, the immigrant does not *cross*.

Arriving at the border in *Mother Tongue*, one is invited instead to join others on a long and sturdy bench for soulfully speaking together. There, all mother and grandfather tongues resonate mellifluously in touching conversation as our narrator and her interlocutor speak, in shared tongues, from memory and present circumstance. Arrested only by a patient, life-begetting-life over-running of all borders, our narrator is not *crossing* any of them.

"The words whose love I tried to grasp," she says. What desire seeks to grasp the love that belongs to words? What desire *takes the scent* of scripts, like the narrator's grandfather tongue, deemed impure or expendable by power? How is speaking a kind of belonging to loving relations, a kind of making and being *in* love? And why are you crying, *too*?

2

POETIC POSSIBILITY

And we'll go on chanting that such poetry is not to be taken seriously or treated as a serious undertaking.

—Plato, *The Republic*[1]

RELEASING POETIC ATTUNEMENT INTO SERIOUS POLITICAL INQUIRY

Ever since Plato derided poetry for nourishing "rule" by the passions instead of reason, the dominant protocols of serious analytical thought have favored dispassionate empirical objectivity, precise de facto stipulation, and pragmatic prescription over the semiotically open, intensely affective, and ethically charged qualities of poetic attunement. And yet, poetic sensibilities are not absent in serious social and political inquiry. Inquirers think and feel deeply about their subject matter. They choose their words in relation to their findings with care, and occasionally they opt for literary expression over crude operational reportage. Spivak's declaration, in her classic essay, that the "subaltern cannot speak" is one such illustration. In response to critics who understood her as claiming subalterns *couldn't* speak, she states that the phrase came to her when she realized the painful "failure of communication" within her family over the purposes of her great aunt's suicide. She writes, "I was so unnerved by this failure of communication that, in the first version of the text, I wrote, in the accents of passionate lament: the subaltern cannot speak! It was an inadvisable remark."[2]

Passionate lament is poetic expression. *Unnerved* is affective response. *Inadvisable*, an almost humorous awareness of the typical and foreseeable failure of serious academic communication.

Poetic expression is not pragmatic assertion with a truth value to be evaluated with precision against firmly established social theoretical principles, such as the capacity of subalterns to speak. Poetic expression—"the subaltern cannot speak!"—*entrusts itself* to the care of the other as it intercepts its audience in a space of *open indeterminacy* wherein *governing concepts* are no longer *in control*.[3] Poetic expression affectively *moves* an attuned audience to receive it and to bear it responsibly in this condition of openness. In this condition, *speaking* and other principles and foundations become matters of *poetic possibility*.

What would it mean for the semiotically open, affective, and ethical qualities of poetic encounter to flourish in explanatory practices of social and political analysis? Whereas hermeneutics and subaltern inquiry make the social sciences receptive to the constitutive meanings and teachings of others, poetically attuned analysis intensifies inquiry by reconfiguring standardized protocols of serious analytical thought. It adds more experience to existing modes of empirical observation and more affective and ethical insight to practices of pragmatic prescription. It does this, in part, by offering a view of power—the central concern of political inquiry—that consistently challenges governing concepts from "outside of" power. I am not advocating that social and political inquirers become poets,[4] although many poems possess acute social and political insight.[5] Rather, I am suggesting that we infuse the practices of social scientific analysis, from the earliest stages of research design through those of culminating professional exchange, with the full potential of the semiotic, affective, and ethical qualities of poetic attunement.

QUALITIES OF POETIC ATTUNEMENT

Probably the most well-known aspect of poetry is what Terry Eagleton calls its "verbally inventive" use of language, in which poetry estranges familiar terms from their ordinary meanings.[6] Poetry plays with or alters the semantic setting of words such that they no longer only mean what they are conventionally or ordinarily understood to mean. "Words leave behind the space of their meanings," explains Gerald Bruns.[7]

Consider the figurative use of "subtracted" in Naomi Shihab Nye's poem "Before I Was a Gazan."[8] A young math pupil was planning on taking his completed homework—"paper with numbers on it,/stacked and lined"—to school to make his teacher happy, "before everything got subtracted," including his uncle, teacher, and "even the best math student and his baby sister."[9] Nye's use of "subtracted" *estranges* us from the word's ordinary meaning. Subtraction leaves behind its strict mathematical meaning as a deduction of one number or amount from another and enters the space of incalculable loss and unsolvable problems. In the final verses of the poem, the boy "would do anything/for a problem I could solve."[10]

The semiotic shift produced by the poetic word opens the familiar signs of language to new possibilities. While readers give words specific meanings in poetic encounter, characteristic of the language of poetry is that it forever postpones any final stipulation of meaning. Poetry "does something in our minds rather than deliver a message," writes Jeffrey Wainwright.[11] It detaches the linguistic sign from its old meaning and places it in a semiotic zone that Hamid Dabashi has referred to as signation.[12]

Dabashi suggests that, in their most elemental forms, the signs of the world do not signify or mean anything. Before they are made to signify something—the lion, king of the jungle; "thumbs up," something positive; or the lightbulb, an idea— the signs of language *signate* or *palpitate* with possibility. Poetic language invites the reader into this place of infinite signation, where meaning may be creatively made, for any sign.[13] In signation, signs palpitate ceaselessly, "falling just short/of arrival anywhere."[14] They "rebel," "interrupt" and "refuse" "attempts to reduce [them] conceptually and instrumentally."[15] Poetic expression "takes itself out of our hands."[16]

Eagleton points out that not all poetic language is verbally inventive. Bruns writes, "Poetry uses language in original and arresting ways; but it does not do so all the time."[17] Some poetic language is "plain and transparent." Poems describe scenes, narrate events, tell stories, and analyze feelings. And, yet, even these seemingly plain and transparent moments are, in the poetic mode, neither plain nor transparent. In Elizabeth Bishop's poem "The Art of One Art the narrator loses their "mother's watch."[18] Read in a plain and transparent way, this might refer to the timepiece they inherited from their mother and then misplaced. Received *poetically*, a mother's watch may, among other possibilities, mean their omnipresence, their concern for safety, or something else entirely. "Mother" may not signify "parent." In the poetic experience of language, the reader encounters the defamiliarizing possibility of semiotic suspension and shift through the artful and unfamiliar use of the familiar signs of language.[19]

This includes signs of punctuation, spacing, and line formation, as in the following lines:

Spacesbetweenwordspreservesenses
Intactbutweneedtomeetineverysense I[20]

Poetic expression is also constituted by a closely related, *affective* dimension. "Poetry is something that is done to us, not just said to us."[21] Poetic language seizes, jolts, calms, unsettles, and surprises—it introduces movement at emotional and embodied levels of experience other than conscious awareness.[22] It sways, steadies, and shocks the reader, making them pause, ponder, wonder, and feel. This affective quality of poetic expression may not be unique to poetry, but it is one of its characteristics. Along with semiotic openness, the affective dimension of poetic encounter has the specific *effect* of altering the *experience* of the poetically attuned, even if only momentarily.[23] "Subtracted in a minute" jolts, moves, and deprives the reader of a prior rhythm or any prior grounding. After the uncle has been subtracted, we are no longer able to use "subtract" meaningfully in a patterned way.

The affective qualities of poetic encounter occur in the challenging dynamics of what Bruns describes, in his study of Hans-Georg Gadamer's writings on the experience of poetry, as the unique intimacy of poetic conversation[24]—"an event of intimacy without identity and perhaps without the [hermeneutical] communication of meaning . . . an intimacy characterized by the 'remoteness of the one nearest to us' (*die Ferne des Allernüachsten*)."[25] Remoteness and nearness relate to poetry's linguistic qualities, but the *intimacy* of the relationship has affective dimensions. Poetic expression is "near" because it addresses and moves us in familiar language; it is "remote" because it estranges. The simultaneity of the near and remote has the *affects* of *pulling* the reader up close as it pulls the reader up short, of *partnering* with the reader as it *resists* the reader's identifications, of *embracing* the reader while also *shifting* them. Bruns connects the affective force of the encounter with poetry to its linguistic estrangement: "The poem is something that *addresses* us, that *intercepts* us, on whatever *way we are*, and situates us in a space of open indeterminacy where the rule of identity and the legislation of concepts are no longer in control."[26]

It is not that the relationship has been reversed and the poem is now "in control." "The poem does not decide," writes Gadamer in his reading of Paul Celan's "Breath-crystal."[27] It does not assume control, and it never claims decisive power, a theme to which I shall return. Rather, the poem invites its attuned recipient into a relationship in which they *let* the poem move and take them elsewhere. Bruns characterizes the disposition of the poetically attuned in this relation using Martin Heidegger's concept of *Gelassenheit*—"letting-be" or "letting-go." Rilke is helpful here as well: "When you have grasped its meaning with your will/then tenderly your eyes will let it go."[28] Such letting is not "a performative act that an agent might or might not take up but a *condition of openness* toward what is outside and uncontainable within what is in our discursive fields."[29] Addressed and intercepted by what Helen Vendler calls the "expressive powers" of palpitating poetic language, the reader lets go and allows the poem to both *open* and *move* them to wander, cognitively and affectively, in the occlusions of the dominant discursive order.[30]

These affective and semiotic qualities of poetic experience undoubtedly require readers to be psychically prepared for, and susceptible to, intellectual and emotional interruption and wandering. Losing one's way poetically can be difficult, confusing, and uncomfortable. But there is more to this intimacy than discomfiting destabilization. There is familiarity. In its

intimate nearness, poetic language addresses the reader, is pur-
posively written *for* the reader, in the reader's language, reflecting or disclosing something different—strange, other, welcome,
and unwelcome—to the reader *in their* language. The poem does
what the mirror (*ayna*), meaning (*anlam*), and lamp (*lamba*) in
Behçet Necatigil's poem "Nilüfer" ("Water Lily") are able to do.
Each shows (from *göstermek*) the reader back to the reader, from
both up close and from a distance, as each is taken away (from
almışlar), leaving the reader to ponder.

> Beni bana gösterecek aynamdı, almışlar. . . .
> Beni bana gösterecek anlamdı, almışlar. . . .
> Beni bana gösterecek lambamdı, almışlar.[31]

The affect here resembles what Stephen Burt describes in his
analysis of John Ashbery's poem "Paradoxes and Oxymorons":
"The same poem that solicits interpretation (asks us to decide
what it means) and solicits companionship (asks you to join it)
also resists those things, pushing the reader slightly away."[32]

> This poem is concerned with language on a very plain level.
> Look at it talking to you. You look out a window.
> Or pretend to fidget. You have it but you don't have it.
> You miss it, it misses you. You miss each other.[33]

Affectively *pushed slightly* away, "miss" palpitates—it "can mean
'miss the meaning,' 'misunderstand,' and also 'long for; regret the
absence of'"—and we no longer "miss" in any singular way.[34] For
Burt, the poetic affect here also involves *wishing*. "The poem
remains over *there*, and you wish it were *here*: more comprehensible, closer to you."[35] This complicated semiotic and affective
enfolding also brings to mind the poet Jorie Graham's description,

in her poem "Prayer," of peering "over a dock railing" and watching thousands of minnows "swirl." The water:

> seems to burst into
> itself (it has those layers), a real current though mostly
> invisible sending into the visible (minnows) arrowing
>   motion that forces change—
> this is freedom. This is the force of faith. Nobody gets
> what they want. Never again are you the same. The longing
> is to be pure. What you get is to be changed. More and more by
> each glistening minute.[36]

Like "wishing," *change* occurs in the intimate, open-ended
indeterminacy of the poem's affective attentiveness to a longing
to be pure.

Poetry "awakens" the feelings, desires, wishes, and deepest
sensibilities of the reader because its language already belongs
to the reader, and the reader, in the throes of poetic inventive-
ness, belongs to it.[37] Readers who lose their way in the glisten-
ing indeterminacy of the address of the poem, on "whatever way
they are," lose their way *with* the poem, in the company of the
poem. This is how poetry moves or compels instability in the
reader, from up close.

The place of radically open indeterminacy in thought and
feeling becomes, then, the space for an intensification of a reciprocal ethical relation of bearing and caring between the poem
and the reader, one in which, as Bruns emphasizes, the reader's
"response or responsiveness" to the poem *as other* becomes para-
mount.[38] Bruns refers to this responsiveness as "an instance of
attentiveness, as if to another human being." It is "not scrutiny,
mere attention to details." It is "an attentiveness of the ear and
of memory"—a way of disposing oneself as expressed by Paul

Celan's concept of *Entsprechung*, which Bruns characterizes as "a condition of attunement in which one is turned toward the other in an event of listening."[39]

ears pressed i listen[40]

Jacques Derrida underscores the ethical qualities of this relation by characterizing it as a kind of responsible *bearing* or *caring* for the otherness of the poem. Reading Celan's verse "the world is gone, I must carry you,"[41] Derrida writes, "The poem still speaks of itself, certainly, but with neither autotelia nor self-sufficiency. On the contrary, we hear it entrust itself to the care of the other, to our care, and put itself secretly within the range of the other. To bear this poem is to put oneself within its grasp, to put it within the other's grasp, to give it to the other to bear."[42]

The poem's otherness derives from its remoteness. As "other," however, it does not only invite semiotic and affective challenge. Because of its otherness, it establishes an ethical relation. In this relation, the poem *entrusts* itself, as other, to the reader—the poem's other—for responsible bearing and care. It *puts* itself—and its otherness—into the bearing and caring grasp of its other.

As it does, the poem "secretly"—quietly, imperceptibly, inconspicuously—puts itself within the range of *another* other, different from the reader. This additional other may be what Celan referred to, in his 1960 speech on poetry discussed by Derrida, as "the wholly other" in whose cause the poem speaks. "I think that it has always belonged to the hopes of the poem . . . to speak in the cause of the *strange*—no, I can no longer use this word—in precisely this manner to speak *for the sake of an Other*—who knows, perhaps for the sake of the *wholly Other*.[43]

Celan moves from the concept of strangeness, with its semiotic connotations, to the concept of the "Other," with its ethical value. The poem speaks beyond its particular expression (autotelia/

self-sufficiency) for the sake of, in the cause of, the wholly other. The "elusiveness of these lines," Bruns remarks, "allows for a good deal of interpolation."[44] I suggest Celan's commentary may be read on at least three related levels. The poem speaks for the sake of the reader's other. It speaks as well for the poem's *otherness*—the inventive strangeness or difference of its signs (e.g., "subtraction")—as they withdraw from the grasp of the reader.[45] And it speaks for all others who share in this difference. Affective and ethical experience in poetic encounter illuminates these levels as three related happenings of poetic encounter.

"Before I was a Gazan" entrusts itself to the care of the other, to our care, at these three levels. It does so in the cause of, or for the sake of, the boy, his uncle, his teacher, the best math student, and his baby sister (the first level). It speaks as well for the otherness of their experience of subtraction (the second level), and it secretly speaks in the cause of, or for the sake of, all uncles, teachers, best students, and baby sisters who get "subtracted" (the third level). Not only those within the immediate "range" of the poem, but all those before and after, who have been or become "Gazans" (where "Gazan" *palpitates* with meaningfulness in relation to "subtracted" others).

The relation between the second and third levels opens a fourth level of bearing care: by placing within the range of our care those others who are spoken for by the poem, the poem, with even more subtlety, places others *of and for* the "spoken for" inexorably within this range as well. Aunts, for example, doctors, accountants, shopkeepers, and, other "bombed" others—other cousins, neighbors, strangers, and their parents and grandparents, who may or may not also be uncles or aunts or teachers or students of math in schools, churches, and temples. . . . All others to the others for whose sake the poem has spoken are also "sent into our arms" for "carrying," as ethical responsiveness, with poetic possibility.[46] Just listen, just *attune*: responsiveness *as* ethical bearing and caring happens "secretly" in poetic encounter. Like "letting go," manifestations of care for the other whose otherness one bears do not appear to be a result of choice or deliberation. Listening and attuning may, at times, require deliberate choice—a theme to which I shall return—but once one attunes to expression as poetic expression, an ethical relation in the cause of all others and their otherness *just happens*.[47]

The ethical dimension of poetic encounter underlies its other two dimensions. To be *affectively* jolted by subtracted uncles, students, and teachers, one must *care*; to let subtraction *palpitate* with this possibility, one must *bear* possibilities for new forms of meaningfulness.[48] Indeed, the experience of bearing and caring for a poem is very familiar to "trained" readers of poetry. While there are different perspectives on poetics itself, formal lessons for reading poetry teach readers to approach what Vendler calls the "imaginative individuality of a poem" with bearing and caring responsibility.[49] To appreciate a single poem, one must open their perceptual, sensual, emotional, cognitive, and imaginative capacities to the fullness of its expression and architecture: the metered positioning; the subtle sound play, weight, and order of the words; the design and organization of space, line, and other aspects of the poem's structure. One must attentively follow the poem's substantive focus and movement, consider its thematic insights, symbolic images, ambivalences, metaphors, rhetorical and ironic turns, and the meticulous detail about things, feelings, scenes, places, persons, etc. that it describes.

"Poems hew to the finely honed discipline," explains Mary Kinzie, "of finding the words to describe the temperature, color, smell, and even the sensation of moving air within waking dreams."[50] One must feel the temperature, notice the colors, imagine the shapes, breathe the aromas, and feel the moving air.

"Taste it everywhere. Wonderland signs."[51] And, along the way, one must also sense and discern the poem's beat, cadence, tone, and diction. One must attend to its either patterned or purposefully peculiar structure, layout, and spacing—its spatial and temporal economy within which words, images, and other marks are artfully placed—the careful ordering of thoughts, the use of repetition, pause and punctuation, the shapes of sentences, and the pace of the language. One should dwell in each line and inhabit, experience, and feel the sudden shifts, pauses, breaks, silences, and enjambments from one line to the next.[52]

> Must read it
> Line by
>   Line[53]

One must endeavor to wander with sensitive and imaginative curiosity where the poem makes you wonder. Some techniques are designed to arouse emotions and others to encourage light cognitive play and ironic discovery.

Poetic encounters, even their most tender and beautiful forms, come with significant cognitive and emotional risk. It is part of the practice of poetry to welcome such risk and require the wherewithal to assume it. In entrusting itself to the reader's bearing and caring, poetry expects to bring a reader's latent and unnoticed feelings and thoughts to the surface—to stimulate attention to previously unconsidered—or underconsidered—connections, associations, questions, and insights that "flash forth," sometimes suddenly, "in recognizable moments" of poetic attunement.[54] Spivak's lamentation, "The subaltern cannot speak!" exemplifies such a moment. As does her reflection, "How much do the Scriptures arbitrate desire?" Both expressions come to her as she bears and cares for the signating signs of her great aunt's "death as text." She does so, as we have seen, for the sake of her great aunt as other, her otherness, and for all women whose desires have been coercively arranged by the scriptures. In *the subaltern cannot speak*, Spivak displays the wherewithal of poetically attuned responsiveness.

Poetic expression—poetry—is thus a fillip for and invitation to a deeply creative, intimate, and transformative encounter. There is an adage in poetic circles, derived from William Carlos Williams's poem "Two Pendants: For the Ears," that even a grocery list may be read as poetry. The adage supports a nonexclusive criterion for poetic diction, which is important to this study: If a shopping list may be received as poetry, so too may violent speech, torture, democratic deliberation, medical care, and scientific data.[55] One may of course read a shopping list in a de facto manner without feeling deprived of a transformative encounter. But if one fails to attune to a poem, one misses the chance for a profoundly open, affective, and ethical experience.[56] To urge that everything should be received as poetic expression—and therefore that the interpretation of politics may be modeled on the happenings of poetic encounter—is another way of saying that everything offers a chance for a poetically attuned relationship, which indeed is my fundamental claim here.

IMPLICATIONS FOR SOCIAL AND POLITICAL ANALYSIS

As suggested in Spivak's example, poetic attunement is not absent in contemporary social and political analysis. In fact, if one listens, it is quite widespread. However, dominant social scientific training and pedagogy focus analytical emphasis on empirically de facto, pragmatic, and strategic assertions.[57] To explore the fullness of the difference that poetic attunement may make, I return to Ahdaf Soueif's autobiographical, postcolonial novel, *In the Eye of the Sun*, whose central character, Asya al-Ulama, exemplifies poetic attunement in at least two senses: She makes sense of experience, including political experience, in terms of poetic verse; and she conveys and composes that sense, like Spivak, in thought that is semiotically open, affective, and profoundly, ethically responsive. Poetic verse and poetically expressive response are, obviously, intimately connected.

Indeed, the novel's title highlights this connection. "In the eye of the sun" is both a verse from a Kipling poem, "Song of the Wise Children," quoted late in the novel, in which the narrator dreams of "undo[ing] what the North has done" by returning to the "wayside magic" of youth "in the eye of the sun," and a comment made by Egyptian general Sidki al-Ghoul, much earlier in the novel, during the war of June 1967, as he questions an order to withdraw his division from the eastern to the western side of the Suez Canal. "Why would I withdraw? And to withdraw at noon, in the eye of the sun, I'd be asking the Israelis to bomb it."[58] Any possible, even incidental, relationship between Kipling's poem and the general's statement is left unexplored in the novel, but their copresence suggests a fundamental role for poetic expression in making sense of life and political experience—Asya's and that of many others.

The novel traces Asya's postcolonial experience as a Westernized Egyptian Muslim woman living through the existential dilemmas associated with European gender emancipation and education; the subaltern pain and difficulties of its accompanying Orientalist, racial, and gender violences;[59] the estrangement that intimate exposure to the West produces in familial, social, and political relationships back home; and the constant presence of deadly regional war and political conflict within Egypt. Asya's character thinks and feels through her experience, the lives of others, and the contexts of their lives with meticulous attentiveness to detail and context that combines empathy, generous literary attentiveness, and constant imagination.[60]

MAKING SENSE THROUGH POETIC VERSE

When she thinks explicitly about politics, verses from poems or songs from Asya's education and life come to her in experience apace with her thoughts. It is as though she speaks another language, that of poetic verse—a character trait not unusual for someone like Asya, who has been exposed to literature from the earliest days of her life, or for persons raised in milieus where poetic verse, song lyrics, or sacred verses are shared and commonly known. In one scene, while Asya and her friends are preparing at her home for their final exam in their English poetry class, Asya invokes verses from the poems of T. S. Eliot and W. H. Auden, and she echoes a famous line from Matthew Arnold's "Dover Beach" to address issues on her mind concerning political oppression, violence, and effective political action.

The first verse enters the story as Asya's classmates discuss whether they will be asked questions about the historical influences on Eliot's poetry. Asya dwells in the verse, "Her hair over her arms and her arms full of flowers" and imagines pausing the study group to attend to this verse. "To say forget the exam and the essay questions and the unseen text. Just listen. Listen":

She turned away, but with the autumn weather
Compelled my imagination many days,
Many days and many hours:
Her hair over her arms and her arms full of flowers.

After rereading these verses, Asya "takes a deep breath"—an affective moment—and reflects, "This *has* to be what matters. Or a large part of what matters. How can people read it and just go on as though they'd been reading the newspaper or some geography lesson that they had to memorize?"[61] The verses are from Eliot's 1917 poem *"La Figlia Che Piange"* (The Weeping Girl). Soueif presents it, as she does many of the poetic references, without this bibliographic information. They are simply in Asya's thoughts. "The Weeping Girl" reflects the semiotic, affective, and ethical dimensions of poetry that I have described. The poem "turns away," inviting the reader to enter into a space of open and imaginative indeterminacy; and, with skillful alliteration, rhyme, repetition, and the alluring image of "her hair over her arms and her arms full of flowers," the poem entrusts the weeping girl to the close, caring and bearing attention of the reader, for many days and many hours.

The second poetic moment occurs when Asya's thoughts echo a line from "Dover Beach." This happens as she wonders intensely about the lives of her study partners, especially Noora and Bassam, a Palestinian born in Nablus in 1949. Noora's father has threatened to disown her if she marries Bassam, and her mother fears disobeying her father. Asya cannot comprehend why. "She's his only daughter," Asya thinks to herself. "How can he disown her? And how can her mother possibly let him?"[62] Asya's thoughts go to Bassam and what it might be like to be him, especially what it would be like to live under occupation, being banned from one's neighborhood and enduring the constant uncertainty of forced displacement. "Any day, any minute, they might come knock on the door and say, 'We are taking over this house. You have one hour to pack.'" Bassam "was living with this," she thinks, and "that was why when you looked at him it seemed, despite his good looks, the mixture of French and

Turkish with curly black hair, green eyes, and a slightish build, he appeared almost—maimed. One of the bruised people. All those bruised people: Palestinians, Armenians, Kurds, and of course the Jews themselves—and who knows what others would be added to the list; what others were in the making right now."[63] At this moment, with Bassam and other occupied others in her bearing care, the verse from "Dover Beach" comes to her thoughts.

> Amazing, really, and frightening, so frightening to think of the things that are happening right now. Right now as they sit here studying for their poetry exam: secret deals being arranged in government departments, counterdeals in secret service meetings, ignorant armies moving silently by night, people being thrown out of their houses, babies being born, people being tortured. Right now. As we sit here. Tortured. And what do we do? We go on studying for our exams. . . . But what else is to be done? What *can* be done? Can you get up right now and rush off to some prison—assuming you know where one is—and hammer at the door? "Let them out, let them out"—or at least, "Stop what you're doing." No. No, well, of course not, that's stupid—and yet how can you just go on sitting here while someone somewhere is having live wires pushed up his rectum, his teeth pulled out of his head, her vagina stuffed with hungry rats, or having to watch her baby's head being smashed against the –
>
> Asya jumps up. She always jumps up when she gets to this bit.[64]

The verse "ignorant armies moving silently by night" closely resembles the final line of "Dover Beach," "ignorant armies clash by night."

> Ah, love, let us be true
> To one another! for the world, which seems

To lie before us like a land of dreams,
So various, so beautiful, so new,
Hath really neither joy, nor love, nor light,
Nor certitude, nor peace, nor help for pain;
And we are here as on a darkling plain
Swept with confused alarms of struggle and flight,
Where ignorant armies clash by night.[65]

The poetically inflected, interpretively open and affective quality of Asya's thoughts models poetic attunement to occupation and the practices of torture that accompany it. In her attunement, Asya imagines the social and sensual experience of those involved, and she is *moved* to rigorously question "just going on" like nothing painfully objectionable is happening. Like Spivak, her thoughts and expression are thoroughly informed by prior study (of other people's lives) and her own experience, and she thinks with the required difficulty about the responsibility that she and others have to those being cruelly tortured right now. She composes brutally vivid imagery of imprisonment and torture. Pushed, pulled, stuffed, smashed. This moment demonstrates what I have referred to as the second aspect of Asya's attuned disposition—poetically responsive thought and expression.

The third poem, Auden's "Musée des Beaux Arts," enters the scene as Asya further ponders how to live within the agonizing juxtaposition between ongoing political violence and the ordinariness of quotidian life. Her thoughts have literally taken her breath away. She walks outside onto the balcony to catch her breath. The lights of the Officer's Club nearby remind her of the night, in May 1967, an army lorry rammed into her uncle's car on the street below, almost killing him—an event described early in the novel.[66] Then:

Across the road on the second floor of the Pharmacie Nou-velle Victoria building, she can see a boy sitting at a table with a book lying open under the light of a desk-lamp—"something amazing—a boy falling out of the sky"—so right, so *right*, it said it all, but apart from poetry—what? What did you actually *do*? Campaign? Where and how and who would permit it, and even if anything worked, by the time it did the people to whom [torture] was happening right now would be dead—or if they weren't dead they would have suffered that much more.[67]

"Something amazing—a boy falling out of the sky." The fig-ure of a boy across the way recalls for Asya the image and story of Icarus escaping from prison with wings made of wax. Ignor-ing the warnings of his father not to fly too close to the sun, however, he falls into the sea. The scene is depicted in Pieter Bruegel the Elder's painting "The Fall of Icarus," the subject of Auden's poem. The painting shows life "going on" while Icarus plunges into the sea. Auden praises "the old masters" of art:

> About suffering they were never wrong
> The Old Masters: how well they understood
> Its human position: how it takes place . . .
>
> In Bruegel's *Icarus*, for instance: how everything turns away.[68]

Asya takes the line "Something amazing—a boy falling out of the sky" into her responsible bearing and care. More turn-ing away but of a different kind: Eliot's girl weeps and "turns away." Bruegel's residents are turning away by "just going on." In Bruegel's painting and Auden's poem, suffering takes place while people "go on" about their business: eating, opening a window, and walking along, and "dogs go on with their doggy life and the torturer's horse/ Scratches its innocent behind on a tree." The ploughman may have heard the splash and cry, but it was not "an important failure," and

> the expensive delicate ship that must have seen
> Something amazing, a boy falling out of the sky
> Had somewhere to get to and sailed calmly on.

So right, so *right*. Poetry *makes* sense. It expresses what *matters*. Or a large part of it. Poetic attunement thus partly involves finding clarifying insight and answers in the poetic experience of the world by letting the constitutive poetic texts of one's life—verses, lyrics, aphorism, adages—have a chance in making sense of experience. "A boy falling out of the sky" is itself Auden's poetically attuned versing from experience, and it comes to Asya in her attunement to the political situation in which she and others find themselves. Verses constitute her understanding of the world and enter the scene of interpretation to make sense, for her, of both her experience and the experience of others. Newspapers and academic textbooks subordinate imagination to stabilized governing concepts; poetry gets it *right*. If people would just *listen* to these verses, they, too, would be intercepted in whatever way they are and *moved otherwise*.

POETICALLY RESPONSIVE THOUGHT

Asya is still thinking about "what else is to be done." And the word "suffered." It had emerged in her thoughts about torture and what form of *doing* might, or might not, "work" to end it. She attunes with ear and memory to "suffer" and lets it palpitate with possibility.

Suffered. How odd it is, this word. "Suffer" the little children to come unto me. You also "suffered" from headaches, from disappointments, from delusions. And people under torture "suffered," too. When Savak forced you down on to a hot steel grid you "suffered." When the Israeli police broke your arms and legs you "suffered." And here? She'd heard that in 1954 men from the Muslim Brotherhood had been pumped up, blown full of water and then guys had jumped on their stomachs and exploded them. . . . Who dreamed up these things? Not the knocking about, the punching, anyone could do that. But the advanced stuff. Who sat there and drew up a nifty little machine that would make pulling out fingernails more efficient: slower perhaps and jerky—oh oh oh. She bends over her stomach then straightens up again. How could you *be* someone who actually does it? . . . You would be a perfectly normal person, eat your breakfast in the morning and drink your tea with two spoonfuls of sugar, see your kids off to school, choose what you were going to wear . . . shave and get dressed—maybe even say your morning prayers—and set off for work. And when you got there you would take off your jacket, roll up your thin-striped sleeves and go into a bare windowless room where you started stripping a guy and blindfolding him, cursing and abusing him as you went along—.[69]

Seeing Asya in pain, Asya's sister Deena joins her on the balcony. The story continues like this, scene after scene.

Asya invokes a fourth poetic verse in her reflections on "suffer": "Suffer the little children to come unto me" paraphrases a verse from the Gospel of Matthew in the New Testament.[70] It comes to Asya as "suffer" palpitates with possibility, demonstrating the generative connection between the first and second aspects of poetic attunement—between evoking poetic verse as explanation and responding, or *co-versing*, with poetically attuned expression. "Turns away," for example, "secretly" pulls Asya close to those turning away, and from this intimate relation she responds with poetically attuned expression, from scene to scene in the eye of the sun. Beyond being meaningfully addressed by poetic verse, therefore, poetic attunement also involves poetic receptivity, reflection, and expression in response to life's happenings.

Each of these recitations of poetic verse is an instance of attunement. Each propels Asya's thought in semiotically open, affective, and ethically attuned ways. Right now/As we sit here/ Tortured. Pulled, pushed, stuffed, smashed. Slower perhaps, and jerky—Oh oh oh. Bruised people—You have one hour to pack. Who knows what others?

Asya's poetic attunement occurs in her inexhaustible efforts, infused with caring and bearing, to find the right expression to describe the texture, sound, shades, and sensations of experience (that is, what says it *all*); in her deeply thoughtful relation to the feel and possibilities of words fitting to grasp and convey a situation; and in her intensely empathetic engagement with Noora, Bassam, Noora's parents, bruised people, the tortured, the torturer, and the conundrums of effective action in the world. What is to be done? How ought one live while so much injustice is taking place? What are one's responsibilities right now? Her poetic attunement lies in her pausing and letting the happenings of her life, like her friends' situations, the violence of torture, or the lives of those who dream torture up signate with possibility, receiving each possibility with more attuned thought and expression. Such expression happens as she thinks, feels, and traces the details of events and scenes that she has either experienced directly or imagines through perception, study, and memory. Her attunement manifests itself in her body: she jumps, loses her breath, and bends over in excruciating pain for and with others brought into range by what she knows has happened and is happening right now.

The semiotic, affective, and ethical elements of poetic attunement may be analytically distinguishable from each other, but, in practice, they are inextricably interrelated. Attentiveness to the rhythms, images, and metaphors of poetic expression stimulates more attention to the details of experience addressed by poetic verse; poetic attentiveness to these details generates more imaginative engagement with what is happening, including, for Asya, a more sustained and spontaneous response and release of unexpected expression in situations in which she finds herself. This expression generates fresh reflections, questions (e.g., "Who dreamed these things up?"), and more attunement—more consideration, more affective response, and more bearing and caring for others who have secretly come into the range of her care.

Poetic attunement is manifested in disposition and composition that strives to be, in Édouard Glissant's terms, "latent, open, multilingual in intention, and in direct contact with everything possible."[71] Asya al-Ulama exemplifies each aspect.

Soueif characterizes such "direct contact with everything possible" as moments when Asya's "heart catches" for others beyond the boundaries of her situation—across and within peoples, groups, classes, and relationships. We have seen her heart catch for Bassam and bruised peoples. Her heart catches for other subalterns throughout the novel.[72] Well into the story, her heart catches for her best friend, Chrissie, whose husband, Fuad, has been disloyal. "But it catches"—even "with the most distant"— "for Fuad as well."[73] And she is aware of moments when a thought is "not catching at my heart."[74] Asya's heart-catching disposition resembles that of Latife Tekin's character Dirmit, the young poet in *Sevgili Arsız Ölüm* (Dear Shameless Death), who, "one by one, . . . took the words from her head and put them into her heart. When a word made her heart pound, she wrote it down at once. When it had no effect on her at all, she cast it out."[75]

Asya wants, moreover, her students to let their hearts catch for poetry, a desire we saw when she was studying with her friends for their poetry exam. Four years later, as a graduate student in England, she ponders the challenges of returning to Cairo and teaching them to "open your heart to" verses of D. H. Lawrence's poem "Piano": "The glamour/Of childish days is upon me, my manhood is cast/Down in the flood of remembrance, I weep like a child for/The past—." If they don't open their hearts to this, she imagines teaching her students, they "will have missed an opportunity to recognize the power of memory, to see how for every one of us there is no escape from our past, to be conscious of terrible tenderness that can beset you for things or people lost to you forever." For Asya, these verses explain so much, just like "Musée des Beaux Arts." Right after she has these thoughts, Asya's heart catches again, but in a slightly different way, for her students. She wishes she could cultivate their attunement in the language of their lives, in Arabic, so they could put aside their dictionaries, recognize the Quranic and other literary and historical references, and "know how the words *sound*, for heaven's sake. What's English literature to them or they to English Literature that everyone must live in torment over it?"[76]

Open, heart-catching caring and bearing clearly does not imply feeling intensely only in one's heart or only feeling intensely. As we have seen in Asya's example, heart catching implies vivid, vulnerable contact and reciprocal expression with everything imaginatively and affectively possible, from the light, pleasant, and inspirational to the cringing, offensive, and heartbreaking. While encountering "Before I was a Gazan," my heart catches for the young pupils, eyes fixed in the sky, with absolute fear, toward missiles raining down upon their schoolmates and their families. I bear the traumas of war and life's most awful reciprocal turns, the end of childhood exuberance, and a terrifying encounter with unsolvable worldly problems. How do solvable problems get displaced by, or become, unsolvable ones? How do solutions become absorbed into problems? (Too easily.) I am conscious of a terrible tenderness that besets me for people or resolutions to problems lost to me and others forever, and my heart aches for other children, teachers, and uncles added to the list of experiencing subtraction right now, while everyone seems to just go on. Strangely but inexorably, in attunement I find my awareness turn to *these* others and the otherness of their staunchly going on as well. This happens almost accidentally, as though they, too, were entrusted to me for some form of responsible bearing and caring. Poetic attunement is *latent* and *open*. It places me *in direct contact* with *everything possible*.

A POETICALLY ATTUNED
THEORY OF POWER

Poetic attunement has implications for the study of power—a central concern of serious political inquiry and, therefore, crucial to our considerations. Specifically, poetic attunement establishes a relation with others and forms of otherness that, like a poem, are vulnerable to power.

People commonly speak of poetry as possessing a capacity to make them feel or think something that they otherwise would not. This understanding of the "power of poetry" resonates with the predominant understanding of the concept of power in the study of politics, namely that power refers to the ability of a person or group "in power" to alter the situation of another— to have another feel, think, or act in a way that they otherwise would not. The legendary political scientist Robert Dahl characterized this form of power as a relation of behavioral influence and control.[77] Thinking of the power of poetry in these terms highlights the affective dimension of poetic experience—the capacity of poetry to move or do something to its reader—but it overlooks the import of poetry's semiotic and ethical dimensions.

Keeping these dimensions in full view, the poetic experience may be better seen not as inviting the recipient of poetry into a relationship of control but rather, as emphasized throughout, as inviting the recipient into a relationship of responsibility. This is precisely because the poem speaks not from a position of power but from the position of the other. By definition, the site of the other is *never* in power. The position of the other is "the strange" in relation to the dominant "normal," the "unusual" in relation to the dominant "familiar," the "excluded" or "occluded" in relation to the dominant "governing," or the "erased" in relation to the dominant "visible." The constitutive meanings and life practices of the other are precisely those positions, meanings, and practices that are dominated by power's manifestations *as* control (exclusion, marginalization, occlusion, and erasure). This is why the other calls forth a sense of ethical and political responsibility. Always the recipient, or potential recipient, of power's violences, the other is not *in* but *out of* power.

The otherness of the poem, therefore, invites its recipient not into a space governed by power relations but rather into one of open indeterminacy and responsibility where no one seeks, or is in, control. Neither the poem nor those to whom it is entrusted desires to impose their will upon the other. Neither seeks governance. Each offers open receptivity to the experience of the other and to forms of otherness that are precisely, and continuously, *not* predominant in their experience: "falling just short/of arrival anywhere."[78] For poetry and poetic expression to be what they are, therefore, they must stay out of power. And it follows that for poetic attunement to *be* poetic attunement, it, must stay out of power, too, with the poetic other. It must stay with, bear, and care for the otherness of the poem and all others that are secretly brought into its range. These are the "power" implications of poetry. They are defined not by power as control of and over others but by intimate relations of responsibility between others. Even poetry of the powerful cannot avoid bringing the other into its range, as I will show in a moment.

Indeed, as other, poetry may be said to anticipate what the marginalized, excluded, subordinated, and erased other already knows: it is always at risk of being domesticated to governing decipherments and significations. As other, it knows and *works against* the diverse violences of power—not being heard, acknowledged, received, considered, asked, or let into meaningful exchange. Poetry, as poetry, knows what power does and wants neither it nor its effects. Poetry that *remains* poetry secretly places its recipient in a permanent position of bearing and caring receptivity to otherness—to forms of life and living that are out of power.

A poetically attuned *theory of power*, therefore, contrasts with the conventional view of power. The poem does not seek to *govern, capture,* or *subdue* readers and their attention, although they may *feel* compelled in these ways and even describe their experience in these terms. Directed explicitly and secretly toward the other, the poem abdicates any constitutive interest in power and privilege. Its interest is in establishing an intimate ethical relationship *between others*, and this happens *outside of power*, if it happens at all.[79] This disposition toward power resembles Hamid Dabashi's principled view of power within the Shiite tradition of Islam. Because Shiism grew from an inaugural act of injustice (the Sunni denial of its claims and destruction of its leadership), Shiism must stay out of power, with the power-less, or lose what makes it Shiism. For Dabashi, a Shiite Islamic Republic is, therefore, a contradiction in terms.[80] Poetic power is similarly an oxymoron. Although poetry has suffered no inaugural act of violence, it anticipates, as I have suggested, violence that always awaits and haunts the position of the other. From the perspective of poetic attunement, therefore, poetry can never be in control or else it loses what it is. It asks its receivers to be out of power with it, permanently out of control on the margins, in the place of open, indeterminate, and indefinite resistance.

When a poem—or poetic expression—moves or resonates with its recipient, therefore, it does so not because of "the power" of the poem. There is no power-full poem. It is the receptive and affective capacities of the poetically attuned to *let* the poem, as other, come into their responsible bearing and care and move them otherwise. In this regard, the power of a poem emanates from the affective and ethical capaciousness of its readers—from *their* capacity to bear, care, endure, and respond creatively to the moving and trusting relation offered up by the poem. In this relation, power as legislative control recedes from the experience. The moment the poem possesses power it is no longer a poem. If one were to imagine a poetic republic, it would be a republic of those attuned in ear and memory, who receive and responsibly bear and care for those who feel the violence of power every day.[81] In a poetic republic, the excellence of the citizen would relate to being intercepted as a poetically attuned listener, always ready to bear and care indeterminately for the signs of otherness.[82] What is seen as the power of a poem is thus the *entrusting* of the poem and all others that are within its range to the bearing care of the reader.

ATTUNING TO VIOLENCE:
DONALD TRUMP'S "POETRY"

DOES TORTURE WORK?

Listen you motherfucker

Not everything is nice

Waterboarding

Sleep deprivation

Me singing "Call me maybe"

I'm not saying it's pleasant but believe me, it works[83]

PERVERT ALERT

Got to do something about these missing chidlren grabbed by the
perverts

#Angels

I own a couple of different guns

I could stand in the middle of 5th Avenue and shoot somebody

Boom, boom, boom

Death to the pervert killer

It makes me feel so good to hit "sleazebags" back

Much better than seeing a psychiatrist (which I never have!)[84]

These are the words of Donald Trump, from *The Beautiful
Poetry of Donald Trump*, in which Rob Sears assembles Trump's
utterances from different times and places and rewrites them
as poetry. In his satirical introduction to the collection, Sears
hails Trump as a "remarkable poet" who uses "lots of declarative
sentences, a staccato rhythm," "deliberate, mesmerizing" repetition, and alterations in voice, from braggadocious to vulnerable.[85]
In remarks following the publication of the volume, Sears notes,

more seriously, that Trump's tendency to speak in "very compact, distilled phrases that tell you a lot about who he is, in a small number of words" is "not far away from poetry."[86]

Sears describes his reasons for creating these poems in terms of the semiotic and affective aims of poetry: he wanted to "defamiliarize [Trump's] words," "allowing us to listen to Trump's patter anew in isolation from his normal baritone," and "help readers get out of the well-worn grooves of response that tired media formats have created."[87] In the same postpublication essay in which he describes those purposes, however, Sears concludes that "the poems are 90 per cent nonsense": "Having wondered at the start if there was another Trump hidden beneath the surface of the one we know, I arrived at an answer. No, there probably isn't. As he's repeatedly said himself, he is who he is. And who he is is a weirdly authentic bullshit artist."[88]

Trump may indeed be that, but, in my reading of the two poems, "Does Torture Work?" and "Pervert Alert," there is more to say about what a poetically attuned reception of "Trump's poetry" might entail, other than being nonsense from an authentic bullshit artist. Sears brilliantly attunes to the ironic, absurd, silly, contradictory, and sometimes unbelievable qualities of Trump's political speech, but poetic attunement is not simply about attending to creative rhetorical style and effects. It requires being intercepted in a space of open indeterminacy and being attentive to the experience of the other against whom violence is done every day. Trump's poetic utterances—or *any political speech received as poetic expression*—speak for the sake of an other.[89] They entrust that other to the bearing care of their recipient, and they secretly bring all others into their recipient's care as well. The poetic quality of the experience may be seen as less legitimate than Asya al-Ulama's encounter with T. S. Eliot, but there are forms of otherness coming through "the beautiful poetry of Donald J. Trump" that deserve close poetic attunement. Attuning to these poems is, as attunement goes, not always pleasant, but difficult forms of bearing and caring are unavoidable in the relationship of trust established by these two poems, independent of the intentions of their authors (Trump and Sears).

In each poem, the speaking other entrusts the poem to the care of others who are intercepted by it, and, as it happens, it places many others and dimensions of otherness in the range of bearing and caring responsibility. "Does Torture Work?" entrusts the speaker-other who believes that torture works to the care of its other, who is addressed as "motherfucker." "Pervert Alert" entrusts the speaker-other who seeks "death to pervert killers" to the care of its others, who may be either perverts or those who may oppose killing them. In its call for violent retribution for "grabbing missing chidlren," #Angels, it also entrusts the #Angels—the missing chidlren and children—to the responsible bearing and care of the poem's addressees.

The shared position of the poems is that severe corporeal or capital punishment ought to be undertaken against others. As such, the verses secretly entrust many others to our care, including, ironically, "pervert killers" and the tortured. "Does Torture Work?" raises the very question of torture's efficacy, and, as it does, it entrusts another other to our care—the other who will hear "Me singing 'Call Me Maybe.'" The poem grimly jokes that singing the acclaimed 2012 hit song would be torture for the poem's others, right up there with waterboarding and sleep deprivation.[90] The threat to sing "Call Me Maybe" both entrusts the other who will be tortured by the singing into the care of its recipient and hesitantly offers to connect with this possibly tortured other—call me, maybe. "Maybe" palpitates: there is much to be borne in the violent relationship between torturer and tortured. Noticeably, the speaking poet-other twice refers to, and understands, themselves as "me." "Me singing 'Call me, maybe.'" Also other to this "me" is the "somebody" the speaker threatens (with onomatopoetic flair, "Boom boom boom") to shoot on Fifth Avenue. One bears those deemed shootable by "me." Under the crowded heading of others entrusted to our responsible bearing and care is also another other of "Pervert Alert"—the psychiatrist. The speaker-advocate of killing perverts is proud not to have ever seen a psychiatrist. This unseen other enters bearing and caring responsibility as never seen.

As an other intercepted by each poem, I bear and care for the speaking other of the poem—the shooter, hitter, killer, torturer—in a relation of dissent, opposition, rage, disgust, and struggle. The raw violence they carry out against others makes it difficult to bear this bearing. As I do, something unexpected occurs. In "Pervert Alert"—secretly, imperceptibly, and strangely—the other's boastful threat to shoot "somebody" also brings other shooters of all somebodies, other mass killers, into the range of my bearing care: school shooters, workplace shooters, store shooters, club shooters, church shooters, mosque shooters, temple shooters. With them are the so-called sleazebag pervert killers, and with them the grabbed and killed schoolchildren, workers, shoppers, clubgoers, and worshippers. They are all in need of care.

What *do* you do with, or about, the pervert-killer as you bear for the grabbed and killed? What do you do with the speaker who wants to put them to death? What do you do for the others who have been killed by the pervert-killers, and for the pervert-killers themselves? Is it possible to be with both the killers and the killed? What are we going to do about all the violent tendencies among all the others who have entered our responsible bearing and care? Kill back? Hit back? What do killing and hitting *do?* Do they *work?* As "what works" *palpitates*, new questions and new teachings from the poetic other arise.

More strangely, does death through killing, or death through punishment, come as joy or relief for the pervert killer, shooter, and other killers?

It makes me feel so good . . .
Much better

Are these verses of the other reaching out for connection—"*call me* maybe" *palpitates*—for treatment and care they have not received from a professional or any somebody? Do killers want others to know how killing makes them feel so good? "So good" *palpitates* with possibility, as the feeling of the killer or all killers. The otherness of that feeling comes into my care, and I bear it. I sustain my focus on that feeling. I stay with it, and responses issue forth. For the killer, hitting and killing, and hitting *as* killing, *feel good.* Is it that torturing not only works but helps, maybe better than a psychiatrist? It works to help the torturer? Killing helps the killer? Shooting helps the shooter? In violence, the torturer-killer-shooter gets help that feels so much better. And what is to be done for the grabbed and the killed? These additional questions arrive as "help" palpitates. Now, I stay with *help*, and with those in need of the help. What *would* help look like, a help that cares to stop the molesting, raping, killing, hitting, and shooting before it all happens to the others in our care? What care *helps?*

Unbearable, the thoughts that come from eye, ear, and memory. The molested, tortured, "writhing with intolerable pain," so that another other may feel "so good."[91] The poem works—believe me, it works. In my bearing and caring for it as other, I experience the immense difficulty of bearing and caring because it is hard to bear and care for those with whom one lives in political and ethical opposition.

I have thus far responded to the verses of these poems without direct reference to Donald Trump. Taking them into my responsible bearing and care with the awareness that he is the speaker-other expands what may happen in their ethical bearing and caring. For instance, in addition to receiving and bearing him as other and the otherness of his views, I encounter and sense Trump's love for hitting and killing, two practices he proudly embraces in his politics as warfare and his warfare as politics. My care enlarges to include those who are most vulnerable to his belligerent hostility and violence—his others, especially others who are banned, others who are belittled, others who are immigrants, others who are women, and others for whom some of these othernesses intersect. Trump's racist, misogynistic, nationalist, and colonial supremacism brings into the range of my care all others on the other end of his verbal and political abuse, seen and unseen in his poetic expression. It also secretly brings all others who share his views, for whom he is their "me," their representative, into my bearing and caring. This is one of the provocations of the poetic encounter. A self cannot enclose itself around itself: whoever you are, listen, and others to you will be entrusted to your care.

Trump's America, other to me, enters my care, and there is much more than can be said here. This is a lifelong embodied experience of intimate challenge. I hear its anthem singing as torture, its fireworks as war. I'm bent over, down on one knee. I am not sure I "like the way Mr. Trump's a-treatin' me."[92] The sign "me,'" that is. With its me, it's hard to "get in a 'you'"—an "other," that is.[93] I return to his "you"—his other, as "[you] motherfucker" who believes he needs real help and whom *he* asks to listen. Yes, the poetry of Donald Trump asks its other to listen. It is not easy, because this "listen" leaves behind the space of its conventional meaning. Trump expects something other than ethical attunement. His "listen" is a "telling" that not everything in life is nice and that torture works. "Believe me." His "listen" is "believing." Do not question. Do not respond. Believe. Fear and believe. His "listen" is follow his command. Again, the poem works, stirs me to question and respond in opposition to him as other, opposition as care. It is us motherfuckers versus him, as other; this is not a parallel situation: us others bear responsibility for other others, all others, before they become his Gazans. He as other is a "me" who curses, tortures, threatens, and kills the other because it feels so good, so much better, and works to ensure the greatness of "me." It is us others (who are with all others) versus the "me-other" (who threatens all others). Each, in disgust, telling their others, listen. Listen palpitates, as shots are fired.

"Motherfucker"—as a sign—unbearably doesn't leave my care. It, too, signates with more possibility. I find myself ready to respond in kind to Trump and those who think and act like him, but "motherfucker" is a term that I do not care to use since it mentions "mothers," and, every time it comes to mind to say, a friend in memory whispers into my ear, "Let's leave the mothers out of this." And here, in the heart-catching call to leave mothers out of this, other others secretly come into range for caring and bearing: the whisperer in my ear who seeks to leave mothers out of this, mothers demeaned in this violent expression, and, again unexpectedly and strangely, the motherfucker that is in me. Not the me that *knows* the insult, although that me is here to be borne as well but the me that is cursed, and curseable, as a motherfucker, by another. How to bear, how to care for this cursed and curseable other, this strange otherness, that is my me, my not-only-me me? The offense here is the one that I cause to the me-other of the poem—the Anti-Other me who is not me—because I care for those who it seeks to torture and kill. How to bear the ill will, the hostility, in me that I create in this other?

Ill will runs deep and in many directions in this intimacy of reciprocal and opposing struggle in which we find ourselves, us others. Most of us only appear to just go on, when we are struggling in and with ill will. What possibilities lie in the relationship between these, us, reciprocally estranged and offending others? What could be *done* politically between them, us, from this bearing and caring? What might *work*?

The more common basis for inquiry during the Trump era (though not only in it) is to proceed on the basis of the assumption, explicit or implicit, that only one or the other of these others is a threat, and their practices should therefore be analyzed almost solely according to their strategic or instrumental goals. Such analyses are narrowly political, not poetically attuned, readings. Narrowly political readings (which have poetic elements), insightful as they may at moments be, rely upon and reproduce enduring antagonisms of unattuned classificatory dismissal (us/them, friend/enemy, free/terrorist, etc.). Poetically attuned readings (which also have political elements) rely upon and reproduce affective listening and a chance for something besides, alongside, or in addition to, antagonism—different and difficult kinds of co-versing within which arise novel, unexpected paths of thought and consideration and, with them, both other antagonisms and relations other than existing antagonism.

Received in poetic attunement, "Does Torture Work?" and "Pervert Alert" move and deprive me of the stable grounding of my prior governing concepts and entrust "Trumpist" others (inside and outside the United States), their otherness, and other others threatened by power, into my bearing and caring responsibility. The intellectually, emotionally, and politically challenging thoughts, feelings, observations, and questions that emerge in that relation give content to the bearing and caring involved. They occur, in their "honesty and wholeness," because of possibilities inherent to poetic attunement and will occur whenever politics is encountered poetically.[94] What happens next is, similarly, a matter of poetic possibility. Poetic attunement offers original paths for consideration necessary to confront violence of various kinds happening *right now*. To struggle in itinerant attunement is to struggle so as *not only* to struggle. At what cost do social scientists *not* encounter politics poetically?

SOCIAL AND POLITICAL ANALYSIS AS POETIC ATTUNEMENT

The social sciences may be methodologically diverse, but they are united around the idea that serious social and political analysis requires empirically grounded and pragmatic assertion and exchange. The reading, thinking, speaking, and writing practices of political inquiry prioritize, for some compelling reasons, the de facto—frank expression of empirically accurate phenomena and pragmatic prescriptions for action and policy. Poetic expression is not absent in political inquiry, but it tends to occur within the pursuit of empirical rigor, or as illustrative appendage, not as an important analytical moment of its own. The disfavoring of the combined semiotic, affective, and ethical dimensions of poetic attunement is visible across the disciplinary diversity of political analysis, not only in its dominant empiricist-positivist mode. One need not be empiricist to be *empiricalist*—to prioritize and promote empirically frank, pragmatic assertion based in fact.

Releasing the qualitative aspects of poetic dwelling, thinking, feeling, and imagining into serious political inquiry opens up the range of responses and responsibilities in explanatory practice, and it entails reading, speaking, thinking, listening, and writing from those responses and responsibilities, from the earliest conceptual stages of research through advanced theorization, and from description to critique. It means fostering a more intimate (remote-near), ethical, and imaginative kind of attentiveness to the familiar signs and scenes of an inquirer's research and writing—the events, causes, patterns, constitutive meanings, structures, discourses, assemblages, forms of power, etc.—and letting them signate with as yet unrealized and indefinite symbolic meaning and significance, moving the inquirer and inquiry in previously unexpected ways. This, in turn, requires letting one's subject matter resist and refuse routine application of established concepts—indeed, letting something original occur, in both the field of concern and in the analyst's own wonder, thinking, feeling, and embodied relation to that field. In this way, poetic attunement intensifies the already existing relationship of care and concern that inquirers possess for the issues and subjects of their inquiry. Finally, it implies reconsideration of the meanings of central concepts of political inquiry, like "power," in relation to a disposition of poetic attunement.

Poetic attunement thus works against empiricalist understandings of objectivity and originality, where objectivity entails a constitutive relative distance between inquirers and the world about which they make authoritative knowledge claims, and originality is understood as replicable contributions to existing knowledge. Poetic attunement, by definition, demands intimate and risk-taking entanglement with the happenings of life, and it refuses to domesticate politics to current legislating concepts. It does not ignore prior expression and knowledge, but in its ongoing intimate, imaginative, and affective relation to the signs of the world, it is prepared to receive the signs very much otherwise and to carry imaginative conversation about them to unusual and unpredictable places. New ways of perceiving, understanding, and explaining political life emerge, so to speak, in the eye of the sun, from an inquirer's conscious tracing and writing the symbolic, affective, and ethical happenings that occur in moments of poetically attuned observation and analysis. All this involves the weighty, sometimes perilous, caring or bearing of the other and all others brought into range by the subject matter because, viewed poetically, every subject matter entrusts itself to the care of those who study it.

Releasing poetic attunement into the spaces dominated by serious political thought need not fully displace existing empirical and pragmatic disciplinary emphases. Rather, the release may occur as a complement, or augmentation, by infusing existing practices with insight that is available only through the poetic. The poetic adds more empirical depth to the existing empirical because poetic attunement is in direct contact with *everything* in an inquirer's sensual and social analytical experience, within which everything *matters*. Stipulated causes or conditions of phenomena to be explained are no longer simply causes or conditions, and observed statistical patterns are no longer simply patterns. Causes are theorized ideas, and quantitative data are numerical signs that, like lines of poetic verse, entrust themselves to the bearing care of their receivers. Poetic attunement also adds more to the pragmatic aspects of political inquiry (e.g., policy critique and proposal) by enlarging an inquirer's attention to the affective and ethical possibilities of every aspect of political life. Bringing the empirical and pragmatic into the imaginative, affective, and ethical space of poetic attunement makes the work of inquiry demanding in new ways. Indeed, research may be judged according to the challenging standards of poetic openness, affective depth, and responsibility. I will demonstrate each of these themes in extensive detail in subsequent discussions. Here are two very brief illustrations, one drawn from studies on the causes of "split-ticket" voting in American politics and the other related to mortality statistics reported during the coronavirus pandemic.

Split-ticket voters are voters who cross party lines in the same election; they vote for, say, a candidate from one party for president and a candidate from another party for congress.[95] Their numbers are diminishing in the era of polarization and hyperpartisanship, but they can play an important role in electoral outcomes.[96] Political scientists have been studying the causes of ticket splitting for decades. From a poetically attuned perspective, ticket splitting gives us a chance to receive split-ticket voters and their votes as entrusted to our responsible bearing care for empirical analysis. Such bearing care reveals split-ticket voters to be precisely those voters who, because they live over and across party boundaries, are difficult, perhaps infinitely difficult, to categorize within a single identitarian, partisan category. "Split," they offer much to bear. They are others to the order of polarization established by the two dominant political parties in the United States. Ticket splitters are not at poles; they are the nonpolarized or unpolarized, the ones who are not able to be polarized. At the polls, they are those of us, wherever we may be, who are not simply this party or that party, but they are not "independent," as such because they may be bi-, tri-, or multipolarized. The ticket splitter threatens the stability of singularly partisan life. Their convictions catch for different sides—at the same time or some of the time. At other times, they may be less split or perhaps split in a different way. Split palpitates as a teaching of nonpartisan others who make nonalignment, or aligning otherwise, possible. And as it palpitates, the split-ticket voter brings into the range of ethical consideration all others outside the established orders, including those who don't even have a ticket to split.

In his 2000 study of electoral data through the 1990s, Richard Born contributed to a body of research that showed the primary cause of ticket splitting to be local candidate incumbency, not, for example, some ideologically driven desire to act as a moderating force in partisan politics.[97] Born measured the rise in ticket splitting from 1956 to 1968 and 1972 to 1992. Most of the rise occurred in districts where ticket splitters voted for their incumbent congressperson and the losing presidential candidate.[98] Presenting multiple tables with data demonstrating these statistical patterns, Born gives empirical content to incumbency as the "potent cause of split ticket growth."[99] In poetically attuned engagement with his study, incumbency as the measurable cause of split-ticket growth entrusts itself for bearing care. It is not simply a cause. It is a *potent* cause, a "powerful determinant" that, like lines of poetic verse, spurs and stirs associations, curiosities, images, feelings, and additional imaginative hypotheses about the convictions, priorities, experiences, and lives of the politically active citizens whose votes are represented in the data: about their sense of stability, trust, and risk in the context of differently mediated, local and distant political relationships.[100] Empiricist political science research explicitly advocates against the kind of intimate, anti-objectivist aims of poetic attunement, but even studies done explicitly on empiricist terms make poetically attuned receptivity available and disclose forms of responsible bearing that can happen in the relationship between analysts and their subject matter. Richard Born's study is one such example, where, in poetic attunement, we are both able to take those who are not aligned by the party order deeply into our care and to receive the researcher's identification of the powerful cause of their behavior as a kind of bearing and caring for their attachment to incumbents. Causal research on the votes of split-ticket voters has profound implications for democratic governance, specifically for understanding continuities in representational power from one election to the next.

As a second initial example, consider the centrality of quantitative data during the coronavirus pandemic. Graphs, tallies, and measurements govern individual and collective experience. The data describe the uneven dangers and suffering of a global public health catastrophe. They clearly show that the world's older, physically vulnerable, and structurally disadvantaged populations are both more likely to die or, in the case of the latter, wait longer for care and vaccination than others.[101]

Among the datasets before me are mortality figures, biological data, and testimonies from those who have survived the virus. As the death tolls have reached one grim milestone after another, many have attuned to the lives of those represented in the numbers and have been pondering their meaningfulness. What might a poetically attuned relationship to these data begin to look like? What palpitates in these numbers for open and affectively expansive bearing and caring responsibility? We have all been with Asya, sitting before our datasets.

Death from coronavirus mostly occurs as the lungs of the sick swell and "fill with fluid and debris."[102] "Oxygen levels in their blood plummet and they struggle ever harder to breathe. On x-rays and computed tomography scans, lungs are riddled with white opacities where black space—air—should be."[103] The gravely ill die of acute respiratory syndrome. "I was coughing like I was going to die," says Nancy Horgus Whitt, a survivor. "Two weeks of incredible headaches and fatigue and pressure on your chest."[104] "I suffered high fever and pains that tortured every part of my body," says Tiger Ye.[105] "It felt, as though I had something sitting on my chest," echoes Naledi Radebe. "As if my—was completely restricted. I couldn't draw a breath of air."[106] "Soso hard to talk," texted Joseph Zielinski in December 2020, two days before he succumbed to the virus.[107]

When the United States reached the milestone of 100,000 deaths, the writer Marc Fisher emphasized that, "these 100,000 are not nameless numbers, nor are they mostly famous people. They are, overwhelmingly, elderly . . . disproportionately poor and black and Latino. Among the younger victims, many did work that allowed others to stay at home, out of the virus's reach . . . transit workers, prison guards and inmates, factory workers and meatpackers. Doctors, nurses and other medical personnel who stepped up to battle an intensely contagious and poorly understood disease . . ."[108]

"It's as if," Fisher wrote, "every person in Edison, N.J., or Kenosha, Wis., died. It's half the population of Salt Lake City or Grand Rapids, Mich."[109] All those lungs filled with debris where air should be.

One hundred thousand. *Cead mile.* One *lakh.*

At the time, the total number of deaths around the world was nearly 350,000. That is half the population of Tunis or Frankfurt. It's as if every person in Campina Grande, Brazil, or Honolulu, Hawaii, died. These are people's relatives, friends, neighbors, and acquaintances. Writing from "the poor black population on the periphery" of Belém, a port city in Brazil, Emerson Roberto da Costa thought, "If I could write this in giant cartoon lettering for you to see I would write that it is terrible. Because, yes, it is terrible. People are dying like water." *Dying like water.* "The hospitals are counting deaths on top of deaths every day. Refrigeration trucks have arrived in Belém to remove these bodies. They are digging more and more graves. . . . Ten of my neighbors have already died. In fact, today, at the exact moment that I am doing this interview with you, I just heard that I lost two friends— two of the oldest people in my neighborhood. I've lost two good friends from work. I lost neighbors—a lot of neighbors."[110] Deaths on top of deaths. Ten of my neighbors. Two good friends.

Even as milestones succeed in memorializing collective pain and loss, they also fail, since mourning the death of each of the deceased may require something other than miles. Even stones separated by inches might be too far apart because many are dying simultaneously, even when they die at a distance. National milestones succeed and fail miserably in this sense. A *total* count, like the virus, knows no borders. There are other measurements and other metaphors to conceive of the proximities between the dead and dying. Like *water*. How much do milestones arbitrate remembrance?

Moreover, the official counts, stacked and lined, are always *undercounts*. They do not include many who died before the causality of the disease was fully understood or at home or otherwise outside the reach of official diagnostics and statistics—such as in nursing homes and ambulances.[111] Arrival at a milestone only happens by counting backward from an indefinite higher number.[112] It doesn't account for the already subtracted, "even my uncle/even my teacher/even the best math student." Deaths off the pages of commemoration. Uncommemorated, untransparent, and inaccessible. Unofficial, out of mind and out of sight, unreported and unspoken for, buried under both mediated statistical clarity and political obfuscation. What matters here concerns bearing and caring, not counting. *Count* palpitates as *mattering*. How to make both the counted and the uncounted *matter*? How to make numbers and statistical data *count*?

100,000; 250,000; 500,000; 1,000,000; 2,000,000; 3,000,000; 6,000,000; and 15,000,000. They look like milestones, but we had already arrived at each number before we acknowledged we were there, that is, where we never should have been.[113] In this regard, the death tolls are also excessive, but it's because of undercaring, not overreporting.[114] They count deaths—easily in the millions—that were avoidable.[115]

The issue here is only partly that numbers misrepresent reality. The deeper issue is that there are teachings to be received in the silence produced by numbering. These teachings emerge from meaningfully open, affective, and ethically responsive immersion in that silence. In their collective silence and the otherness of their experience, the counted and uncounted in the official toll teach, perhaps, the *experience* of rapid decline and demise, of unimaginable isolation and fear. They "speak" of societal failure, needless death, and preventability. They teach to keep nothing about living and no one that matters at a distance, not ever. They teach missing forever and that living requires constant care. They teach the solvability of seemingly unsolvable problems.

Received in poetic attunement, both quantitative and qualitative data do not only inform or misinform, govern or misgovern. They offer the chance for attuned dwelling within the data's silenced teachings. It is possible to receive both kinds of data as entrusted for one's bearing and caring responsibility, to let them palpitate in their meaningfulness and significance and, in this intimate and deeply concerned receptivity, to allow them to move both the inquirer and the inquiry in unexpected and profoundly important ways. In poetically attuned inquiry, this is not a matter of choice. It is what happens when one receives data in a disposition of poetic attunement. The data entrust themselves to the undivided care of the inquirer.

Critical analyses of reductive data discriminations rightly seek to end datafied injustices, but such critiques must take care not to reproduce philosophically narrow understandings of data. There are other ways to conceptualize data, alternatives to the data analytics of the empiricalist sciences, and other forms of justice than seemingly raw observational counting or accurate reporting. It is not enough to revise the algorithms and correct the counts. Receiving data in attunement makes it possible to *know* the data otherwise and to respond affectively and ethically with a depth of open empirical consideration unavailable in dominant nonpoetically attuned data analytical discourses. Poetic attunement challenges analysts to attend closely to the teachings of the silenced and erased lives of the data.

At the heart of serious social science has always been a readiness to bear so much about the lives of others and to take any subject matter—appealing, bleak, curious, offensive, etc.—into its care. And so poetic attunement matters for the same reason social science matters. Poetically attuned social science does not turn away. It receives, for deep and nuanced consideration, cerebrally and affectively demanding questions of human experience: simple, complex, confusing, thrilling, surprising, scary, imaginable and unimaginable issues of life and death, possibility and impossibility, agency and necessity. Such issues are sometimes truly inexplicable, but they call forth the human effort to explain—to interpret and misinterpret, to understand and misunderstand. Contemporary social and political analysis favors accurate de facto expression of facts, cases, causes, meanings, structures, systems, ideologies, discourses, assemblages, and forms of power, as well as pragmatic prescriptions for political action and intervention. But underneath its discursive objectivism, it is seized by an aspiration to make sense of layers of human experience that animate poetic attunement: the scope and limits of human imagination and meaning-making, the textured subtleties of human conduct within relationships and institutions that shape collective life, the psychological and practical import and impact of sociohistorical force and context. The just and the unjust. The right, the wrong, and the expedient. The scrutable and the inscrutable. Human trial, error, and experiment. Social scientists want their categories to correspond to a stable reality, but in constantly generating new research and investigation, they betray their uneasiness with how things are and how things are understood. They often seek to compel and move their audiences to think, feel, and act otherwise in relation to diagnosable improprieties and injustices within a status quo.

Poetic attunement thus discloses the experiences of palpitating explanatory possibility and responsible bearing care that occur in the relationship between inquirers and their subjects. It foregrounds and centers the underlying semiotic, affective, and ethical motivations and aspirations constitutive of social scientific practice. The existence, depth, and analytical significance of these motivations and aspirations are occluded or dismissed by dominant empiricalist disciplinary emphases. When social scientific inquiry is compelling, it is often the very qualities of poetic attunement that make it so.

3

DOCTORING THE DATA

Where there is possibility there is error...
—Della Pollock[1]

POETICALLY ATTUNED DATA ANALYSIS

In cultivating an open, affective, and ethically attuned relation with its subject matter, poetic attunement offers a new understanding of the data analytical relation in the social sciences. The internationally acclaimed film *Once Upon a Time in Anatolia* offers a compelling site to explore the "knowledge constitutive" purposes and aspirations of poetic attunement, especially in the film's culminating autopsy scene.[2] The film presents a fictionalized account of an all-night search for the body of a murdered man in the fields of the Turkish countryside. During the search, in conversation with the state prosecutor, the doctor in the search party solves the mystery of another death—that of a pregnant woman who predicted the day she would die—through painstaking, empirically de facto causal inquiry. In the final scene, however, while dictating the official autopsy report of the murdered man's cause of death, the doctor shockingly conceals the truth of the presence of dirt in the man's windpipe and lungs. Evidence of suffocation in the lower respiratory system implies that the man was buried alive by his murderer, who had let it slip in an evening of drinking that he, not the murdered man, was the father of the dead man's son.

The doctor's apparent departure from de facto analysis makes some sense in the context of the scene. Awareness in the community of the man's true cause of death could ruin the lives of his wife and son. In the context of the broader overnight story, however, the concealment marks an astonishing reversal of the doctor's dedication to empirically rigorous data analysis and causal inquiry. I will argue here that this apparent contradiction may be resolved by recognizing the unchanging constitutive purpose in the doctor's analytical practice: *to profoundly support and make possible the "living on"* of the lives represented by "data." These lives may be understood as the *subaltern others* of the data, and receiving their teachings with empirical accuracy *requires* poetically attuned, social scientific data analysis.

Several studies discussed thus far exemplify this data analytical purpose or aspiration of poetic attunement. Gayatri Chakravorty Spivak's account of Bhubaneswari Bhaduri's death profoundly supports and makes possible the living on of the latter's intervention in the field of *sati* suicide. In dominant records or databases of female suicide, Bhubaneswari's death may have otherwise remained in history as another casualty of illicit love. Emine Sevgi Özdamar's narration of migrants as living on after life's accidents supports and makes possible their *survivre* in reciprocal and loving, multilingual relationships with other survivors of accidents. In dominant migration databases, the "migrant" constantly enters history as a "border crosser" of one kind or another. The very title of Ahdaf Soueif's *In the Eye of the Sun* supports and makes possible the living on of subaltern others. It invokes General Sidki al-Ghoul's perspicacious opposition to grueling troop relocations in the scorching desert heat of the war of June 1967. The general protested orders that soon left his soldiers vulnerable to unguarded attack. With "a rocket for each tank followed by a burst of napalm," his entire division was "wiped out."[3] In poetic attunement, Soueif recasts a war that enters the databases of the Arab-Israel conflict in temporal terms—six days in June—as avertable chemical warfare carnage "in the eye of the sun."[4]

These poetically attuned efforts are each constituted by the principal aspiration to support—sustain, attend to, care and provide for, and carry—and make possible the living on of their subaltern teachings. This living on occurs as a *chance* in the data analytical relation for those teachings to enter the discursive field of social and political thought. To situate this constitutive purpose within the diverse landscape of the dominant methodological purposes of contemporary political analysis, the subaltern hermeneutical, poetically attuned inquirer is not only engaged in empirically de facto quantitative or qualitative causal analysis, ethically neutral pragmatic or strategic prescription, or transformative critique of ideology, structure, discourse, or coloniality. The subaltern hermeneutical, poetically attuned inquirer is an *agent for living on.*

Nuri Bilge Ceylan, the director of *Once Upon a Time in Anatolia*,[5] has been described as "among the most profound and poetic filmmakers of our time."[6] The search upon which the film is based occurred in the mid-1980s, in the early professional life of Ercan Kesal, the film's main screenwriter and a physician by training. During his government medical service in Kırıkkale, Turkey, a small town in central Anatolia, Kesal was part of the search party that was guided to the body by the murderer. The group also included the state prosecutor, the local police commissioner, and several other town bureaucrats. They were escorted from field to field in the dark Anatolian countryside by members of the gendarmerie.

Kesal has stated that the screenplay was partly inspired by Gabriel Garcia Márquez's *Chronicle of a Death Foretold*.[7] Based on a true story of an "honor killing" in a small Latin American town, *Chronicle of a Death Foretold* revisits the day of the murder and allegorizes the complicity of the townspeople who knew it was about to happen and did nothing to stop it. *Once Upon a Time in Anatolia* similarly attunes to essential facts, events, and signs in memory that pulsate with meaning, ones that people shroud or conceal from themselves and each other.[8] "The truth lies in what's hidden, in what's not told," the director Ceylan avers. "Reality lies in the unspoken part of our lives."[9] The allegorical quality of *Once Upon a Time in Anatolia* relates especially to Kesal's creative innovation in the final, "most key scene of the film," to make the doctor, Cemal Bey, a "partner" or "accomplice" to the crime by having him bury the evidence of the dirt in the dead man's lungs.[10]

Thinking of the poetically attuned inquirer as a partner in profoundly supporting and making possible the living on of others has additional implications. The idea brings underexplored, affective qualities of the intersubjective relation between poetically attuned inquirers and those whose lives they explain into sharp focus and suggests that the intense issues of life and death with which inquirers engage resound with meaningful significance in their own lives as well. Profoundly supporting and making possible the living on of others becomes a kind of *shared receptivity* to the teachings of life's accidents that challenges boundaries between the domains of social scientific practice and life. This indeed may be regarded as something like a crime in empirically objectivist, professional academic circles. To become partners or accomplices in life, however, is to make both life matter more to social science and social science matter more to life. It is to realize that inquirers share a world with those they study, that we are all living on after—and even before—life's many untold social and political accidents, and that meaningful explanatory exchange about those accidents is possible at a level of depth unreachable without poetic attunement. This is an important aspect of the significance of the final scene in the movie.

The final scene and the doctor's motives for concealing the dirt in the dead man's lungs have been subject to a great deal of interpretation. To show that the doctor's act exemplifies the constitutive purposes of poetically attuned data analysis, I enter conversation with these interpretations, the moments in the film upon which they are based, and their contrasting theoretical and political implications. I further discuss aspects of the doctor-patient relation that make doctoring a particular kind of scientific practice, one that lends itself to what might be understood as ethical deviations from strictly empirical analysis. I detail the doctor's attunement throughout the film and the broader teachings his practice offers for poetically attuned, social scientific data analysis.

DUTIFULLY DE FACTO

It is not explicitly clear until the penultimate scene of the movie that the unnamed woman who announced the timing of her future demise is the prosecutor's wife. Until then, the prosecutor discusses her as "the wife of a friend" and as one of many *inexplicable* deaths he has encountered in his job. "This is nothing," he tells the doctor, referring to the search for the body of the murdered man. "How many more examples, only worse!

With some of the deaths I come across in this job you need to be less a prosecutor than an astrologer to find *the cause* (*neden*) [emphasis added]."

The prosecutor invites the doctor to try to solve the mystery of the woman's death. In seemingly cold, calculated scientistic form, the doctor eventually does so by identifying the precise heart-attack-inducing pill the woman had access to and likely taken, as well as the reason she had done so—to punish her husband, the prosecutor, for his infidelity.[11] She had caught him with another woman, he tells the doctor in a gripping scene in which the prosecutor visibly struggles to come to terms with the doctor's persuasive explanation. The prosecutor initially rejects the doctor's hypothesis that his wife had been suffering from his betrayal, but he succumbs eventually to the doctor's meticulous and steady empirical logic. In one final, emotionally wrenching effort to preserve his prior understanding and shield himself from the truth, the shaken prosecutor asks the doctor whether a person would "really kill themselves to punish someone else? Would they do that, Doctor?"[12] The doctor responds, "Aren't most suicides intended to punish someone else, Savcı Bey [Mr. Prosecutor]?" The prosecutor nods, "Yes, aren't they? Bravo, bravo. That's what I thought. That's it, of course that's it."

This realization breaks the prosecutor, who, a moment later, reveals what has become obvious: the dead woman is his wife. At the same time, the doctor's forthright asseveration of the underlying interpersonal causality of the woman's suicide displays once more his thorough dedication to the empirical analysis of causal truths at all costs—so much so that his concealment of the dirt in the lungs of the murdered man in the very next scene appears as a stunning abandonment of that dedication and a departure from both his scientific accuracy and his duty.

EXPLAINING DEVIATION:
NIHILISM, REVENGE, CORRUPTION,
AND PATHOLOGY

Astute scholars of film, including Nuri Bilge Ceylan, have suggested that the reasons for the doctor's concealment of the dirt lie in his "nihilism."[13] This interpretation stems from the doctor's emotionally aloof, lonesome, and introverted manner, as Kesal describes it, making his character especially perplexing and open to many interpretations.[14] He is divorced, childless, and wistful, as made visible in a scene where he flips through photographs from his vital youth and happier married times.

In their study, *The Cinema of Nuri Bilge Ceylan*, Bülent Diken, Graeme Gilloch, and Craig Hammond suggest that the doctor's confident display of de facto analytical rationality in resolving the death of the prosecutor's wife masks his deeper struggle to find meaning in life. He is "a morbid disciple of rational and rationalizing knowledge (in his case, medical knowledge)," "befallen by relational homelessness and an emptiness of life," for whom "the inner and sublime landscape of spiritual growth and metaphysical home remains elusive."[15] Diken, Gilloch, and Hammond do not comment specifically on the autopsy scene, but their strong implication is that the doctor's act emanates from his being a wanderer haunted by past wounds: "Memorial shadows and echoes of fallibility, of loss and regret puncture the seemingly emotionless demeanor of [Dr.] Cemal's fragile armor."[16]

The doctor's nihilism emerges most prominently during a heart-to-heart exchange with the burly and amiable local bureaucrat, Arap Ali, as the two men wait by the cars while the search team looks around for the body at a third location.[17] A strong wind blows the tall grass surrounding the two men, who are illuminated by bright beams from the gendarmerie's army jeep and the dimmer yellow headlights of the search party's two old Turkish-model cars. Claps of thunder erupt from the direction of nearby Iğdebeli. As their exchange deepens, the thoughts expressed by the two men are heard but not visibly spoken. The visual modification achieves the director's characteristic, phenomenological focus on "what's happening inside humans" in their "inner worlds."[18] A conversation—initially about the sculptures in the area and overtime salaries—takes place, but the audience can only hear it, not "see" it taking place.

As they stand by the cars, Arap Ali explains to the doctor that he comes to these parts often to let off some steam with his gun. "So you have a gun," says the doctor. Arap Ali says that one needs one around here because it is hard to tell "the good" from "the bad." "If it comes to it, you have to be ruthless." You need to "take matters into your own hands" and "shoot them right between the eyes."

ARAP ALI: I know, I'm telling you. You have to stay in the circle, and keep an eye on the center. . . . The thing is . . . if it comes to it, you also have to be able to give up. None of us live forever, do we, doctor? The Prophet Solomon. He lived to 750. Gold jewels. . . . Well, he died in the end, too. Right doctor?

This is one of a series of lessons in life that the local officials give the doctor in the course of the search. At different points, Arap Ali, the prosecutor, and the police commissioner, Naci Bey (Mr. Naci), offer him advice about everything—from the outlooks of the local villagers and townspeople to the difference between buffalo yogurt and hard cheese.[19] These scenes highlight the ways in which the doctor is, for the men of Anatolia, a man from the city and a stranger and visitor in their midst.

In the scene with Arap Ali, the doctor listens and then, in a deep voice, pensively reflects:

> DOCTOR: It's raaiining in Iiiğdebeli. Leeet it [*Yaaağsın*]. It's been raining for centuries. What difference does it make? But not even a hundred years from now, Arap. Neither you, me, the prosecutor nor the police chief. . . . Well, as the poet said, still the years will pass and not a trace will remain of me . . . darkness and cold will enfold my weary soul (*yorgun ruhum*).[20]

The camera is positioned behind the doctor as he speaks. As he turns his head toward Arap Ali, the audience realizes that he has not been speaking aloud; these are his inner thoughts. But when he says, "Isn't that so, Arap?" Arap Ali responds, smiling, as if he had heard every word the doctor has just said.

"Hey, steady on, doctor!" Arap Ali exclaims. "We're not done yet! And you've buried us before we're even dead. You shouldn't think like that." The Turkish expression for "we're not done yet" may be literally translated as "we have a world of things still to do."

When the doctor responds, he sounds like a nihilist. "I don't know. It's dragging on. It's the boredom getting to me."

Arap Ali tries to raise the doctor's morale. The subaltern bureaucrat with ominous advice waxes poetically:

> ARAP ALI: "Yo yo. No, no. Don't you know. Maybe you're bored to death now. But one day you may get a kick out of the stuff going on here. When you have a family, you'll have a story to tell. Is that so bad? You can say, "Once upon a time in Anatolia . . . when I was working out in the sticks I remember this one night which began like this." You can tell it like, *ne biliyim*,[21] a fairytale. Isn't that right doctor?"
> DOCTOR: "*Oyle. Oyle tabii*. Yes. Sure."

Assuming that the doctor is nihilistic, commentators differ, however, about the relationship between his nihilism and his concealment of the dirt in dead man's lungs. In their analysis of the film, Zak Bronson and Gözde Kılıç suggest that the doctor's "choice" or "decision" "to ignore the evidence" or "to hide the truth" demonstrates his "growing nihilism."[22] Like a hero in the genre of the American Western, he "rejects the formalities of the law in order to achieve what he sees as a measure of justice" for the "victim's wife," saving her from "humiliation" that might follow the disclosure of the true cause of her husband's death.[23]

Ceylan, the director, sees the doctor's concealment of the dirt differently—not as evidence of growing nihilism but rather as part of the doctor's existential and moral awakening *from* his nihilism. He says, "We really don't know the doctor's real motivation" for concealing the dirt.[24] Ceylan speculates that the doctor "takes Kenan's [the accused murderer's] side" for several possible reasons—to reduce his sentence, not to cause more pain for the woman and her son, or to take revenge against the local officials for humiliating him during the search, as in "the cigarette scene" when Naci Bey scolds the doctor for being "too soft" by giving Kenan a cigarette before he leads them to the body. More fundamentally, Ceylan draws our attention to the morning the search team returns to town with the body, after the doctor briefly visits the hospital, and before the autopsy. The scene depicts the vivid sights and sounds of the town beginning a new day: the steamy inside of the nearby *hamam*, the exhausted doctor pouring hot water over his head to revive himself, a loud slap of the hand of one of the *hamam*'s attendants as it lands on the back of another man to whom he is giving a massage; the brightening sky and a loudly squawking flock of birds startled from their perch by a sudden bang nearby; shopkeepers sweeping away the clutter in front of their stores as they prepare to open shop for the day; birds chirping in a rain gutter above the fluttering ice-cream banners above a small market, in the bright early morning light; and morning traffic and the calm visage of the doctor as he walks through the narrow alleys and along the main street of the town. Given the suspense of the prior overnight search, the scene is remarkable in its ordinariness. For Ceylan it is loaded with meaning.

> I wanted to show this man has the potential to change, even though actually he is the kind of person who is actually dead inside. He has a nihilistic attitude; it's hard for him to create meaning in life. He senses life is meaningless. But a nihilistic person is also in a position to create his own meaning, not accepting any other meaning from outside himself. At the end of the night, in the morning, I carefully tried to put that in the walking scenes in the town, which show that he has the potential to change. He looks at the town like he's seeing the details for the first time in his life. Meaning is created from zero—and at certain important moments I have myself felt this happening. I look at the street where I live every day but most of the time I don't see anything. Then suddenly I see the details, but generally it's only after some important, changing event. So I wanted to show this potential for change in the character during the town scene: the birds and the smoke and the shutters on the shop windows. And also the sounds, which are the same every day but sometimes your ear selects different ones in these moments.[25]

The scene is a poetic bearing and caring for the doctor. Ceylan is supporting the living on of a nihilist, all nihilists, who sense life is meaningless, showing the potential for a sudden change in one's fundamental attitude toward life.

Whether or not, in the later autopsy scene, the doctor is disregarding formal legal standards or experiencing an existential awakening, these views of the doctor's nihilism nonetheless converge to suggest that the doctor's concealment of the dirt in the lungs is a just, compassionate, principled, well-intentioned, and meaningful good deed. To suggest that the man was buried alive could mean a harsher sentence for Kenan; intense pain, humiliation, and tumult in the lives of the dead man's wife and son; and, in general, a more devastating experience for them, and others, with the death. The doctor saves them from this. When he chooses or decides to hide the truth, to use Bronson and Kılıç's terms, he is, somehow, thinking, focused on, or concerned with justice and the well-being of others.

There are other readings of the doctor's act that complicate this reading. These relate to the relationships that the doctor has with the state and the bureaucratic officials around him, not with the accused or the family. One reading relates to the possibility, suggested by Ceylan, that the doctor may have been taking revenge against the local officials for humiliating him: "The doctor feels humiliated . . . and that creates a kind of violence hidden inside him."[26]

Ceylan's specific reference is to the tumultuous scene that occurs at the search party's fourth stop, where the prosecutor asks the doctor to solve the mystery of the woman who predicted her own death. While they are talking, Naci Bey erupts in anger down the hill in front of them. Frustrated about coming up empty-handed once more, he curses, threatens, kicks, and punches Kenan, bloodying his nose. He remarks that this is the "language" that Kenan "understands." The prosecutor runs down the hill to upbraid Naci Bey, telling him that he'll get them both in trouble if he continues like this.

When things settle down, the doctor attends to Kenan's injuries and wipes the blood from his face. Before they get back into their cars, the doctor lifts Kenan's face to see if his nose is still bleeding and then starts to walk away. As he does, Kenan asks the doctor if he has a cigarette. "Got a cigarette?" is the subtitle, but in Turkish he also says "*abi*": "*Sigaran var mı abi.*"[27] The doctor turns, looks back, and responds, "Did you say something?"

"Can I have cigarette, if you have one?"

The doctor pauses, thinks for a moment, and then nods and says, "*Tabii.*" "Sure."

It appears that the doctor doesn't have a cigarette, so he asks Arap Ali, who is standing a few feet away, for a cigarette. Arap Ali gives him one, which they light together. The doctor takes a few drags as he walks over to Kenan. As he holds it out to Kenan to take into his mouth (his hands are handcuffed), two things happen almost simultaneously. Kenan says, "*Sağol abi,*" ("thank you, abi"), and Naci Bey intervenes from the other side of the car.

"Hang on, Doctor. Don't give it to him. What do you want with that cigarette, ha? What do you want with that cigarette?

Kenan does not answer.

"I'm talking to you![28] What do you want with it?"

Kenan, whose head has been bowed, stays completely still and doesn't utter a word. (He had just been roughed up by Naci Bey.) Instead, the doctor answers, "He wants a smoke, what else?"[29]

Naci Bey rejects the doctor's answer and says, "No wait," and then directs himself to Kenan: "You tell me. What do want with the cigarette?"

Kenan remains quiet, his head still lowered.

The doctor's eyes, however, are focused on Naci Bey, who continues:

Oğlum,[30] look, if you want a cigarette, first you have to earn it. Nothing comes for free anymore. Look at the prosecutor. The guy studied law, he's worked. He can smoke and he can give people hell. Why? Because he's earned it. What have you done? You've made idiots of us.[31] No, none of that. No more free cigarettes. We're tuned to another channel now. Doctor, doctor, you don't know these guys. They're such bastards they'd rob you blind, the assholes. He's seen you're a pigeon.[32] He's plotting now as we speak. *Yok.* It's over. From now on, I'm talking a different language to you.

This is the moment of humiliation to which Ceylan refers. But the scene is not yet over. After they all get back into the car, Kenan looks briefly at the doctor, lowers his head again, and then lifts it and softly whispers, "*Sağol.*" "Thanks."

Like the story of the search, the dynamics of this scene draw upon the life experience of the filmmakers. Ceylan's father was a local bureaucrat in the small Anatolian town where his family lived until he was ten years old. As a child, he would visit the government building where his father worked and observe the squabbles and quarrels in the hierarchical relations of a "small-town bureaucracy."[33] He describes the relationships as mutually degrading, as if everyone would try to seize the first opportunity to humiliate one another.[34] This experience lies behind Ceylan's proposal that "maybe he [the doctor] just wants to get revenge on the other bureaucrats because the police chief humiliated him in the cigarette scene by saying to him that he is unspoiled, too innocent [a "pigeon"]. So maybe it's a response to that humiliation, or maybe it's because Kenan said 'thank you' after the cigarette thing."[35] This moment seems crucial because, despite efforts by the local officials to instruct the doctor on the viciousness of men like Kenan, there appears to be some humanity in the murder suspect. Perhaps the doctor empathizes with

Kenan as a target of abuse by the police commissioner. As the filmmaker, Ceylan keeps the interpretative possibilities open. "We don't know exactly what the motivation is, but it could be one of these."[36]

The bureaucrats in *Once Upon a Time in Anatolia, as* bureaucrats, like all bureaucrats, are, in varying degrees, serious and knowledgeable about their jobs. At the same time, they are at times quintessentially inept or clumsy in relation to expectations of linear bureaucratic discipline. One could say that, like Hayri Irdal in Ahmet Hamdi Tanpınar's classic *The Time Regulation Institute,* they "don't *believe*."[37] That is, in their *way of living*, they are meaningfully unregulated by standardized protocols of bureaucratic officiality. For example, while the prosecutor is reprimanding Naci Bey for beating up Kenan, Arap Ali is jumping up to shake a few apples off a nearby tree for a snack. In this scene, the film wanders, too. It follows one of the apples that falls from the tree as it rolls away—filling the audience with the expectation that it will bump into the missing corpse. But nothing of the sort happens. The apple tumbles across the field, bounces into a shallow rocky creek below, and spins slowly with the current over the rocks until it comes to rest alongside a few other fallen apples that appear to have followed the same path.

The unregulated attitude of the bureaucrats does not always show up in innocuous ways. As they perform their jobs, they distance themselves from the situation and its gravity. They quarrel, forget important things, and make mistakes, some gravely consequential, some less so. And they innovate along the way. They joke and taunt, sometimes when events suggest that they should be more serious and engaged, as when they discover the body at dawn.

They are sober as they encounter the shallow grave in a grassy field and exhume the body. When they discover that the murdered man, Yaşar, was buried hog-tied, with his feet and hands tied together behind his back, Naci Bey again curses Kenan, who is standing nearby but looking away in shame. Naci Bey says Kenan is an "inhuman sadist" who lacks respect for the dead and now deserves the same. The prosecutor again pulls Naci Bey to the side to calm him down.

With the exception of the doctor, the state prosecutor is probably the most consistently serious among all the men, but he nonetheless gets stuck almost right away in a classic bureaucratic entanglement. As he begins to dictate the official report, he asks the accompanying gendarmerie official for the name of the administrative district in which they have discovered the body. The sergeant, who values precise measurement to a fault, says, "It is simple," except for the fact that the body has been buried exactly on the boundary between one district and another, which he names and repeats in a convoluted statement. The prosecutor loses patience amid the tortuous verbiage, interrupts the sergeant, and declares the district to be one of the two named places.

Meanwhile, the others have untied the dead man's hands. The body had been buried face down. As they roll it over, the camera shows the gruesome look on his face, his mouth agape and his eyes, glaring, still open. Without any visible reaction, the prosecutor unhesitatingly continues his report: "Now, open a new paragraph." He describes the clothes on the body, the man's approximate height, weight, and age, and while he does, the camera cuts to Naci Bey and Arap Ali, who are standing by a small spring on the edge of the field near the road. Naci Bey takes a spiteful shot at the prosecutor. "He's twittering. We slog all night, you just revel. The thing to be in life, Arap, is a master of the revels."[38] These are the mutually degrading bureaucratic relations in a small town, just as Ceylan described them.

Even the serious prosecutor dabbles in moments of light humor and candor with the men, who, as his subordinates, follow his instructions as best they can. While dictating the description of the body, for example, the prosecutor says that the man "looked like Clark Gable" and estimates his weight. He pauses as the stenographer, Abidin, types away. Then he looks toward the men, cracks a smile and a laugh, and is joined by the others in laughter. "Abidin, you got that word for word, huh?" and the laughter continues. There is another pause, and Abidin replies, "You look a bit like Clark Gable, you know, Savci Bey." There is a more laughter. The prosecutor smiles and nods as if to say, "That's enough." Abidin apologizes and the prosecutor proceeds. "Let's go, let's be serious now."

He soon turns to the doctor to ask for an official statement about performing an autopsy at the state hospital given the "unsuitable circumstances" where the body was found. The two men together dictate a very formal legal statement: "Due to circumstances being ill suited to the performance of an autopsy and because hospital conditions would be more appropriate it was decided to have a conventional autopsy performed to transfer the corpse to town to establish the exact cause of death (*ölüm nedeninin tam tespit icin*), to drive the corpse to town in one of the investigation vehicles."

The prosecutor asks Hayrettin, one of the assistants, to prepare the body to be placed in a body bag and to run and get one from the car. In the moments before he returns, the men are preoccupied with everything but the death right before them. Arap Ali is picking ripe melons off the ground in the next field, and the prosecutor tells the men, "At the university, people used to call me Clark Nusret, by the way." Abidin says, "But really you look like Clark Gable, Savci Bey." The prosecutor nods and smiles.

Hayrettin returns from the car and quietly tells Abidin that there's no body bag. Abidin looks to Tevfik, one of the courthouse drivers, who shrugs his shoulders. "You didn't bring the bag?" "Did you?" "But I told you!" The prosecutor asks, "What's going on?" and Abidin says definitively, "Tevfik forgot to bring the bags." Tevfik quickly retorts, "Why, bringing the bags is not my job, *arkadaş*,[39] and a quarrel erupts. "I told you to get them though." "When did you tell me to get them?" "Before going to the courthouse." The prosecutor steps in and scolds them. "How could you forget the goddamn body bag? You knew where we were going?" He asks Hayrettin to run quickly and grab a blanket from the car. As he does, we hear Abidin turn to Tevfik and insult him. "When did your village ever turn out any real men?" "Look who's talking!" Tevfik responds. "Ratting at the first chance."

The men wrap the body in a blanket, gather the evidence from the scene—Naci Bey says "don't forget the evidence (*deliler*)"—and on the way back to the car, the prosecutor approaches Kenan and says, "*Oğlum*,[40] I'm really curious, you know. Seeing that you killed a man, why did you go and tie him up like this?" Kenan responds, "He wouldn't fit in the car otherwise, *efendim*."[41] "Hmm, really," says the prosecutor, his curiosity satisfied.

When the men get to the cars they face another dilemma. The ambulance that was expected has broken down. They decide to load the body into the trunk of one of the cars, but it appears it won't fit. In order to make it fit, the prosecutor matter-of-factly suggests that they tie Yaşar's hands behind his back.

Naci Bey looks at him in slight disbelief. "What?"

"He won't fit unless he's tied up, look."

Naci Bey suggests there is no need for that if they bend him forward, and that's what they do. It takes all the men to lift the heavy body and squeeze it, with difficulty, into the trunk of the car. They close the trunk, and, as the men are getting into the cars, Arap Ali looks around cautiously. He goes back to the trunk, opens it, and throws a few melons into an open space beside the head of the dead man.

The doctor's later concealment of the dirt in the lungs during the autopsy may be a response to the scattered attention of these men. He is surely different from them—a difference that is highlighted once more just before the autopsy begins, in the doctor's interaction with Şakir, the autopsy specialist who actually dissects the body at the direction of the doctor. Şakir appears oblivious to the drama of the night's activities. He carries on about not having the most up-to-date instruments like they do in a town nearby. "We have such lousy equipment," he complains.[42] "How can you do an autopsy with this kit, for God's sake?"

The doctor responds impatiently, "What's the problem? We do it all the time."

But Şakir prattles on about the need for "the first-rate equipment" and derides those who stand in its way:

> For instance, they got an electric version of this saw. The saw is electric but rechargeable too. Two hours on charge and use it for 24 out in the wild, wherever you want. I tell the prosecutor let's get the kit and he sends me to the accountant. Fine, talk to the accountant, but he's a real jerk. He's totally clueless. All he's worried about is chasing skirt at the courthouse. And he can't even get it up!

The doctor interrupts. "Şakir!" He has heard enough.
"Yes?"

The doctor lifts his head toward the body, "Take off that sheet and let's start *Allah aşkına*.[43] I'm worn out. I need sleep."

"Okay," says Şakir, "but I mean I just wanted to share my troubles with you, Doctor."

The comment humanizes Şakir and suggests that Ceylan has been poetically bearing and caring for the bureaucrats all along. These are the characters Ceylan grew up around. Making light of their quirkiness and their rough relationships reminds us that poetic bearing and caring can take many forms, such as parody, satire, and irony for creative artists like Ceylan, or light humor, sarcasm, and squabbling for coworkers like the film's state officials. In these ways they hold each other close in the context of the many accidents in life they experience personally and encounter as government officials. Affective and ethical bearing and caring is a broad and capacious space of feeling and life. It occurs in sharing a joke, a cigarette, or a meal. It happens between strangers on a nighttime journey or while passing each other in a corridor. It takes place in serious decisions or in the playful kick of a ball between friends.

The doctor has shown himself to be one with whom others can commiserate, but he is exhausted when Şakir wants to share his troubles. Şakir appears not to notice. Nor does he seem sensitive to the destroyed life lying before them on the autopsy table or the suffering of Yaşar's survivors—his wife Gülnaz and their young son, Adem. Just before the exchange over autopsy equipment, Gülnaz had stood, deeply upset, among the men, to identify the body of her husband and to answer the prosecutor's standard questions. During the questioning, while the prosecutor pauses to correct several errors Abidin has made in the report—"Last thing was 'identified the body.' No! You don't type it there. How many times have I told you? Type above, leaving the space below"—Adem opens the door and peeks into the room. Şakir is facing the door and deftly performs a quick magic trick for the boy. He slides a cigarette into his nose and pulls it out of his mouth. Şakir has a magician's performative flair, but the trick misses its mark. The boy just stares at him, literally just stares, and closes the door. The doctor smiles at Şakir, but it's awkward. Gülnaz is standing there, a waiting widow, with tears in her eyes.

The local officials are not uncaring, but they sometimes turn away from the violence and suffering happening right before their very eyes. Their priorities lie elsewhere; their ways are fixed no matter the issue before them. If the doctor's decision to conceal the dirt in the dead man's lungs is, as Ceylan suggests, an act of "revenge," it is revenge against the routinized detachment he experiences in this bureaucratic order. The doctor's concealment is a retaliatory affirmation of the humanity of those on the other end of its reifying power—Gülnaz, the boy, Yaşar, and Kenan. If it is revenge, it is a just act of counterviolence against the systematic indifference of bureaucracy.

Yet other interpreters view the doctor's concealment not as revenge but as a dishonorable act of corruption, either singular on his part or symbolic of a larger corrupt order. Either way, he has overstepped the limits of a doctor's—a *state* doctor's—formal authority.

This abuse of power violates the tenets of a political order founded upon standards of legal and scientific neutrality. Legal neutrality requires the uniform, unbiased application of law to each and every case without privilege or favor. Scientific neutrality requires reporting facts "as they are" without a similar admixture of personal judgment or favoritism. To the extent that the doctor's act relates specifically to the official governing ideals of the Republic of Turkey, it may be seen as a fundamental abrogation of the state's *laicist* foundational principle (*laiklik*), requiring that public decisions are guided by positivist science, not personal judgments. Turkey's charismatic founding president, Mustafa Kemal Atatürk, famously declared, "Science is the true guide for life"—a maxim that is taught in every laicist school in the country.[44] In practice, however, the nationalist ideals of the state have taken precedence over its positivist commitments, often in violent Anatolian conflicts throughout the Republic's history. For audience members familiar with this background, the scene symbolically evokes a known pattern of official corruption and cover-up.[45] As Şükrü Argın poetically suggests, the blood that suddenly spurts from the dead man's body onto the doctor's face during the autopsy, right after he falsifies the record, hits not only his face.[46] Arap Ali's circle of fire "encircles all of us."[47] The doctor's decision serves as a heavy dose of a collectively falsified reality. Until that moment, he is honest, pure, and reliable.[48] One commentator on the Turkish social media forum *ekşisözlük* summarizes this view very well.

> oh man doctor I liked you from the start of the film. you had an innocent, incorrupt (*bozulmamış*) way. you only struggled with your own loneliness. In addition, in my eyes you had a quiet, calm, harmless personality (*kişilik*). but what you did during the autopsy. what was that, pride? . . . did you develop extreme empathy for the killer? well, didn't you have any respect or feel hurt for the slain man, for his existence? isn't there a huge difference between a person who is buried alive and a person who is buried dead? Maybe you were dirty in fact and I was searching for a bit of goodness and honesty. I put that on you, ahhh.[49]

The main writer of the film, Ercan Kesal, takes a view somewhere between those already expressed.[50] In his book about the film, *Evvel Zaman*, he describes two features of the doctor's character that are especially relevant to our study.[51]

Kesal explains that the decision to make the doctor a "partner to the crime" was a way of giving the doctor more *kişilik*. The word (also used by the *ekşisözlük* commentator in the previous quotation) may be translated into English as either "character" or "personality."[52] The filmmakers had already decided that the doctor would sit next to Kenan in the back seat of the car, where, in Kesal's description, the doctor would become "*suçluya sempati*," sympathetic to the criminal. The screenplay emphasized that Kenan's handcuffs were not to be shown.[53]

More provocatively, Kesal describes the doctor's concealment of the dirt in Yaşar's lungs as "a pathological good deed" (*patolojik bir iyilik*).[54] The term is recorded, without elaboration, in Kesal's written notes from December 7, 2009, the day the autopsy scene was filmed: "The doctor makes a decision sympathetic to the accused as a 'pathological good deed.'"[55] Kesal knows something about the decision. The filming took place in the same hospital where he completed his government service twenty-five years earlier.[56] To describe the decision as "pathological" highlights its dysfunctionality relative to both the state's authority and the doctor's profession. The word implies an unhealthy, insufficiently reflective compulsiveness constitutive of the act, perhaps a disregard for rules in the doctor's *kişilik*. At the moment he conceals the truth, he undermines an institutional order that depends upon his honesty. But Kesal does not only say the act was pathological; he says it was a pathological *good deed*. The combination of "pathological" and "goodness" places the decision to conceal the dirt in a space of constant ethical ambiguity and keeps it there. Was the deed actually a good deed? Was it healthy for the doctor? Did it feel (so) good to reduce the severity of the crime? The multilayered and complex scene artfully withholds answers as it prompts deep psychological speculation.

Kesal writes extensively about the psychoanalytic relevance of the film. The making of the film served as therapeutic processing of events that have deeply affected him.[57] The original title of the film was *Mavera*, meaning "the other side," because the story exhumes, dissects, reveals, and encourages examination of dimensions of human experience that people conceal from themselves and each other.[58] It excavates metaphorically buried corpses in our lives that haunt the happenings of everyday life.[59] We all have them, Kesal observes.[60] He consequently sees *Once Upon a Time in Anatolia* as a timeless story of universal existential significance.[61] The dramatic visual depiction of concealment in the autopsy scene is so central to the film's provocation that, at one point in production, Ceylan suggested that the title should be *Otopsi*.[62] "Autopsy" is a metaphor for psychoanalytical excavation.

Calling the act pathological thus partly relates to the characterization of the doctor as a nihilist. It implies that the sources of the doctor's nihilism are the reasons for his compassionate concealment. Specifically, the weariness, loss, and regret he has suffered in life psychologically *cause* the "good deed" of concealing the truth. They manifest themselves *in the moment of decision* as an effort to compensate for difficulty in his life by doing something good for others. This requires violating the rules of a political order indifferent to human suffering (including his). The doctor transgresses and deviates from the law and ethical codes of honesty and truthful reporting to do what he may think and feel at that moment is a good deed.

Symbolically, all of these interpretations make the doctor an ambivalent figure of modernity, constituted by the ideals of scientific rationality and, for various reasons, not fully aligned, in his being, with them. In the first autopsy there is a smooth and successful functioning of those ideals, securing the ultimate legitimacy of the doctor's diagnosis; in the second, there is a profound break from them, and the doctor, embedded experientially in affective attachments with the murderer and the family of the murdered man, comes to signify defiance as well as a refusal of or threat to the order of scientific rationality.

DOCTORING

In the vast technical structure of our civilization
we are all patients.

—Hans-Georg Gadamer[63]

Let us rethink the doctor not only as a subject of modernity's various forces but as consistently disposed toward inquiry and the other characters in the film in a poetically attuned manner. The two autopsies that the doctor performs remain distinct, but his apparent deviation from rigorous scientific analysis becomes a revolutionary, poetically attuned intervention in the social practice of autopsy "reporting" that supports and makes possible the living on of the subalterns in the film. The doctor, too, emerges as a subaltern figure. In concealing the dirt in the lungs of the murdered man, he commits an "ethical error"—his "crime"—that, I suggest, interrupts the intergenerational transmission of the most painful forms of betrayal and violence that mature human beings carry out against one another.

My interpretation eludes both strict classification according to modernity's binaries and a unitary focus on the doctor's subjectivity, an emphasis in other interpretations that extracts the doctor from the intersubjective domain of his practice as a physician. Understanding his actions during the autopsy scene requires broadening our sense of what he may be up to. As a physician, the doctor is dedicated not, as such, to the objective analysis of cause-and-effect relationships but to such analysis as part of the ethically motivated practice of healing. The rationality and medical knowledge of the doctor do not neatly equate to the positivist rationality of scientific modernity. In the autopsy scene, when Şakir asks the doctor if he thinks Yaşar had been buried alive, the doctor pauses, reflects, and makes a clear decision. To the extent that, at that moment, the doctor is thinking and reasoning, I want to suggest that not all thinking and reasoning in the context of social scientific inquiry—not all rationality—is positivist, instrumental-strategic, or bureaucratic, especially that of the doctor. From one scene to the next, his disposition implies an entirely different relation to life, nature, human beings, death, and, therefore, data, evidence, and the facts as they are—a different data analytical relationship.

My view here draws partly on Hans-Georg Gadamer's distinction between the primary constitutive aims of modern scientific inquiry and those of the practice of medicine. "When it is a question of applying scientific knowledge to our own health," Gadamer avers, "it is clear that we cannot be treated solely from the perspective of science."[64] Although modern technical and instrumental rationality has shaped contemporary medicine, the practice of doctoring in both its historical inheritance and contemporary possibility implies something more.[65] Doctoring *incorporates* scientifically generated causal knowledge, but is not exhausted by it because it requires an ethically attuned relation, constituted by a "peculiar unity of theoretical knowledge and practical know-how," between doctor and patient.[66] Gadamer identifies ancient Greek precedents for this unity, especially Aristotle's concept of *phronesis*, or practical wisdom. Phronesis is a kind of know-how that integrates ethical and instrumental human capacities that have been increasingly differentiated in modernity. Practical wisdom is a single capacity to appreciate the moral quality of any decision and to act *well* in practical affairs, that is, to act responsibly in one's relations with others.[67] Doctoring is such a relation. It is an encounter "with another human being."[68]

In this encounter, the doctor fulfills their responsibility by attending sensitively to the personhood of the individual patient.

"What takes place between the doctor and patient is a form of attentiveness, namely the ability to sense the demands of an individual person at a particular moment and to respond to those demands in an [ethically] appropriate manner."[69] This calls forth the gamut of sensory activity on the part of the doctor. "It is not only a question of the skilled hand," writes Gadamer, "but of the sensitive ear which is attentive to the significance of what the patient says, and of the doctor's observant and unobtrusive eye which knows how to protect the patient from unnecessary distress."[70]

During treatment, doctoring involves knowing when to intervene and when to let nature take its course. Doctors "must be capable of reflecting on their own medical intervention and its probable effect on the patient. They must know when to stand back."[71] Indeed, "success" in medicine has the unique consequence of ending the doctor's intervention. If health is achieved, the doctor withdraws. "All medical efforts at healing are already conceived from the outset in light of the fact that the doctor's contribution consummates itself by disappearing as soon as the equilibrium of health is restored."[72]

Letting life happen again, letting patients "live on" is the philosophical rendering of the medical goal of restoring health. Philosophers disagree over whether health constitutes a restoration of a prior equilibrium or the creation of a new one.[73] Gadamer emphasizes the intersubjective significance of the former because the "equilibrium of health" pertains to both the biological and social contexts of a patient's life.[74] "For sickness, and loss of equilibrium, does not merely represent a medical-biological state of affairs, but also a life-historical and social process."[75] Health concerns the patient's life as a whole. The healthy return to "the general equilibrium of the life in which they were formerly active and could be themselves. . . . Doctors must be able to look beyond the 'case' they are treating and have regard for the human being as a whole in that person's particular life situation."[76] Gadamer stresses the importance of conversation in precisely this context,[77] as well as the "fragile and intermediate position" this responsibility creates for doctors—between "enjoying a particular professional existence just like any other" and "participating in something that is binding upon our very humanity."[78]

A doctor's practical responsibilities do not end when health fails and death occurs. Doctors remain participants in the treatment of the body after its death. They have the social responsibility of explaining the death. Consider the practice of forensic medicine and the centrality of the autopsy as a site of medical practice. Doctors' responsibilities include making death comprehensible to the deceased's survivors.[79] Gadamer comments in this context on the historical importance of meaningful, after-death rituals: "Those who were left behind were helped through such rituals to continue their lives and be reincorporated into the community. . . . Even in age of growing mass atheism such rituals are still sustained by people who are not believers."[80] For survivors, the rituals of death bridge the experience of death and life.

Both Ceylan and Kesal emphasize the importance of the autopsy as a bridge between death and life. They draw on their own experiences in the towns and villages of Anatolia. They "wanted to show," Ceylan states, that "death is within life in the provincial areas. . . . They don't hide it like we do in the cities."[81] In one interview, Kesal mentions a visit the filmmakers made to the Istanbul Council on Forensic Medicine, where they observed a modern autopsy. He describes the world of difference between an autopsy carried out by specialists under perfectly sterile conditions and projected on a screen, like the one they observed, and those he performed during his government service in Kırıkkale. His were more like "field procedures." On the one side, "you do the autopsy, on the other side, the relatives are crying, they're boiling hot water to clean the body after the autopsy, and the imam is waiting." In these socially intimate conditions, it is impossible to maintain the identity of a doctor as a (bureaucratic) performer of a specialized task. "The deceased may be someone you know, maybe an old patient. You hug the relatives on the one hand, and you do the autopsy on the other." "And when you're finished with the work, you go to pray together with the imam, and so forth." "It is lived differently now."[82] Gadamer concurs: "The local doctor who was virtually a member of the family is a thing of the past."[83]

These observations are crucial to understanding the constitutive relationship between the doctor and Yaşar's survivors in *Once Upon a Time in Anatolia*. The practice of doctoring in a small Anatolian town or village is constituted by a unique expectation of closeness. Hence, the importance of Gadamer's central observation that the practice of medicine, from its earliest moments of diagnostic treatment through the autopsy, involves attending sensitively to the individual and social life of the patient. The practice of doctoring and its constitutive rationality are distinct from other, more objective forms of scientific inquiry precisely because they involve intimate relations with people. Employing both causal knowledge and attentiveness, the doctor has the ethical responsibility to restore health and community life. In medicine, there is room for decisions and reports that are grounded in, but not equivalent to, the biological facts of any case.

A more refined concept of doctoring, however, still leaves open the issue of the doctor's possible wrongdoing. For all their practical know-how, and sometimes because of it, doctors make errors and bad judgments. In order to evaluate whether or not the doctor in *Once Upon a Time in Anatolia* is in the wrong, we need to examine in more detail the conditions under which he decided to conceal the presence of dirt in Yaşar's lungs. At this point it is possible to say that, to the extent the doctor *errs*, he does so in a way that exceeds conventional expectations of honesty and duty. This is one of the reasons why Kesal's concept of the pathological good deed is so provocative and probably correct. However, there is a bit more to say about the specifically pathological dimension, and about errors. As Georges Canguilhem observes, "In the end it must be admitted that the notion of error, like the concept of pathology, is polysemic."[84]

The theorist Della Pollock analyzes the ethical qualities of *performative* errors. These are errors that interrupt the smooth repetition of a practice and, therefore, the identities and relations produced by that repetition. Performtive errors—like subaltern interventions—rupture normalized expectations and introduce chances for new identities and relations to enter the field of experience. The doctor's concealment of the dirt is a performative error in the context of the practice of doctoring. On the one hand, he "refuses the discursive hold" of the performative expectation that his report will comply with formal, de facto rules and codes of honesty.[85] It is dishonest where honesty is expected. On the other hand, he fulfills the discursive expectation that he will profoundly support the living on of those in his care. His concealment of the dirt, therefore, is an error in one regard, and it is very ethical in another. It is not being a doctor, in the sense that it departs from what doctors are expected to do, and, at the same time, it is being a doctor, in the sense that it fulfills precisely what doctors are expected to do. It is an ethical error, and that is the reason why it is profoundly instructive as well. His nonrepetition of empirically de facto reporting is an intervention in the practice of autopsy reporting for ethical ends because ethical determinations made for the survival of those in his care are as important as causal diagnoses. This is not to say that he is exempt from critique, but it is to locate his decision to conceal that dirt in the lungs in a different discursive space, wherein it may be viewed as a completely consistent, ethically motivated error—as an ethical error.

This deed has *transformative* significance in the story and in the context of the philosophy of social inquiry more generally because, as Pollock puts it, "Where there is possibility there is error: the mistake, imperfection, or transgression that challenge the normative repetition of the same . . . invite correction, punishment and recrimination."[86] In the eyes of the law, the doctor's deviation from expectations constitutes a violation. Even sympathetic interpretations consider his decision to be objectively tainted, either as pathological or related to the doctor's purported nihilism. "And yet," Pollock continues, "where there is error, there is possibility"—for new subjectivities and relations between human beings, including, I will emphasize, between inquirers and the "datafied" subjects of their inquiry.[87] The doctor's responsibilities include those he has, as a doctor, for the death *and* life of the persons under his care, in an bureaucratic institutional context wherein, importantly, errors already abound. When he conceals the presence of dirt in the lungs, he joins the other fallen apples and attunes poetically to Yaşar's "death as text" as an agent for the living on of the subalterns in the film.

SUBALTERN LIVES

One of the first moments of the doctor's poetic attunement occurs in the scene with Arap Ali, where the doctor muses, "Still the years will pass and not a trace will remain of me. . . .

Darkness and cold will enfold my weary soul." The Turkish for "weary soul" is *yorgun ruhum*. *Yorgun*—weary. *Ruhum*—my soul. My yorgun *ruh, ruh* like *Ruhe*. The doctor and Arap Ali converse on Emine Sevgi Özdamar's bench in the middle of the nightlong search for another victim of life's *kazalar*. If the narrator of *Mother Tongue* exemplifies poetic attunement in her speaking with those who have survived such accidents, and Asya al-Ulama does so in her imaginative bearing and caring for subaltern suffering, the doctor exemplifies it in his intimate bearing and caring for the personhood of subaltern bodies under his care as a physician. Almost all the film's characters are subaltern. They "cannot speak or be heard"—their voice consciousnesses are not acknowledged—in dominant discourses about them, and they offer teachings to be received through attentiveness to their silenced subject positions. For the purposes of this analysis, I view Yaşar, Kenan, Gülnaz, her son, and the prosecutor's wife as subaltern in relation to the discourses represented as dominant in the film and to the doctor's decision to conceal the dirt in Yaşar's lungs.

For most of the film, Yaşar is a corpse, but he makes two "live" appearances. In the very first scene of the film, he shares an evening meal with Kenan and Kenan's younger brother, Ramazan, in the office of Yaşar's old tire repair garage on the side of the rural highway. The camera peers into the office through a scratched and smudged window. As the camera gradually zooms in, the setting becomes clearer. Yaşar is leaning over the table talking, and the others are listening intently. They appear to be enjoying eating, drinking, and an evening of conversation at the end of the workday. Yaşar hears a dog barking outside, and before stepping outside, he peers through the window. It is a gray and stormy night. Thunder crackles above as the dog whimpers. A storm is coming. Yaşar walks outside. The dog is his, chained in front of the shop. He says some things, feeds and pets the dog, and then walks inside as a tractor trailer slowly passes by. The title of the film, *Bir Zamanlar Anadolu'da*, appears in the next image.

Yaşar's second appearance occurs in a hallucination in the house of a village *muhtar*, where the search party stops to rest and eat after failing to find the body at several sites. As they finish their meal, the electricity goes out, at which point they are served tea by the *muhtar*'s youngest daughter, Cemile. She carries the tea on a candlelit tray. As each takes a glass, their eyes gaze in amazement at what the doctor later describes as Cemile's "angel-like" countenance—her mesmerizing beauty, which shocks the doctor in relation to her much less attractive father. "But what a waste," the prosecutor later tells the doctor. "She'll just fade away in the godforsaken village. The beautiful usually have bad fortune, doctor." Cemile is a subaltern figure as well in this male-centered film, permeated by masculinist attitudes and filmed primarily by men, in a patriarchal setting, a point to which I will return momentarily.

Kenan is, of course, a central subaltern figure. As suspect and murderer, his subjectivity is frequently and simultaneously represented and erased in the official discourse of criminal justice as one of the "twisted fools," "assholes," "rats," "bastards," and manipulative "sadistic inhuman" "criminals" of Anatolia.[88] Further, if Cemile represents physical beauty in the aesthetic discourse of the film, Kenan is just the opposite. He is played by a Shakespearean actor who is also known as Turkey's John Lennon. He resembles the late Beatle, and he is a musician. But, in the film, he is a small, thin, disheveled, and ugly man who looks like he has been through the ringer after a night of drinking, literally, to death—the death of his friend Yaşar.

The sight of Cemile affects Kenan, too. After he takes his tea with his cuffed hands, he sobs quietly in the darkness at the edges of the dimly lit room. During this time, the camera shows only one other character—the doctor, sitting across the room, who hears Kenan and turns his head in Kenan's direction. The next person to whom Cemile offers tea is Yaşar. We are in the midst of Kenan's hallucination. Yaşar nods in gratitude as he takes a glass from Cemile's tray. Kenan looks to Yaşar in utter disbelief and asks, "Yaşar Ağabi, aren't you dead?" Yaşar does not respond. He stirs his tea slowly, clinking the inside of the glass. Then, the worst occurs: Yaşar looks out the window and starts to gasp for air. He tries to loosen his shirt as his breathing gets harder. (The scene anticipates the blockage in Yaşar's lungs.) Kenan stares at him in shock. The next moment, Naci Bey, who has finished his tea, stands in front of Kenan, calling to him and waving his hand in front of his face. Naci Bey is about to take Kenan out back for another interrogation.

Cemile is one of only a handful of female characters in the film, who all have very little screen presence. Their minimal visibility is, perhaps, deliberate. Each of the film's central storylines involves a severe breach between men and women in a highly patriarchal society. Every female character—Gülnaz, Cemile, the prosecutor's unnamed wife, Naci Bey's unnamed wife with whom he speaks on his cell phone, and the doctor's unnamed ex-wife who appears in photographs—is a subaltern figure, in several senses. Some of the scenes, quite simply, display patriarchal attitudes. For example, as the search party drives to town after the body is found, Naci shares a sexist interpretation of the causes the murder. He quotes an old boss who used to say, "Wherever you find a can of worms, be sure to look for an issue with a woman. And truly, all these years—the guy hasn't once proved wrong." (Why not look for an issue with those who have an issue with a woman?) Naci Bey's comment occurs shortly before Gülnaz's first appearance in the film and, therefore, effectively introduces her. She is standing with her boy outside the hospital when the search party arrives with the body. Finally, among the subalterns, we must consider other young people in the film, in particular Kenan's brother Ramazan, Naci Bey's unnamed son, and Adem. Ramazan appears to be in his late teens. He accompanies the search party and, at one point, near the grave, anxiously squeals responsibility for the murder: "I'm the one who killed Yaşar Ağabey." Kenan hushes him quickly. ("Shut the fuck up, moron.") Naci Bey's boy suffers from a chronic condition, and in a phone conversation his wife reminds him to get a prescription from the doctor for their son's medicines. Adem is the subject of the question of fatherhood that lies behind the murder. When the police lead Kenan out of the car at the hospital, Adem hurls a rock in "rage and revenge" that hits Kenan in the face.[89] Kenan is stunned and hurt. He looks toward Adem in agony. Adem glares back with anger in his eyes and clings to his mother, who shields him, glowering as well.

EXEMPLIFYING ATTUNEMENT

Throughout the nighttime search, the doctor tends closely to Kenan's injuries. After the first beating Kenan receives from Naci Bey—and just before Kenan asks the doctor for a cigarette—the doctor approaches Kenan in the background and gently raises his jaw to view it in the light. With his hand resting on Kenan's shoulder, he wipes and examines Kenan's bloodied nose and face. He talks to him and examines Kenan's previously bandaged hand, taking it into his and making sure Kenan can move his fingers.

In the foreground, Tefvik and Arap Ali squabble over where the search party should take their break. Tefvik tells the prosecutor that the village of Ceceli, where Arap Ali's wife is from, is closest, but Arap Ali, who appears to want to avoid the place at all costs, says Kösgher is closer and that the roads to Ceceli are flooded. When the prosecutor announces that they are going to Ceceli, the police officer İzzet leads Kenan to a spring and wipes Kenan's face with water. His perfunctory splash and dry contrasts with the gentle touch of the doctor. İzzet walks Kenan to the cars, near where Naci Bey is drying his feet from the wet fields. While Kenan is standing by the car, he and the doctor see each other. Kenan lowers his head shamefully as the doctor approaches and says, *"Bir bakayım"*—"Let me have a look." He lifts Kenan's head slightly, turns it toward the light and checks Kenan's bloodied nose for a second time. Kenan nods as if to say that he's fine, and the doctor lowers his hand and starts to walk away. The nose has returned to its bloodless equilibrium. All this *doctoring* happens just before Kenan asks, "Do you have a cigarette, abi?"[90] These moments display the doctor's unassuming manner in his care for the film's subalterns.

The doctor also offers medical advice throughout the night. In one conversation between search sites, the men in the car discuss the number of times it is normal to urinate at night. The prosecutor has stopped the convoy often to relieve himself. The doctor invites Naci Bey, who seems most curious about this topic, to come in for a prostate exam sometime soon. Despite Naci Bey's self-professed enlightenment, however, he declines because he "know[s] how it's done." The second topic is Naci Bey's smoking habits.

DOCTOR: *Ya komiserim, siz sigaraya başladınız herhalde yine.* Too bad, chief. Looks like you started smoking again.

NACI BEY: *Ya Doctor, ben bırakıyorum da o beni bırakmıyor şerifsiz.* Well, Doctor, I give up, but the damn thing won't give me up.

DOCTOR: *Iyi gidiyordiniz.* You were doing so well. *Ne oldu birden-bire?* What happened all of a sudden?

NACI BEY: *Birdenbire değil, Doktor.* It wasn't all of a sudden, Doctor.

The doctor appears to enjoy a reputation for being caring and concerned. Just after the members of the search party sit down for the meal in Ceceli, the *muhtar* comments, "It takes a death to get you to our village, Savcı Bey [Mr. Prosecutor]. The doctor came the other day to vaccinate the babies, bless him."[91] The doctor smiles as he eats and nods vigorously with this recognition. The *muhtar* adds, "But his thing's different" (*ama o başka, sizinki başka*).[92] It is a very subtle line. The *muhtar*—played by Ercan Kesal—*knows* that the affairs of the doctor are not like those of the others. He knows that the doctor attends to different matters, that the doctor *attends*, and he blesses him with gratitude for that attention.

Scene after scene, the doctor's disposition is attentiveness. One of his most attuned moments occurs just before the autopsy, after he has returned to the hospital from his bath and breakfast. He is walking down the hallway to his office and notices Adem eating breakfast in the small hospital kitchen. The boy is sitting at a table near the window while Hamit, the cook, prepares the day's meal. The doctor pauses by the open door. As he does, he turns to glance back down the hallway. Gülnaz is sitting on a bench, next to an older couple. She had been there when he walked by. It is difficult to say whether he noticed her. The hallway is lit only by tinted rays of sunlight coming through a large window at its very end. When Gülnaz leans forward, the light shines on part of her face; when she leans back, her face is obscured by the hallway shadow.

She glances very briefly in the doctor's direction and then looks away. Hamit greets the doctor.

HAMIT: *Hocam buyrun. Hayırdır.* Come in, Doctor. What's up?

DOCTOR: Morning, Hamit Usta.

HAMIT: Morning. How are you? Fine, thanks, have a tea. *Gel bir çay iç.*

DOCTOR: No thanks, I was just passing. What are you making for lunch?

HAMIT: *Ne olsun işte.*[93] Green beans, soup, and salad.

There's a long pause. The doctor turns his head and looks toward Gülnaz. He's absorbing the situation. It is clear that Hamit has taken the boy into his care. The doctor looks back into the kitchen.

DOCTOR: *Fasulye mi dedin?* Did you say green beans?

HAMIT: *Ha fasulye?* Yes, green beans.

More pauses.

DOCTOR: *Etli mi?* With meat?

The boy is eating heartily, looking ahead toward the kitchen cabinets, not the doctor.

HAMIT: *Yok.* No, no meat.

It is quiet. Now the doctor is clearly focused on the boy. He asks Hamit Usta, "What's he up to? *Ne iş?*"

Hamit understands. He nods and says with a warm smile, "He was hungry, so I gave him breakfast." It is a grayish scene; the colors of the food on the plate stand out.

"Good for you," says the doctor.

The boy fills his glass with water from a pitcher on the windowsill. Then, one of the most poetic moments in the entire film occurs. It lasts only ten seconds, but it shows the doctor's attentiveness to Yaşar's aggrieved son and wife, about whom so much had been said during the search. The camera turns toward Gülnaz, who very briefly glances again at the doctor. She is sitting with her legs crossed, her top leg slightly bouncing. The camera leaves her face and zooms in on the jet black, block-heeled shoe she is wearing as it moves up and down with her leg. We imagine that this is the doctor's gaze. He watches her shoe bob up and down for a few seconds and then lifts his eyes. Then he glances down and back toward the kitchen. The scene abruptly ends there, and the film cuts to the doctor's office upstairs where he meets the prosecutor and resolves the mystery of the woman who had predicted her own demise.

The doctor's disposition is so focused that it is never clear if any of these scenes affect what he does from one scene to the next. But the moment he sees the boy eating heartily and Gülnaz *waiting*, they affectively enter his responsible bearing care, just as others have before. A few minutes later, he is conversing with the prosecutor about the prosecutor's wife's death, and soon after that watching Gülnaz choke up in tears as she stands before the body of her husband in the autopsy room. When she leaves the room, he will stand where she had, next to the body, to dictate his findings for the official autopsy report. The signs of their lives and deaths signate continuously from one moment to the next.

AUTOPSY I

The formal discourse about the prosecutor's wife is that "she was a smart, educated woman, not in the least superstitious," "gorgeous," and "the loveliest woman" whose family "saw no need for an autopsy, [for] carving up a beautiful young woman for no reason." She was also "serious" and clear about her intention to die after giving birth to the baby. Despite all this, her husband, the prosecutor, "thought his wife was joking."

"It's no joke," she apparently responded, "I'm serious (*çok ciddiyim yani*). I tell you, I'm going to die after having the baby."

"Annoyed naturally," the prosecutor says, attributing her words to "gloominess" caused by her pregnancy: "As you know, [Doctor,] women tend to be a bit volatile when they're pregnant. They can get terribly gloomy. So the guy put it down to that. He didn't dwell on her words." The prosecutor, her husband, did not dwell with her. And "the next day, it was the same words again." The day of the birth came. "They had a healthy baby girl. Before long, the woman was at home lying in bed and wanted to cuddle the baby. So they brought her the baby a kiss and a cuddle and so on. And afterwards, she said, 'Well I can die now (*artık ölebilirim*).' And sure enough, she died soon after right in front of everyone's eyes."

These are "the facts (*olay böyle*)," the prosecutor tells the doctor. "Let's see what sense you can make of them now (*anla, şimdi analyabilirsen*), Doctor."[94]

The prosecutor continues to believe until late in the story that the death was "most bizarre" (*cok tuhaf*) and that "there was really no cause for it," while the doctor methodically proceeds to solve the mystery by identifying, with airtight precision, both the biological and social or interpersonal causes of the woman's suicide. He does this by receiving and letting the signs of her life signate with possibility in a weighty relation of ethical bearing and caring, similar to what Spivak does in accounting for the suicide of her aunt, Bhubaneswari Bhaduri. Whereas her husband, the state prosecutor, saw her as lovely, volatile, and joking, the doctor sees everything she does as constituted by her seriousness (*ciddilik*). He takes her seriousness seriously.[95] He takes her words seriously, he takes her pregnancy seriously, and, like Spivak, he takes her *waiting* to take her life as serious and purposeful. He proceeds tenaciously, ultimately earning from the prosecutor the backhanded compliment that he's "the most skeptical" (*pireli*) man he's ever met.

The film reveals this compelling contrast between the prosecutor, who betrayed his wife and left the fate of her death to the musings of astrologers (no doubt accurate on their own terms), and the doctor, who remains *with* her in the condition of her death, as *autopsy*. He engages with her "death as text" as a receiver of her teaching and agent for her *survivre*, her living on as a serious person who ended her life with justification, and who waited, with purpose and responsibility, to ensure the life of her child. The doctor's inquiry is thus not simply a scientistic pursuit of the biological causes of her death, even though the language of his exchange with the prosecutor throughout the film—"cause of death"—lends itself to empiricist thinking. The doctor repeatedly demonstrates that his responsibility is to the person and life of the woman—both to her heart attack and what attacked her heart. His explanatory tenacity is itself an ethical embrace, a *staying with* the body of the dead woman, in her life, in her death, and in her life after her death.

This inquiry models causal data analysis infused with a physician's care. "Maybe there was a personal problem she couldn't deal with," he hypothesizes. "She wanted to kill herself and be spared." *Maybe she wanted to be spared. How does such inquiry happen?*

The doctor says that he does not know why he speculates the way he does. He says he's just "guessing" (*tahmin*), but his substantive guesses emerge as attentiveness to the conditions of the woman's life in the context of her shared life-world. The doctor allows those conditions to withdraw from the prosecutor's authoritative signification as "nothing to it" and palpate with other possibility.

For the prosecutor, the idea that his wife may have killed herself is absurd. The social causes (or reasons) of her death emerge in a dramatic encounter between the two men in the doctor's office.

PROSECUTOR: If the woman was so troubled, wouldn't she show it?

DOCTOR: Yes, of course. Her friends . . . her husband [the doctor nods emphatically], for example, should have realized. Were they on good terms?

PROSECUTOR: Huh?

DOCTOR: Did they get along well?

PROSECUTOR: Sure. Very well. Why?

DOCTOR: I don't know, just asking.

PROSECUTOR: True, they had a few minor problems. But I mean, the kind you get in any family.

DOCTOR: I see.

PROSECUTOR: Only . . . one day, she caught her husband with another woman.

DOCTOR: Ohhh.

PROSECUTOR: They didn't make a thing of it. She forgave him right away.

DOCTOR: But women don't easily forgive such a thing, Savcı Bey.

PROSECUTOR: She did, though. She really forgave him. They didn't even mention it again.

DOCTOR: Well, there you go. The woman made up her mind to kill herself right back then. She waited until after the birth so as not to harm the baby.[96]

PROSECUTOR: No, come on! I really don't think so. For one thing, the guy did nothing really wrong. It was some ridiculous thing that happened when he was drunk. Nothing to write home about. You couldn't call it cheating. The woman must have thought the same because she forgave the guy right off.

DOCTOR: No one dies just like that. There's no such thing in medicine.

"In medicine," the cause of death is a combination of biological and social causes. One must *attend* to both. Pained deeply
by the betrayal of her husband, the doctor explains, the woman
intervened in the social text of her marriage and departed from
it, without taking the life of her daughter.

There is a pause in their conversation, after which the doctor
identifies a drug, digoxin, which, taken in a strong enough dose,
can induce a heart attack. The prosecutor tells the doctor that
he knows the drug well. His father-in-law had been taking
it. He knows it comes in small yellow tablets. The mystery is
solved. At that point the phone rings. The doctor answers. It's
from the autopsy room downstairs—everything is ready for "the
conventional autopsy" of the murdered man.

The prosecutor has already risen from his chair and walked to
the other side of the room, where he stands deep in thought, his
head slightly lowered and facing a window. The doctor rises and
calls the prosecutor to join him, but the prosecutor doesn't turn
around. The doctor calls to him again. This time, the prosecutor
slowly turns. He smiles as he raises his head, but his face is shiny
with perspiration, and his eyes are glossy and bloodshot. The
prosecutor stares at the doctor and nods in agreement.

"Shall we go?" says the doctor. He opens the door, but the
prosecutor doesn't move.

"Look, Doctor, would a person really kill themselves to punish someone else? Would they do that, Doctor?"

It is important to keep in mind that it is a state *prosecutor* asking this question of the doctor. If anyone should know
about killing and punishing, it's him. (It is also important to
remember that the prosecutor has not yet explicitly said that
the woman they have been discussing is his wife. It has only
been very strongly implied.) But, in this moment, he is not asking as a prosecutor. He is asking as *a survivor* of the deceased.

The autopsy has penetrated the armor around his past. He is exposed, showing confusion where there had been clarity, asking questions he never thought he would ask. A pained smile comes across his face. He is looking to the doctor to make the incomprehensible death of his wife comprehensible. *Would they kill themselves to punish another?*

With a nod and a faint, knowing smile, the doctor calmly responds, "Aren't most suicides"—he pauses—"intended to punish someone else, Mr. Prosecutor?"

The prosecutor smiles back. "Yes, aren't they? Bravo, bravo. That's what I thought." He takes a deep breath and refastens his armor. "That's it, of course. Let's go," he says, as he joins the doctor with a laugh and a pat on the doctor's shoulder. The doctor smiles. "What are we waiting for?" says the prosecutor as he opens the door.

The doctor appears to have forgotten something and turns back inside, but then he pats the pocket of his sport coat and realizes he has what he needs. In the doorway, the prosecutor faces him. The prosecutor is crumbling, near tears. He struggles to speak and then manages, "My wife . . ." There is a pause, and then, with an injured smile on his face, the prosecutor says, "Women can sometimes be very ruthless, Doctor. Really. Very." Broken momentarily by the realization of his role in the death of his wife, the state prosecutor lashes out at (all) women.

By contrast, the doctor has taken the wife of the prosecutor into his bearing care along with other women who have experienced the devastating pain of spousal betrayal. Their internal pain, their seriousness, and their responses come through him as a doctor. In his replies to the prosecutor's questions, he is not simply averring a causal relation between betrayal and punishment qua suicide. He is *doctoring* the record of her death. He is passing on her subaltern teaching that deeply betrayed and pained beings do not die mysteriously. They take their own lives because of life-shattering suffering and disappointment they incur in their living, and they do so with the purpose of punishing the person who has wronged them. His diagnosis restores justice to the wronged. The prosecutor's wife's declaration that she was going to die was her "death sentence" for her husband. And it was a harsh one. The prosecutor's guilt is written all over his face.

The doctor maintains his steely composure throughout this exchange, but the prosecutor's reaction affects him, as is evident as the two men exchange looks in the autopsy room in the very next scene, just after Gülnaz identifies the body.

"Let's move on to the doctor," the prosecutor says. "The doctor was admitted to view the body. He was duly sworn in. He was shown the body. He was asked the cause of death (*ölüm sebebi*). He answered, "Because the cause of death cannot be established within the scope of the evidence"—the doctor nods silently in agreement and the prosecutor continues—"there is a call (*gerek vardır*) for a conventional autopsy."

Just then, the doctor, who is intensely following each word, interjects, "*Kesinlikle.*" "Absolutely."

The prosecutor was not expecting this. He turns and glances at the doctor, smiling.

The two men look at each other. They say nothing, but the prosecutor's final words reverberate. The Turkish translated as "call" (*gerek vardır*) may also be translated as "is required or necessary." A conventional autopsy is required. *Kesinlikle.* It has been required for *both* unresolved deaths.

The prosecutor slowly nods his head. "Yes, Doctor. That's it. The ball is in your court. I'm off. Send me a copy of the report," he says as he tosses the file on Abidin's desk. "*Kolay gelsin.*"[97] "Thank you," the others respond. The prosecutor pauses at the door and looks back toward the doctor across the room, who, for the first time in their exchange, *lowers his head and looks away.* The prosecutor departs as the doctor lifts his head.

The two autopsies are coming together. The doctor has just observed the prosecutor's dramatic collapse as he learned of the unknown, true cause of his wife's death. The doctor's subsequent concealment of the cause of Yaşar's death may be a belated moment of ethical bearing and caring for the prosecutor as a survivor, and for all survivors, as they are confronted with unexpected truths about the deaths of their loved ones.

AUTOPSY II

The doctor's falsification of the report partly demonstrates his sympathy for Kenan, whose representation in the local official discourse as one of the "bastard assholes" of Anatolia crumbles in several scenes already discussed. The discourse falls apart even more after dinner at the *muhtar*'s house, when Naci Bey again interrogates Kenan, who tells him that he is the father of Adem. "He says on the night of the incident he was drunk and it just slipped out," Naci Bey tells the prosecutor, with the doctor listening. This revelation appears to soften even Naci Bey. After the interrogation, *he* gives Kenan a cigarette, and they stand next to each other as they smoke. It is another remarkable image: the handcuffed suspect and the police commissioner who has just beaten the truth out of him, smoking together.

After the body is loaded into the trunk, on the ride back to town, Naci Bey reveals Kenan's impact on him. He tells the others that, in his twenty-five years of police experience, he's never been certain whether the people he has encountered are "men or beasts."

Then there's the likes of Kenan. I mean they're different. They're, how can I say. It's like they get you with that nerve, that thing they have. At the mayor's place, the guy says, "He's my brother. My mum left him in my hands." "Don't do this or that to him." He's almost saying "Let him go." I whacked him around again and said "Stop giving us the run around!" And you know what he says to me? "You're a decent guy. That boy's mine. Can you watch out for him while I'm in jail?"

For Naci Bey, Kenan is one of the beasts; for Kenan, the officer whacking him around is a decent guy. Kenan confides in him and asks that he go easy on his brother and look after his son. Perhaps Kenan experiences the beating as a *sign* of Naci Bey's concern. Maybe getting whacked around *is* a language he understands, because after the beating, he entrusts his son to the caring responsibility of his other. The two men—"other" to each other—smoking cigarettes together after the beating is made possible by their interpersonal poetic attunement. In that moment, the one's brutality and the other's alleged lack of humanity recede. Later that morning, Kenan's face falls in shame when he sees the raised mound of earth at the burial site. His humanity reaches and catches Naci Bey by surprise: "Do you laugh or cry?" he says in the car, "I beat the guy up, and he makes me responsible for his son."

This conversation continues with the doctor before the autopsy, when Naci Bey stops by the doctor's office to get the prescription for his son. Naci Bey urges the doctor, because he's still relatively young, to find a better place to live. Life in the town is difficult, he says, "especially if you're a boy and your dad's never around." Except it is not clear if he's talking about his boy or Kenan's. "That's why I feel a bit sorry for the kid," he says. The doctor asks Naci Bey if he really thinks Kenan is the father. "I have no idea. But after the kid threw a stone at him he cried all the way to the courthouse. It's the kids who suffer in the end, Doctor. Everyone pays for the things they do. But kids pay for the sins of adults." In attunement, Naci Bey, a small-town police commissioner and father of a child with chronic medical needs, receives subaltern teachings from the stone and tears and conveys them to the doctor. This kid, these kids, *all* kids pay for adult sins. It is morning and the doctor is awakening to the meanings constitutive of the world around him.

If Kenan is Adem's biological father, Gülnaz may be one of the sinners in Naci Bey's mind. The doctor has taken careful notice of her as well, both in the hospital hallway and when she identifies the body in the autopsy room. There, she weeps quietly as she gazes down at Yaşar's body, stretched out before her in his soiled work clothes. When the prosecutor asks if this is her husband, Gülnaz does not speak. The prosecutor repeats the question, and, continuing to look straight at the body, she nods and says, "Mmm." Her affirmative gesture remains inadequate for the prosecutor, for the law: "I'm asking if it's your husband." Choking up, she speaks. "*Evet.*" "Yes." The prosecutor asks if she's sure. She replies, "Emhum." "Okay," he says and asks Şakir to cover the body. The prosecutor then continues with the formalities of the report, ascertaining from Gülnaz that she went to the police because he had not come home for two days and that she did not know how he died.[98] Of course, of all those gathered in the room, she may not know how Yaşar died, but she may have an idea about why. For her, having seen Kenan taken away, she may know enough about the crime already, so no autopsy is necessary.

Her head is bowed as the men do their jobs. The doctor, off to her side near a window, looks in her direction. This is when the prosecutor reprimands Abidin about his typing errors and Şakir performs his magic trick. The boy is unimpressed, but the doctor smiles—an odd change of expression for him. He glances toward Gülnaz, who is looking away. The prosecutor resumes the proceeding: "Okay, young lady. You're done. You can go. My condolences to you." The heels of her shoes click on the tile floor as she leaves the room. The sound recalls the earlier image of her shoe bobbing up and down, a palpitating sign in a space of open indeterminacy.[99]

By the time the ball is in the doctor's court, many "causes" of Yaşar's death seem *possible*. There's even a possibility that Kenan is not the killer; his brother Ramazan appeared to confess to the crime at the burial site, but it is not clear whether the doctor heard or knows of this confession. If true, however, this would alter the picture significantly: Kenan may be understood as taking the fall for Ramazan, perhaps to fulfill the promise he made to their mother to care for his younger brother.

It is also possible that Kenan, if not *the* killer, is also not *a* killer because it is possible that the death was a drunken accident, and the doctor therefore sees him, and everyone else, as survivors of a terrible accident. The accidental quality of Yaşar's death is suggested precisely when the doctor hesitates to confirm Şakir's suggestion that they "buried him alive." The doctor says, "No, it's not like that," and it may *not* have been like that. They may never have intended to bury him alive or to kill him.

The ball is in the doctor's court, and "court" palpitates. Who are the judges and what are the evidentiary criteria? At the suspenseful moment of deciding what to report, the doctor may be thinking of his responsibility in courts of judgment other than those of the state. In the autopsy room, the doctor is trying to make sense of Yaşar's death as text, and Yaşar's body is not the only body under his care. His courtroom is full with survivors of this horrible accident, each awaiting his judgment. The doctor is about to give them justice as an agent of their living on.

The autopsy commences with another display of bureaucratic indifference and squabbling. When the men discover, as the doctor states, that "the body was determined to be wearing no underpants," Şakir coldly remarks, "The old man went around ready for action," and Abidin lets out a laugh. The doctor, losing patience, casts a stern glance in Abidin's direction.[100] That is not all. As Abidin and Şakir gather Yaşar's belongings to give to Gülnaz, Şakir pulls rank over Abidin, snidely saying, "Don't hang around" and "Make yourself useful" even as Abidin, to his credit, is carefully doing just that. He walks out of the room with the bag for Gülnaz. While he is in the hallway, the doctor stands by the window looking outside. Şakir, after adjusting something near the body, swaggers to the side of the room, folds his arms, and leans against the wall.

In the next image, the doctor and Şakir are leaning over the body from different sides of the autopsy table. Şakir slices into the body and, off camera, blood pours into a bucket below. Şakir rips, tears, and cracks the body open. The doctor focuses intensely on moving the procedure along. He speaks in a commanding voice, with forceful authority.

"The cerebrum and cerebellum were removed. Extensive subarachnoid hemorrhaging, epidural hematoma, and contusion were identified on the cerebral and cerebellar surfaces." The doctor wipes his forehead with his forearm.

"The thorax was opened. Open it up, Şakir." Şakir cuts, cracks, and rips the throat open.

The doctor points down: "Keep going down to the end." He waits as Şakir works.

"Lift off the valve." Şakir groans as he does.

"The sternal valve was removed. Neither free fluid nor hemorrhagic fluid were identified in the thoracic cavity. Take the heart out. The heart was removed."

"The whole thing, Doctor?" "*Komple kes.*" Cut it completely.

"The cardiac valves were found to be normal. The lungs were removed. Take them out, Şakir." As he does, the doctor walks over to the window and looks outside again. He wipes his forehead with his sleeve.

The camera turns to Şakir, peering inside where he has just removed the lungs. Something puzzles him. He looks further inside the body and then in the doctor's direction.

"Doctor! (*Hocam!*)"

"Hmm?"

"Doctor, can you look at this? *Hocam, bir bakar mısınız?*" he says softly.

The doctor walks over.

"Doctor, there's a. . . . Look, there's dirt in the windpipe." He pauses briefly. "In this lung, too, actually."[101]

"Hold on."[102]

Both examine the lungs closely. The doctor leans over the body to see them from a different angle.

"Doctor, dirt in the lungs . . ."[103]

The doctor interrupts. "Okay, just hold on."[104] He looks inside the body and takes a deep breath.

"Doctor, you don't suppose they buried him alive?"[105]

Continuing to peer inside the body, the doctor nods his head, seemingly agreeing that there is something there, but he is thinking hard. He seems to nod yes.

Şakir says, "Hmm?"

The doctor eyes Şakir. They both gaze into the body again. Şakir furls his brow in confusion. Again, he asks, "I said, you don't think they buried the guy alive?"[106]

"*Yok, yok yok* . . . No, no no, it's nothing like that, but . . ." Deep in thought, the doctor lifts his head and glances in the direction of the window (not at Şakir). He takes a few breaths and thinks some more.

The camera spins to show Abidin leaning back in a chair in the corner of the room. He is adjusting his sport coat and twiddling his thumbs in front of his laptop.

The camera turns back to the doctor, who turns his head to view the body again.

Abidin says, "Yes, Dr. Cemal. What are we saying here?"[107]

This is the second time that morning that he has been in the position of disclosing the hard truth about the cause of a person's death. He is thinking, hesitating, nodding, and thinking again. His eyes move from Abidin to the body to Şakir and to the window, but he is "keeping an eye on the center."

"Let's say this."[108] He pauses briefly, still eyeing the body. "No abnormalities were encountered in the trachea, esophagus, or soft tissue of the neck."[109]

Şakir looks right at him, but we see only his raised head and back; the camera faces the doctor, who glances briefly at Abidin, then Şakir, and back to Abidin.

The doctor is ready to continue. He nods slightly and, in a slow, deep voice, directs Şakir: "The abdomen was then opened. Open it up, Şakir." He casts a pointed look at Şakir and walks back to the window.

Şakir wipes the side of his face with his shoulder (his hands are a mess). He pauses and looks into the body. Confounded, he glances in the direction of the doctor, then the body, and finally Abidin. There is little doubt that, for him, something is wrong.

The doctor returns to his side of the table. "Go on."

Şakir proceeds, and, as he makes the next incision, blood spurts from the body onto the doctor's face. A large drop lands on his right cheek and a smaller one on his left. He flinches.[110]

He wipes away the larger spot with his surgical glove, steps back, and stares sharply at Şakir.

"Doctor, why don't you step back a bit or you'll get stuff on you."[111]

The doctor steps back a bit more and then walks back to the window as Şakir plumbs further into the body.

Outside, a school bell rings nearby and children are heard playing in that direction. The doctor glances out the window and looks back at Şakir, who is lifting and arranging squishy body parts. The camera shifts to the doctor's view outside, where the boy and his mother are walking down a grassy slope alongside the hospital, in the direction of the school playground, beyond which lies the center of town. The boy is leading the way, stumbling with youthful agility down a dirt path. Gülnaz is moving more slowly, carrying the bag of Yaşar's belongings.

The doctor glances briefly toward the autopsy table but turns his gaze to follow the two as they make their way down the hill. The camera draws close to the doctor's face and the stain of blood on his left cheek, while children's voices resound in the background.

Suddenly, a soccer ball from the playground flies up the hill behind the boy and Gülnaz. The boy runs back, snatches the ball, and with a few steps of forward momentum, kicks the ball high in the air and back onto the playground, as his mother walks on. He sprints to catch up with her, and they disappear on the path to town. At the window, the doctor bows his head slightly in deep thought. He remains there for a few moments, glances briefly in their direction one last time, and then turns and walks away. The camera remains at the window. The children shout and cheer in the background as the credits roll.

A POETICALLY ATTUNED DATA RELATION

The doctor does not aspire to achieve empiricalist precision about the biological cause and effect relations that ended Yaşar's life. For him, the events of the nighttime search signate in a realm of open indeterminacy. He has observed, touched, heard, thought, felt, analyzed, related, questioned, adjusted, guessed, suggested, and pondered in his relations with the wounds, desires, and feelings of Kenan; the health concerns, advice, reprimands, anger, and wisdom of Naci Bey; the bitterness, trials, tragedies, taunts, skepticism, and collapse of the prosecutor; the pain, determination, sadness, generosity, seriousness, and depression of the prosecutor's wife; the loss, tragedy, youthfulness, sadness, worry, and grief of Adem and Gülnaz; and the scattered and routinized indifference of his bureaucratic colleagues. The morning scene is a kind of existential awakening because he has quietly and confidently attended to all these lives *in their particular life situations.*[112] When he looks in the mirror of his office and flips through pictures from his youth and marriage, he views his own life through the prism of all he has absorbed.

"It is nothing like that," he tells Şakir, who sees the dirt in the lungs and presses the doctor to state that Yaşar was buried alive. Perhaps at that moment, the doctor recalls Arap Ali's earlier advice not to "bury" them too soon. "Hey, steady on, doctor!" Arap Ali had insisted in their conversation about mortality. "You've buried us before we're even dead. You shouldn't think like that. We're not done yet!" "Buried" and "alive," as poetic signs, palpitate with possibility. Perhaps the doctor reflects that he should not have buried himself or others while they are still alive: that he shouldn't think like that, that no one should think like that, that no one should let others think like that, that no one should believe that others *would* think like that, that is, that they would bury someone before they are even dead. He shouldn't think like that: *there are other ways to think* about—to *analyze*—the dirt in the lungs.

The events of the night have affectively moved the doctor from attending to death to attending to life. Yaşar is a person, another human being, a life embedded in relations with others who "are not done yet!" They have "a world of things still to do." There is dirt in Yaşar's lungs, but there is also something other than that. Yaşar is not a measurable or objectified body given for narrowly biological data analysis. *How much does empiricalism arbitrate desire? The question of scientific and social scientific explanation.* Yaşar is a subaltern body, with teachings to convey. He is not done yet. He has a world of things still to do. Incidentally, the name Yaşar in Turkish means "lives," as in one who lives. He is literally exhumed because, figuratively, he has a lot of living left in him and teachings to teach. The doctor is attending to the silence of his death at text.

What does the subalternized datum, "dirt in Yaşar's lungs," teach? How may it give rise to an appropriate diagnosis of the cause of Yaşar's suffocation? Where is the source of the pain, and what skills are necessary to find it? Will the newest instruments of Şakir's desires work any better than the ones that fail him now? What, in Gadamer's terms, is the "sphere of judgment and experience out of which the right practical decisions are made?"[113] "The German word for treating a patient," Gadamer observes, "is *behandeln*, equivalent to the Latin *palpare*. It means, with the hand (*palpus*), carefully and responsibly feeling the patient's body so as to detect strains and tensions which can perhaps help to confirm or correct the patient's own subjective localization, that is, the patient's experience of pain."[114] Once the source of the pain has been found, once the cause of the disequilibrium has been located, what does one say, write, or report to others, *all* others, about it? *Report* is from the Latin *reportare*, meaning to carry or bring back. How is the doctor to carry what is happening in Yaşar's body to his others? Their world is gone, how is he to carry them? The doctor is their interlocutor, who is in between Yaşar's death and their living on. Whatever he will say, write, or report is subjective, but it is not only that. It is inter-subjective, and relational, and the doctor knows this. One cannot report by oneself.

What does the dirt in the lungs speak, write, and report to others? What ought to be reported to them? Notice the immense distance between the discovery of the dirt in lungs and all possible legitimate responses to Abidin's question, "What are we saying here, Doctor?" There is as much distance between the two as there is between the dirt and a clear intention to bury Yaşar alive. If what is said about any piece of data always "goes beyond the data"—a central tenet of postpositivist philosophy of science—there is so much more that goes beyond the dirt.[115] There is both other data (other dirt, like the uncertain father-hood of his son) and something other than dirt in the lungs, like *survivre* made possible by the doctor's intimate, atten-tive treatment of the murdered man in the context of his life-world. If the dirt and lungs are data, they are also more than data because other things are happening. The friendship and betrayal between Yaşar and Kenan, for example, does not come into view with the dirt. Even were the doctor to report the blockage in the lungs, whatever happened the night of the murder as it relates to the experience and lives of the persons involved will remain unknown. And yet the data, the dirt in the lungs, gives all this to the doctor for his bearing and caring responsibility.

Ercan Kesal made the doctor an accomplice or partner to the crime. Viewed as an effort to minimize the severity of the crime (and reduce Kenan's sentence), the doctor does indeed share in the guilt. The reasons for this lie in his attunement, as a doctor, to the pain human beings endure in the course of life's injurious accidents: a suicide that follows an affair and a murder that occurs after a hurtful truth slips out. As the doctor attunes to one life, it is as though he attunes to them all. He lets their collective darkness enfold his weary soul and partners with them in an ethical embrace. It is his *personality* (*kişilik*), his *character*, to bear and care for the vulnerable.

The main teaching of every subaltern figure in the film is that the causes of death, bereavement, and suffering lie not only in biological causality but in the pain that human beings inflict upon one another in their most intimate relations. It is the awful reality that the causes of the two deaths are the same: betrayal. Indeed, nothing abnormal there. One might want to point to intervening causes, but those of us who have lived the fragility of human relations know that infidelity and betrayal can destroy foundations of trust needed to survive, to live on, in the world. It is not too difficult to imagine the life-shattering anguish that Yaşar must have felt when he encountered the possibility that neither his son nor his marriage were what he believed them to be. It is not hard to imagine that the conflicts over fatherhood and honor were the primary social causes of Yaşar's chronicled death. To report that he may have been buried alive is to open up a can worms that could harm Gülnaz and her son. Does the doctor feel the need to save *their* lives by *not* evoking the trauma of betrayal that claimed Yaşar's? The doctor receives the lives of these survivors of life's accidents into his ethical bearing and care and intervenes to rewrite the practice of autopsy reporting. He does so to spare them. Adem had peeked into the autopsy room. Maybe he wanted to be spared the pain and consequences of the sins of those adults around him. Maybe this is what the prosecutor's daughter would want. Maybe this is what all the children playing on the playground would want. The goal of emphasizing their innocence was part of the intentions of the filmmakers.[116]

The doctor has turned the postmortem pathology into a pathological good deed for the sake of the living on of Yaşar's survivors. The deed lessens their suffering and gifts them a chance to continue their lives and be reincorporated into the community without the additional pain of believing he was buried alive. "No abnormalities were encountered" is *profound support* for their healing and living on after Yaşar's living and dying.

As the search party arrived at the hospital earlier that morning, an angry crowd of men had clamored for revenge, furious and ready to inflict more violence. On his own the doctor cannot disrupt these enormous forces and restore a prior equilibrium— *what* prior equilibrium? But he is sensitive to these societal pathologies, and he can, as a doctor, reduce the harm they engender. If his decision to conceal the dirt is a pathological deed, it is a pathological *de*-pathologization of the world outside the autopsy room.[117] In this regard, he is attuned to, caring for, and bearing the fate of the entire community. He doctors the record, not in the sense of falsifying, but in the sense of addressing the many ills that have presented themselves to him for judgment, treatment, and explanation.

The pathologies of the bureaucratic order within which the doctor works are relevant here as well, as emphasized by the filmmakers. Bureaucracy is not only pathological because it depersonalizes human relationships. It is pathological because it is founded on the pessimistic premise that human beings cannot organize or address their collective affairs without specialized expertise. The state rationalizes a mythology of bureaucratic objectivity as essential to sustainable life. But does it *sustain life*? The doctor uses his authoritative expertise and specialized position within the bureaucratic order in the service of short- and long-term social healing. Its order in Anatolia does not encourage errors, but, crucially, provides room for them. Naci Bey shares a cigarette with the accused murderer, and Arap Ali drops a few melons next to the head of the body in the trunk of his car. There's room for unexpected relations, for the cigarette, for the melons. And there's room for a little bit of humor, bickering, and nomadic conversation. Decisions like the doctor's add a little bit more life to the life that flourishes in these moments of poetic possibility.

The technocratic autopsy specialist wants better instruments, but the doctor insists that they have what they need to analyze the body. They already have what people under their care need: the capacity for poetic attunement. "What are we saying here, doctor?" In the silence of the moment of decision, when he pauses and thinks hard about what to say, the doctor teaches the importance, and risks, of being an agent for the living on of the lives of others. In that profound pause, he bears empiricalist expectations and simultaneously undermines them in his bearing and caring for their others: he releases a poetically attuned relationship to data into the protocols of professional neutrality and bears and cares for the lives of those to whom he is responsible. In the theoretical expression of *Once Upon a Time in Anatolia*, analyses of the lives of others are only always *once* upon *a* time. In other words, analytical efforts are always unique and singular. In the Anatolias of our research, there is no absolute requirement that, at any given time or with any given data, what is said, written, or reported from the data must be said, written, or reported in a uniform way. Uniformity is not the norm—attunement is. The doctor *knows* this and, in the final autopsy scene, carries out a bold act of poetically attuned support. Characterizations of his act as erroneous, nihilistic, or symbolic of his subjective, existential awakening obscure the deeply relational, poetically attuned meaningfulness of his intervention in the practice of social scientific explanation.

A close friend and I met with Ercan Kesal for coffee in Istanbul in November 2018. I had gone to meet him at a book signing a few weeks earlier. As he signed my collection of his books, I introduced myself and told him I've been teaching Once Upon a Time in Anatolia *for years and would love to talk with him about what he meant when he described the doctor's decision as a* "patolojik bir iyilik"—*a pathological good deed. He looked me straight in the eyes and said, "It was just like that." Before I could finish my introduction, he had written his email and cell phone number on the title page of* Aslında . . .

When we met a few weeks later, Ercan Bey told us about some of the experiences behind the story, such as the sympathetic liking he had taken to the suspect during the early part of the search. The man was handsome, polite, and respectful, he said. But he also described a total loss of hope for humanity when the search party discovered the annihilated body of the murdered man. The handsome, polite, and respectful man and his companions had "torn the body into pieces." He also said that he didn't like the local officials at all. He recalled his days as a rebel in the local bureaucracy, where he was once scolded by the local kaymakam, *an old friend of his, for tossing useless official paperwork into the trash.*

We urged him to help us understand the meaning of a pathological good deed. He recalled writing the phrase and said that he had initially thought of the doctor's decision as a good one, but he added "pathological" to "weaken it" a little bit. The deed has some goodness in it, he said, but it is not a complete good. The good and the bad, the optimistic and the pessimistic, travel together in Once Upon a Time in Anatolia.[118] *He insisted that without consent,[119] an act that affects others "is not good." "In fact, it's a bad deed"* ("Aslında bir kötülük"). *Moreover, he added, the consequences of the doctor's action are not so clear. A lighter sentence for Kenan, for example, could have harmful, even dangerous, consequences for Yaşar's survivors.*

I explained to Ercan Bey that I have been teaching the doctor's act as an illustration of subaltern, poetically attuned data analysis. So, I pressed him further on other possible teachings *in the doctor's decision not to report the dirt in Yaşar's lungs. What made the deed pathological?*

Ercan Bey registered my deeper curiosity. He told us another story from his service in the town. The mother of a family died, and the son went to another town for work. While he was away, the father sexually abused the daughter. The son returned, found out, and killed his father. The son's representatives came to him, Ercan Bey, to ask him for a mental incompetency report for the son's legal defense. He provided it—but immediately added that, if the same circumstances presented themselves, he's not sure if he would do so again. His implication was that he did something that was sympathetic to the son, that it was a good, compassionate, and just deed. What he wanted to emphasize, however, was that what he did was not as such a good thing. It's more complicated than that. What he did was—now he turned the subject to the doctor in the film—what he did was about his own journey (kendi yolculuğu), *process, or place in life; his own reckoning* (hesaplaşma); *his own development or sense of where he was and was going* (ilerleme). *He did something in the moment that, at that moment, he just did. These are things in this life that we do to make ourselves feel good* ("Bu hayat içinde kendiminizi iyi hissettiğimiz şeyler bunlar"). *At the end of the film, the doctor feels he has done right; but what he did was not objectively good. It was deeply* subjective (öznel)—*the central existential theme, as we have seen, in the filmmakers' interpretations of the doctor's decision.*

In the conversation, I struggled at moments in my rusty Turkish to explain what I hoped to write about the autopsy scene. My friend Gürol, one of my closest on earth, picked up the conversation and told Ercan Bey about my careful hermeneutical work with texts and more about me as a teacher. "He asks his students what is in their understanding as they read and talks with them," my friend said. "And he doesn't grade them. He converses with them about their learning experience." Ercan Bey needed to get going—his son had a basketball game—but just before he stood up and invited us to return for more conversation, a wide smile came across his face. He gestured toward me and said, "He's in pursuit of pathological goodness, too!"[120]

4

THINGS GIVEN

If we are not to remain lost in the present we have little choice save to retrace our steps. By uncovering and recovering lost meanings, conceptual histories enable us to escape the politically stultifying confines of a parochial and increasingly dangerous present.

—Terence Ball, James Farr, and Russell L. Hanson[1]

A POETIC HISTORY OF DATA

In his "historical sketch" of "the early history of the concept of data," Daniel Rosenberg discusses Joseph Priestley's 1788 *Lectures on History and General Policy*, in which Priestley "refers to the facts of history as 'data.'"[2] Rosenberg contextualizes Priestley's observation: "Priestley was an early innovator in the field we now call data graphics. His 1765 *Chart of Biography* is a great achievement in this field, an engraved double-folio diagram displaying the lives of about two thousand famous historical figures on a measured grid. It was one of the earliest works to employ the conventions of linearity and regularity now common in historical timelines and the most important work of its kind published in the eighteenth century."[3]

Rosenberg reproduces an image of the *Chart*, from the Rare Book Division of Princeton University Library, and underscores Priestley's other contributions to the history of empiricist science. He mentions "the isolation of oxygen from air in 1774" and Priestley's "interest in aggregate phenomena" (or "large constellations of information"). Priestley "examined fields of scientific endeavor quantitatively, grouping historical figures by their domains of achievement and plotting their lives on a measured timeline in order to observe patterns of occurrence and variations in density"—like Dr. Cemal in *Once Upon a Time in Anatolia*.[4]

The doctor also received aggregate phenomena as entrusted to him for his bearing and caring responsibility. He grouped historical figures—the woman who predicted the timing of her own death, Yaşar, Kenan, Gülnaz, and Adem—by their domains of achievement, plotting their lives on measured and palpitating timelines. An innovator, he intervened in the scientific endeavor of autopsy by observing, in attunement, "patterns of occurrence and variations of density" in the subaltern lives of those under his care.[5] In other words, Doctor Cemal's poetically attuned data analytics are also significant to the history of data.

As the *history* of data recedes from its conventional empiricist associations and welcomes poetically attuned data encounters like the doctor's, a need for clarity about the *meaning* of "data" in poetically attuned data analysis arises. What conception of data underlies poetic attunement, and how might this conception alter the history of data?

To address these questions, I propose three related engagements: First, a sketch of the wide variety of meanings data has had over time; second, an extensive interpretive analysis of data's earliest usages, including in landmark, seventeenth-century texts of the history of science and social science; and third, a poetically attuned engagement with salient aspects of that history that receives the otherness of data's historical usages as entrusted to the care of the other, to our care. Taken together, these three engagements prove immensely fruitful in revealing data's *foundational poetics*.

THE GIVENS

Jonathan Furner's clarifying historical essay, "Data: the Data," shows that "data" palpitates with various meanings and usages across time and context. At least since its sixth-century link to the word "date," "data" has never only meant "things given." And, even when it has, that which is given has varied considerably, from gifts given by another person, nature, or God to premises and values used in scientific, theological, or philosophical reasoning. Furner's account provides a valuable reference point for our discussion. He classifies and dates nine different historical "lives" or interpretations of data: classical (ca. 100 BCE), documentary (ca. 100 BCE), ecclesiastical (ca. 1614), geometric (ca. 1645), mathematical (ca. 1704), epistemic (ca. 1648), informational (ca. 1630), computational (ca. 1980), and diaphoric (ca. 2000) interpretations.[6]

The classical interpretation refers to data's meaning in the Latin language, "the form of the language used in the period roughly between 100 BCE and 200 CE," to mean "things given," from the Latin *dare* ("to give").[7] Furner points out that *datum* literally means "that which is given," or "gift," "the plural *data*, then, maybe translated as 'things given' or 'gifts.' "[8]

The documentary interpretation refers to a different conjugational possibility of *dare* and means "things sent," "in the specific sense of a statement at the beginning or end of a letter—a statement not only of time at which, but also of the place from which, the letter was sent."[9] Furner observes that the *Oxford English*

Dictionary etymologically connects the Latin *data* to the English word "date." The primary etymology of "date" links it to the French *dat*, but the *OED* notes as well that the word for date in postclassical (sixth-century) Latin was *data:* "the feminine singular of *datus*, past participle of *dare*, to give (see datum, n.)."[10]

The ecclesiastical interpretation elaborates the substantive meaning of "given" in a theological context to mean "that which is given by God." God is the "Giver."[11] Furner quotes Thomas Tuke, an early-seventeenth-century clergyman, who wrote, "Every Sacrament is a Mysterie, but every Mysterie is not a Sacrament. Sacraments are not *Nata*, but *Data*: Not Naturall, but by Divine appointment."[12] Furner further archives the use of several early-seventeenth-century Latin phrases, like *gratia gratis data* ("grace freely given") and *data desuper* ("given from above") "that occasionally appear in religious texts of early-seventeenth-century England."[13]

The related geometric, mathematical, and epistemic interpretations view data as the "things given" or "known" in order to deduce, determine, or know other things that are given as well. Furner traces these still very familiar meanings to Euclid's second-century BCE work, *Dedoména*, written in Greek, which "opened with" a "form of the passive perfect participle of δίδωμι (dídōmi, 'I give')," and the language of "the given" pervades the text.[14] *Dedoména* addresses "the nature of that-which-is-given in geometrical problems, and ways of deducing what additional facts are also 'given' (i.e., determinable) once the known facts, the premises, are taken into account."[15] The latter givens are sometimes referred to as the *data quaesita*s (from *quaero*, "sought").[16] *Dedoména* was translated into Latin in the twelfth century and "was given the title *Data*"![17] "The first English translation of *Data*, by 'two students of mathematics' (John Leeke and George Serle), was included with an edition of Euclid's *Elements* in

1661; the work would have been known to some English writers before then, of course, through the various printed editions that existed of the Latin translation."[18] Furner follows the *OED* and notes the earliest written usage of the geometric meaning in English appears to be in 1645 by "the Scottish maverick" Thomas Urquhart, who defined "data" in the lexicon of a work on trigonometry, as "the parts of a Triangle, which are given us, whether they be Sides or Angles, or both."[19]

Furner's epistemic interpretation of data generalizes the geometric and mathematical usages, such that data means any "things," "conditions," or "truths or premises" that are "given" "in order to find out other Things . . . which are unknown, or sought for" in *any kind* of knowledge- or truth-seeking argument.[20] Furner dates this usage to the mid eighteenth century but also cites Daniel Rosenberg's reference to a 1646 usage listed in the *OED* by the clergyman Henry Hammond. Rosenberg argues that Hammond's usage of the phrase "heap of data" in a "theological tract" refers to "a list of theological propositions accepted as true for the sake of argument—that priests should be called to prayer, that liturgy should be rigorously followed, and so forth."[21] Rosenberg finds in Hammond's usage an early example of the "irreducible," *rhetorical* meaning of data as "facts or principles" that are agreed to be "beyond argument" in any argumentative context.[22] "In mathematics, theology, and every other connotative realm in which the term was used," Rosenberg writes, "[data] was something given by the conventions of argument."[23]

According to Furner's informational interpretation, data are "attribute values" that appear as the "content" of "systematically organized tables of numerical values."[24] These values—like numerical data reported on statistical charts or tables—"record and report the frequency and quantities resulting from observations and measurements conducted in accordance with the principles and standards of scientific method."[25] Informational data are "manipulated as 'givens' for statistical analysis."[26] This clearly empiricist-quantitative interpretation also originates in the seventeenth century and evolves in the nineteenth century to include nonnumerical information or the "attribute values" of qualitative social science.[27]

Furner's final two interpretations, which he describes very briefly, are the contemporary computational interpretation of data as binary digits (or "bits" of os and is) "processed" by computers "at the most fundamental level" and the diaphoric interpretation that "treats" data at different objective, subjective, and expressive "levels" of linguistic and informational analysis.[28] In his discussion of the computational interpretation, he issues a more generally useful caution against conflating different meanings of "data." "A source of misunderstanding" in contemporary discussions of data, he writes, "is a tendency to conflate three related but distinct interpretations: data as evidence; data as (typically numeric) attribute-values; and data as bits."[29]

ANOMALIES

1630: W. Batten, *Most Easie Way Finding Sunnes Amplitude* (*table*): Data.[30]

1645 T. Urquhart, Trissotetras 53, The verticall Angles, according to the diversity of the three Cases being by the foresaid Datas thus obtained.[31]

1646 H. Hammond, *Let.* 4 Nov. in Copy of Papers betwixt Author of Pract. Catechisme & Mr. Ch. (1647) 83. From all this heape of *data* (if they were *concessa* too) it would not follow that it was necessary . . . to abolish all set Formes in the publique service of God.[32]

1691 W. Petty, *Treat. Naval Philos.* in T. Hale, *Acct. New Inventions* 128,
Out of what Data arises the knowledge.[33]

1691 *Philos. Trans. (Royal Soc.)* 16, 498, From these data . . . the time of
this Invasion will be determined to a day.[34]

These five entries represent the "earliest known" usages of
data or datum in the *Oxford English Dictionary*.[35] One salient
feature of the conceptual histories of "data" we have reviewed
is their use of the *OED* as an authoritative source. Furner discusses several usages from the *OED* in constructing his classical and documentary interpretations, and he and Rosenberg
describe early usages listed in the *OED* by Thomas Urquhart
(1611–1660), Henry Hammond (1605–1660), and William Batten
(1601–1667).[36]

Two other, earliest known entries in the *OED* include an
anonymous 1691 entry, under the first entry for "datum" as "an
item of (chiefly numerical) information, esp. one obtained by scientific work, a number of which are typically collected together
for reference, analysis, or calculation."[37] A Google search of this
entry identifies its author as the renowned Astronomer Royal
Edmond Halley (1656–1742), after whom Halley's Comet is
named. The second usage is by William Petty (1623–1687),
another major figure in the history of science, under the second
definition of "datum," as "something given or granted; something
known or assumed as fact, and made the basis of reasoning; an
assumption or premise from which inferences are drawn."[38]

Further review of these five seventeenth-century *OED* entries
taken together reveals several curious anomalies in "the history
of data" that invite additional hermeneutical inquiry.

Furner cites Hammond's "heap of data" in his account of
the ecclesiastical interpretation but provides an earlier, explicitly theological precedent for that usage—Tuke's "Not Nata, but

Data."Tuke's absence in the *OED* is perplexing. It also overlooks the 1661 use of data in the translation of Euclid's *Dedoména*. Also odd is that Rosenberg provides a different title for Hammond's work than the one provided by the *OED*, and Furner's citation to Urquhart's contribution to the geometric interpretation of data differs from the one listed in the *OED*. In subaltern, poetically attuned terms, the latter is especially peculiar.

Urquhart's usage in the *OED* is "datas," not "data." It is listed under the very first definition of data as "a count noun: an item of information; a datum; a set of data."[39] Datas appears to be a plural rendering of data, but, according to every etymological reference point in the history of data, data is already plural.[40] The significance of this discrepancy grows because Urquhart's 1645 usage is the *first* seventeenth-century usage of the concept in written prose. (Batten's 1630 usage is a heading in a table.) Nowhere in the given histories or authoritative sources on data is datas part of its early English language history, except in this particular entry. Datas cannot be read in relation to the standard grammatical information. In the discourse of data, datas may be read as a deviation, a typographical error, or a predeveloped form or spelling of the word that must be corrected. Neither datas nor its *teachings* can be recognized or acknowledged in their difference.

DATA'S OTHER LIVES

Even when the usages of data in its early Anglophone history lend themselves to classification according to Furner or Rosenberg's organizing schemas, those usages palpitate with additional meaningfulness in the contexts of the varied purposes of the texts in which they appear. With no exaggeration, it may be said that these texts touch on monumental matters in the history of human efforts to know and navigate life in the world—issues such as mathematical precision, scientific objectivity, salvation, empire, pedagogy, and literary creativity.

Petty and Batten used "data" in their advocacy for the use of modern scientific techniques to enhance the nautical capacities and maritime interests of the British Empire—Batten through a proposed logarithm for calculating, with unprecedented precision, one's location on the surface of the Earth, and Petty with guidance for the construction of seaworthy ships. Petty's usage has additional significance. Research on the text in which he employed "data" suggests that this renowned champion of neutrality in social science viewed his social scientific work as a means to promote his own standing within the hierarchies of British power in Ireland, adding explicitly instrumental and strategic dimensions to the use of "data" in the history of the concept. Halley's usage more closely parallels objectivist scientific research. He used the word as part of a dedicated effort to apply modern scientific techniques to the resolution of questions left unanswered by traditional historical sources. Like Batten, Halley's "value-free" analysis is backgrounded by British national and imperial curiosity: the particular historical puzzle to which Halley applied his scientific knowledge was the identification of the accurate date of the first Roman invasion of Britain.

These usages differ significantly from those of Hammond and Urquhart. The cleric Hammond writes "heape of data" in a significant argument with a representative of church orthodoxy over forms of worship requisite for the salvation of a Christian believer. While his usage is rhetorical, the content of the theological argument in which he was involved discloses data's additional *ideational* importance, according to which data are not "what is given" or "taken for granted" in any general or abstract sense. Rather, the things that are given are *ideas*—heaps of them—that interlocutors exchange in the heat of philosophical arguments. Urquhart's usage similarly exceeds prior categories. He combines what can only be described as *scientific* and *poetic* qualities in a self-conscious effort to innovate the terms of geometric learning with ingenious literary flair.

DATA, KNOWLEDGE, POWER, AND STRATEGY

"Data" appears as a heading of the four tables in Batten's 1630 work, *A Most Plaine and Easie Way for the Finding of the Sunnes Amplitude and Azimuth, and Thereby the Variation of the Compasse, by Logarithm.*[41] In the essay, Batten—mathematician, "English naval officer and Member of Parliament"—offers a logarithm to calculate the magnetic declination of the Earth.[42] The declination is "the difference between the true *Meridian* of the world and the *Meridian* of the *Loadstone*, which is pointed out by the Compasse or Needle." The latter, Batten observes, "is for the most part *variable* as you sayle to different places." The loadstone—literally, "way-stone," the magnetic element of the compass—did not consistently show "the way."[43] Hence Batten's promise, in the title of his essay, to show the "most plaine and easie *way*" (emphasis added) to calculate the declination. That way is logarithmic arithmetic, which Batten describes as "the most easiest of all *Arethmaticall worke*."

In the specific context of Batten's calculations, the meaning of "data" may be said to be "chiefly numerical, navigational measurements for the calculation of the declination." "Data" is written as the heading of tables that indicate latitude coordinates, their direction, their mathematical complement, and the declination.[44] Batten's first "example" includes the coordinates "40.deg.30. North" for the "Complement, Latitude" and "20.— 40. North" for the "Declination." Similar tables with increasing amounts of information follow. Batten's attribute values include geometric figures. Mathematical operations pervade the essay.[45] Furner aptly cites this usage as an early example of data's informational interpretation.[46] Noteworthy is Batten's explicit use of the language of "the given" to describe the geometric bases for his calculations. The meaning of data is there—as things to be given—even when the word is not.

> It is to be considered that in the Doctrine of Triangles, it is required in the solution of any question there are three thinges to be giuen in any Triangle, before the question can bee answered, which in this for finding the true Azimuth of the Sunne; you are to know or imagine your Latitude, the Complement thereof is one side of a Triangle (which is the distance betweene the Pole and the Zenith) the Complement of the Sunnes Declination is another side of the same Triangle (which is the distance between the Sunne and the Pole) then is the Complement of the Almicanter the other side (which is the distance betweene the Sunne and the Zenith.)

Batten's contribution may be situated in the broader human scientific effort to develop precise measuring tools to know one's location on the Earth, as that location changes. According to the geophysicist William Lowrie, the difference between the geographical meridian and the magnetic meridian had been known "to vary according to place" since the sixth century:

> It was known to the Chinese around 500 A.D., in the Tang dynasty, that magnetic compasses did not point exactly to

geographical north, as defined by the stars. . . . By the 14th century, the ships of the British navy were equipped with a mari-
ner's compass, which became an essential tool for navigation. It
was used in conjunction with celestial methods, and gradually it
became apparent that the declination changed with position on
the globe. During the 15th and 16th centuries the world-wide pattern of declination was established. By the end of the 16th century,
Mercator recognized that declination was the principal cause of
error in contemporary map-making.[47]

Batten's use of "data" is thus part of a time-immemorial, scientific endeavor to ascertain true, fixed, and permanent geographic knowledge. "Fixt and permanent being the same, always
in one and the same place; (although there may be difference
in the touch of the *Stone*, and in the obseruations of different
men)." Mathematics, with data as its heading, is the new way to
correct for imprecision in limited geographic techniques.

In both Batten's 1630 and Urquhart's 1645 usages, "data" gains
early currency in the English language in Euclidean intellectual
circles. Batten's usage, however, relates more closely to the meanings that Petty and Halley give to the concept than to Urquhart's.
Petty and Halley, major figures in the history of science, use it
in discussions directly related to developing more precise knowledge of nautical affairs—Petty to describe, in elaborate engineering detail, sturdy shipbuilding practices for the British Navy, and
Halley to achieving precise knowledge about Caesar's naval invasion of Britain's coast in 55 BCE.

The *OED* dates Petty's usage as 1691; however, he died in 1687.
The text cited by the *OED* appears at the end of a posthumously
published essay, "A Treatise on Naval Philosophy," written and
shared by Petty with his friends in 1671.[48] In the words of the
intellectual historian Ted McCormick, the treatise was "a sort of

prospectus or set of heads [lists] for a [longer] treatise on naval matters of all sorts."[49] Petty's friends "hoped that one day he might be persuaded to expand it."[50] As it turned out, he never did. The twenty-odd pages (in today's length) were "all that ever existed of the 'Treatise.'"[51]

The work has three parts: "A Phisico-Mathematical Discourse of Ships and Sailing"; 'Of Naval Policy"; and "Of Naval Oeconomy or Husbandry."[52] Each part has several chapters, and each chapter contains short, numbered assertions. The usage of "data"—in 1671, the fourth written usage recorded by the *OED*—appears in chapter 4 of the first part, in the fourth assertion (of five). The first part is the most lengthy and focuses, as its title suggests, on the physics and mathematics of shipbuilding and sailing. Its first three chapters offer extremely detailed technical observations and commentary on nautical physics, the design and construction of naval ships, and considerations of navigational circumstances. The text displays Petty's naval, shipping, engineering, and nautical competences.[53] McCormick observes that Petty was "an inveterate inventor" and that "his most famous invention was a 'double-bottomed boat' designed to sail faster and with a smaller crew than conventional ships of the same tonnage."[54] He knew the subject matter.

"Data" emerges in a set of assertions where Petty applies what he calls the "speculative" considerations of assertions in the prior chapters to the actual practice of shipbuilding—"the practical part of Ship-Carpentry, which is the Art of imitating the moddel afore-mentioned, and of composing a Ship, not out of one but several thousand pieces of Wood and Iron." Petty offers five analytical guides. He uses "data" in the fourth:

1. The History of the Practice of the best Shipwrights in England, Holland, and Portugal, in their building Ships as aforesaid.

2. Supposing that a Ship commonly reckoned 150 Tun, be a fit size to sail in round the World: And that the just strength of every part of the same were certainly known and determined, 'tis desired to know of what size and scantling each correspondent Timber must be of, to make a greater or lesser Vessel of equal strength, and to compute the difference of strength between greater and smaller Vessels of the common Built.

3. How to make practical Equations between the strength of Timber and Irons, and between Trenailes and Bolts, &c.

4. Out of what Data arises the knowledge of the strength of Knees, Bolts and Nails.

5. That vast Ships of 1500 Tuns, do require a different way of Carpentry of Masts and Yards than what is used, and particularly in no Case a Mast above 30 inches through and above ¾ the present length, is requisite.[55]

Data's usage here, like Batten's, aligns with what Furner calls the epistemic and informational interpretations. Petty asserts that ship construction requires "determining" or "certainly knowing" quantitative values corresponding to the strength of the ship's knees, bolts, and nails. Those quantifications would be the "[informational] data" out of which "arises the [epistemic] knowledge of" the said strength.[56] As with Batten's calculation for the Earth's magnetic declination, Petty's calculations of the strength of knees, bolts, and nails has useful maritime consequences: strength is one of many particular "requisite" conditions for constructing vessels that are commonly reckoned to be of the size that "can sail round the world."

The idea of sailing round the world discloses additional purposes of Petty's treatise, about which he is explicit in the closing entries of the work. In the fifth and last chapter of the first part, he endorses the comparative and historical study of "improvements in shipping" construction for purposes of trade and warfare,[57] and, in the second and third parts, he offers recommendations to meet the "interest" of "the King of England, being not only by Right and Custom Soveraign of the Narrow Seas, but having also the best Means and most Concernment to be more considerable at Sea, than any other Prince or State." Only a few pages in length, these latter parts of the treatise offer suggestions for determining "the number of the Tuns of Shipping of which the whole Navy is to consist"; amounts of materials, ordnance, and seamen; and "matters of cost" so that "the same may be done with the least Charge, and with the least Expence of forreign Commodities."[58] Petty further enters into specific considerations of economic "benefits" and "advantages" of trade to the "Shipping Trade in General," "the Fishing Trade," "the Commonwealth," and "the World": "Of what benefit to the World is the Discovery of new Countries, new Passages, new Mines of Gold, of Silver, and of the Longitude itself."[59] Ships built with strong knees, bolts, and nails according to the most advanced knowledge of the day will secure these many benefits. The usage of "data" in Petty's treatise thus resides within the larger purpose of advancing England's economic interests and enlarging the realm of imperial exploration and colonial domination of the world.

According to McCormick's research on this specific text, Petty wrote the treatise with additional concerns in mind, namely his own personal political ambitions. This constitutive interest calls into question Petty's inherited reputation as an early proponent of value-free social science. A friend of Thomas Hobbes and unfavorably named by Karl Marx as the "father of English political economy," Petty is especially known for his work *Political Arithmetick*, written in the 1680s.[60] This classic text in the history of social science established the analytical template for politically neutral, "objective" policy studies in the field of political economy: "quantitative analysis of human and natural resources, advocacy of economic and social policies based on empirical criteria, and numerous practical schemes for improving infrastructure, agriculture, manufacture, and trade."[61] In the book's preface, Petty famously articulated the fundamental presupposition of empiricist social science, namely that all legitimate knowledge derives from empirical observation, where empirical is understood as experienced through the five senses or instruments used to enhance them.

> The Method I take to do this is not yet very usual; for instead of using only comparative and superlative Words, and intellectual Arguments, I have taken the course (as a specimen of Political Arithmetick I have long aimed at): to express my self in terms of *Number*, *Weight*, or *Measure*; to use only Arguments of Sense, and to consider only such causes as have visible Foundations in Nature; leaving those that depend upon mutable Minds, Opinions, Appetites and Passions of particular Men, to the Consideration of Others.[62]

McCormick contests Petty's objectivist reputation by highlighting the explicitly political aims of Petty's most significant social scientific works, *Political Arithmetick* and *The Political Anatomy of Ireland*. They were, McCormick avers, "instrument[s] tailor-made" for the "social engineering" purposes of "a composite monarchy and a colonial empire."[63] He quotes Petty defending "the use of rough estimates in a variety of practical contexts."[64] "The accuracy or precision of the actual numbers Petty used was much less important than the possibilities for action that the kinds of figures he employed—demographic proportions in particular—opened up."[65] Such analysis "was not just actuarial, but 'political' in a transformative sense—not simply to describe the nation's lands but to show the sovereign how to manipulate them."[66] This pattern clearly applies to his treatise and its goal of promoting British imperial supremacy at sea.

Moreover, Petty placed texts like it into circulation in order to secure patronage among officials who could advance his career. According to McCormick, all of Petty's "papers" were "schemes" to "sell economic, political, and social projects to a carefully selected and assiduously pursued audience of powerful men."[67] "Rather than publication as we think of it, this was Petty's goal": to "impress upon the relevant authorities a sense of Petty's ability, both conceptual and, potentially, administrative."[68] Petty apparently sent the "treatise in 1671 to the Accountant-General of Ireland, Robert Wood, a close associate, because Wood "was in a position Petty might have envied."[69] Wood circulated the work to his superiors, who

> read it over with much greediness, crying out several times Excellent things! Rare! &c. and then fell to commend you, & asked what you would have him to do, whether to write to the King about it, or to send to those Heads, or expect the Booke it selfe, (which he hopes you would let him see) or to send you a letter to give the King with the Booke? any thing he would do to promote that which he thought tended so much to the public good. I replyed, I knew nothing more of it then what I had imparted to your Lordship from your letter, nor whether things were yet ripe for publication. He then desired me to remember him unto you, & asked shall we see him in Ireland again? & when?"[70]

McCormick relays that, in 1676, "Petty ultimately received a judgeship in the Admiralty Court," but it "ended badly," and he resigned several years later.[71]

It would be an overstatement to read the usage of "data" exclusively within the context of Petty's personal political ambitions, but these ambitions are nonetheless part of the history of data. With both the king's and his own position of power in clear view, Petty's epistemic usage of the word as a term of engineering and technical knowledge appears to be constituted *as well* by political passion. However the relation between Petty's data-based knowledge and his constitutive political aims is characterized, their connection in the history of data is obscured by any attempt to assimilate Petty's usage to the dominant objectivist-scientific discourse. His strategic ambitions, and the ambitions of his audience, were also *given*, prior to and within the analysis of, his argumentation.

MODERNIST INTERVENTION

More thoroughly consistent with the presuppositions of scientific objectivist discourse is Halley's usage of data in the *Philosophical Transactions of the Royal Society*. In his short paper, the famous mathematician calculates the exact date of Caesar's invasion of Britain in 55 BCE. Although the *OED* entry suggests that his usage was contemporaneous with Petty's, Halley's was actually about twenty years later. Interestingly, Halley's work over time evidences intellectual connections with both Batten and Petty. In 1698, Halley received a temporary commission as captain of the Royal Navy so that he could set sail and measure variations of the compass.[72] By the 1680s, Halley and Petty were apparently aware of each other's work through the Royal Society, Petty as one of its founders and Halley as a prolific contributor to its publications.[73] In one essay, Halley revisited Petty's coauthored work, "Bills of Mortality of London," to rectify through significant mathematical analysis "deductions" that "seemed, even to their authors, to be defective."[74] Petty is, likewise, reported by McCormick to have "traded thoughts" on Halley's "pronouncements on the origins of Mankind and the history of population since the Flood."[75] Halley had earlier "initiated direct discussion on the natural historical accuracy of biblical texts" by using his scientific skills to offer natural scientific, causal accounts for humanity's origins.[76] The biblical stories, in Halley's view, provided only "the moral context," not accurate scientific explanation.[77]

Halley's commitment to achieving greater historical accuracy through modern scientific methods is precisely what produced the 1691 text in which he used the concept of "data." Entitled "A Discourse Tending to Prove at What Time and Place Julius Caesar Made His First Descent upon Britain," Halley declared his purpose to be "the great use of Astronomical Calculation for fixing and ascertaining the Times of Memorial Actions, when omitted or not delivered by the Historian."[78] Halley names Caesar and the Roman historian Dion Cassius as "the authors that mention this expedition with any circumstances" but did not "deliver" on the exact date.[79] The year is certain, he says. It was "in the year of the consulate of Pompey and Crassus," which was "Rome 699, or the 55th before the usual era of Christ."[80] He then retells what is known about the invasion through the available sources, including Caesar's account of the condition of the sea as "*celerem atque instabilem*, quick and uneven."[81] Halley's knowledge of astronomy is central to his dramatic retelling of the invasion: Caesar had only been in Britain for four days. His ships were about to land, "when a sudden tempest arose, with contrary winds, so that some of the ships put back again, others were driven to the westward, not without great danger and coming anchor, they found they could not ride it out: so when night came on, they put off to sea, and returned from whence they came. That same night it was full-moon, which makes the greatest tides in the ocean, and they being ignorant thereof, their galleys, which were drawn on shore, were filled by tide, &c."[82]

Halley reports that, with the autumn equinox approaching, Caesar decided to return to Gaul, postponing a fuller assault until the following year. Halley notes that Caesar's commentaries offer additional details about the location, conditions, and timing of the failed invasion. Halley also translates some of Dion Cassius's reports concerning the site of landing. At that point, Halley uses all this data to deduce the date of the invasion as April 26:

From these data, that it was in the year of the Consulate of Pompey and Crasses; that it was *Exiguâ parte aestatis reliquâ* ["with a little part of the summer still remaining"] and four days before a full-moon, which fell out in the night time; the time of this invasion will be determined to a day: For by the eclipse of the moon, whereof Drusus made so good use to quiet a mutiny in the Pannonian army, on the news of the death of Augustus, it follows that Augustus died Anno Christi 14, which was reckoned anno urbis conditae 767; and that this action was 68 years before, viz. in the 55th year before Christ current. in which year the full-moon fell out August 30, after midnight, or 31st in the morning before day; and the preceding full-moon was August 1, soon afternoon; so that this could not be the full-moon mentioned, as falling in the day time; nor that in the beginning of July, it being not 10 days after the summer solstice, when it would not have been said *exiguâ parte aestatis reliquâ*. It follows therefore that the full-moon spoken of, was on August 30, at night, and that the landing on Britain was August 26, in the afternoon, about a month before the autumnal equinox; which agrees to all the circumstances of the story in point of time.[83]

"Data" here means evidence to calculate a measurement—the numerical date—with precision. This usage is most evidently consistent with Furner's epistemic and informational interpretations. Halley approaches the received evidence as "conditions" that have been "given" "in order to find out other Things . . . which are unknown, or sought for," namely the exact date and place of Caesar's invasion.[84] But his assertions are also a palimpsest of one of data's earliest meanings in the Latin language, as a synonym for the word "date." Recall that *data* was "the first word of [a] formula . . . used as a term . . . referring to the time and day on which a letter was sent." "From these data," he may have said, "the *data* the ships were sent will be determined."

Halley's usage of "data" exemplifies the *modernism* of the modern scientific enterprise. He espied omissions in traditional (biblical and classical-historical) accounts and sought to replace them with up-to-date knowledge using the day's most advanced concepts, theories, techniques, and instruments of measurement. Allan Chapman characterizes Halley's method as a combination of "astute textual criticism and the interpretation of physical evidence."[85] Halley viewed such "combined" historical and natural scientific research as part of "the overall investigation of nature."[86] In such investigation, "the [historical] scholar must be scientific, and the scientist must also be a historian."[87]

Halley addressed his contributions to knowledge to those he described as "the curious"—presumably fellow believers in the powers of modern scientific analysis. "The whole argument," he writes in the conclusion of the essay on Caesar's landing, "will t'is hoped be admitted by the Curious."[88] Similarly, in his critique of Petty's essay on mortality rates, he complements the "curious Sir William Petty" and concludes with hope that "the curious in other cities would attempt" an analysis similar to the one he proposes.[89] "Data" thus gains its meaning in this context of supplying critically updated knowledge for the curious. Out of such data, one might say, arises modern historical knowledge.

In comparison with Petty, who explicitly connected knowledge and the pursuit of power in his use of data, Halley constitutes his historical findings with no other explicit ambition than that of the modern scientific enterprise. In this regard, it is comparable to Batten's, in a very particular sense. Batten used modern scientific knowledge to close the gap and "fix" inadequate understandings of the relation between human beings and nature; Halley uses it to close the gap and fix inadequate understandings in the relation between human beings and their history.

IDEATIONAL DATA

The two remaining seventeenth-century English usages are those of Thomas Urquhart and Henry Hammond. These are the second and third earliest usages of "data" in English writing according to the *OED*, separated only by a year, and their constitutive purposes differ substantially from those reviewed thus far. Furner describes Urquhart as a "maverick" and mentions a usage other than the one listed in the *OED*, and Rosenberg characterizes Hammond's usage of data in a theological context as evidence for his view that the meaning of data since the seventeenth century is "rhetorical."

Hammond's usage indeed occurs in the context of a complex theological dispute, in October and November 1646, with Francis Cheynell (d. 1665) over assertions in Hammond's work, *A Practical Catechism*—"a manual for the young people of [Hammond's] parish, summarizing his understanding of the basic truths of Christianity."[90] Hammond had published the work

anonymously in 1645. Cheynell gave several sermons condemn-
ing it as "contrary to Christian truths."[91]

Their dispute involved different views of Christian salvation
in light of the Fall—God's punishment of Adam and Eve for
their disobedience. *A Practical Catechism* maintained that "it was
still possible to hear, understand, and believe the Gospel even
after the Fall without any special grace" from God.[92] Good works
through dutiful obedience to God's commands mattered in the
life of the Christian believer. Cheynell represented the orthodox
puritan view of the council of the Westminster Assembly that
believed that such obedience was not possible prior to God's
grace.[93] Neil Lettinga summarizes the significance of Hammond's intervention: "If the key question in Christianity is 'what
must I do to be saved?' . . . Hammond said Christians were saved
because God accepted their sincere attempt to obey his commands as sufficient for eternal life; puritan divines said Christians were saved because God accepted Christ's obedience as
sufficient for the salvation of the elect. The importance cannot
be overestimated; it reached down into the heart of their respective understandings of Christianity itself."[94]

Angered by Cheynell's public criticism, Hammond wrote
to him to demand "an exact account in writing . . . of all that
you said in publicke," vigorously contesting the latter's "accusa-
tions" and "false suggestions."[95] Cheynell's response is equally
severe, stating initially that *A Practical Catechism* "does in effect
overthrow the sum and substance of the Gospel."[96] Their
lengthy back-and-forth contains several disputes of theological significance. The concept "data" emerges in an exchange
over the legitimacy of the so-called "set forms of prayer" in the
church—forms of prayer "prescribed" and exemplified initially
by Christ that were conveyed in the liturgies of the apostles
James and Mark.[97]

Cheynell criticizes *A Practical Catechism* for restricting legitimate ministerial prayer to the set forms and thus trying to
standardize church practice according to them. He demands
Hammond "show him the Liturgy which you say was formed in
the Apostles times, and to be continued in the Church."[98] Indeed,
in *A Practical Catechism*, Hammond defends the lawfulness of
the set forms, especially against attempts to make them "unlawful," but he does not restrict all forms of prayer to them.[99] The
set forms, he states, are "ways and forms of serving God publicly,
and . . . means to preserve the true religion from all corruptions
in doctrine,"[100] but "other forms" of prayer may be used by the
church, under conditions of prudence, piety, reverence, and edification.[101] He thus finds Cheynell's demand for clarification to be
"wholly impertinent," summarizing his view as: "Saying that the
holy Ghost enabled the Ministery in the very Apostles times to
forme a Liturgy to continue in the Church, doth not conclude
that that very Liturgy was to bee continued. . . . You see, I said
not, and professe not to have meant in those words 'to continue'
but onely that it might continue (i.e., if the Church thought
good) either so as it was, or with such additions or alterations as
the Church should thinke fit."[102]

Cheynell does not oppose the set forms but wants to make
room for ministers who either question their necessity or pray
without the use of Liturgy (with "ordinary" prayer). He further
asks Hammond to "prove it necessary that any whole entire set
Platforme of Liturgie should bee rigorously imposed upon all
the Ministers of these three Kingdomes of England, &c? Is not
that the thing which you doe so passionately long after, and ear-
nestly contend for?"[103]

In his lengthy response, Hammond consistently reiter-
ates that exercises of "the miraculous gift of prayer" "different
from the set Formes" are permissible, even "alterations" of the

forms are allowable, but he continues to insist that this does not "give the present Church of England . . . leave to cast out all set Forms."[104] Hammond thus distinguishes between abolishing the set forms and seeking their imposition. If their imposition is Cheynell's worst fear, then their becoming unlawful is Hammond's.[105]

At this point, Hammond enters into a set of hypothetical considerations to reiterate and "prove" (Cheynell's term above) his central contention, namely that a change in practice is possible without the abolition of the set forms. He makes two emphatic arguments: one short and one multilayered. The use of "heape of data" emerges in the second. Interspaced between the two is Hammond's terse rejection of Cheynell's demand for original liturgical evidence.

To understand Hammond's use of data—and the reason why Rosenberg finds it rhetorical—it is important to note the *logical* quality of Hammond's assertions. Asked repeatedly to defend and prove his position, he is clearly engaged in a philosophical argument (over theological matters). The "heape of data" are several premises he grants Cheynell so as to affirm, through logical inference, a conclusion that follows from those premises. Substantively, Hammond defends his views in both *A Practical Catechism* and *The View of a New Directory* that the set forms are lawful "in the public service of God." No church deviation if granted or conceded would alter the basic point that the set forms serve God and should not be abolished. No "heape of data" could refute that:

> You see now how little right your conclusion of that fifth *Sect.* had
> to bee induced upon any words of mine: and yet let mee tell you,
> that if it were granted you possible, That *a Minister may pray as in*
> *a Congregation without the use of the Liturgy formed in the Apostles*

times, &c. nay, without the helpe of the late Common-prayer-booke, yet will it not follow from thence, that it is well done to abolish (with this Liturgie) all set Forms, much lesse that it was necessary to abolish this.

To your sixth you already discerne my answer, that neither I nor the Author of the View are obliged to shew you any Liturgie, and avouch that it is (I suppose you meane) that formed in the Apostles times without any interpolation, &c.

In your seventh you will not spend time about the *miraculous gift of prayer*, (which if you had done, and observed the use that I there made of that doctrine to the present purpose, it would have stood you in some stead, at least kept you from being ignorant of my sense, and (the consequent of it) your asking of more questions,) and I will not spend any more time about your severall questions then to tell you, that all that I now, or the Author of the *View* contend for, doth not prove us concern'd in those new *quaeres*: for were it granted, that there were *an ordinary gift of prayer, and that to be stirred up and exercised, that Ministers should study to pray seasonably,* (which I suppose is not to pray *ex tempore* because you say *study) that he that hath not ordinary wisdome to pray as hee ought, is not called by Christ to bee a Minister of the Gospel,* (and yet sure hee that hath that ordinary wisdome to pray as he ought upon premeditation, may pray as hee ought not, upon sudden effusion; and the Liturgie would a litle prevent that, and perhaps enable him to pray more to the edification of the people, then hee is able to doe, who yet is able in some degree to pray as hee ought) and *that it doth not follow that the Liturgies under the name of* St. James and St. Marke *should be rigorously imposed, nay, that it were true that there are some endewed with the spirit of prayer,* (as that is by you set, for somewhat more then the ordinary gift, and which it will bee heard for any man to demonstrate to others that hee is truly possest of) were, I say, all this granted to you, yet sure from all this heape of *data* (if they were *concessa* too) it would not follow that it was necessary, or so much as tolerably well done, to abolish all set Formes in the publique service of God, which was the prime thing by that *View* insisted on.[106]

Hammond's usage of "data" here is fully logical and philosophical—that is, it has the specific meaning of premises that are agreed upon in this context of argumentation, as Rosenberg discerns. Hammond's likening the data to *concessa*, or concessions, further supports this interpretation. Hammond is *conceding* Cheynell's premises—they are *givens* for him—to underscore his central claim that is not refuted by them, namely, that there is no justification for abolishing the set forms, and that these should be understood as undertaken in the service of God. Hammond essentially says, I grant, concede, or allow as "given" all that you have said, and it still would not follow that it is necessary to abolish the set forms.

This is not Hammond's only usage of the word "heape" (or "heap") in this text. Earlier, he describes a "heape of exceptions" in reference to other objections, and, in the heat of their argument, Hammond writes that Cheynell makes a "heap of mistakes" when Cheynell describes Hammond as being "too angry" for being "reproached and slandered."[107] (Hammond counters that he was "reproached without being too angry" and distinguishes between "being reproached" and a "reproach.") The meaning of "heap/e" is something like "a great amount." It expresses an assertive intensity in Hammond's response to what he takes to be Cheynell's unwarranted criticisms.

The intensity of this clerical dispute recalls the issues at stake—the salvation of the Christian believer—and indicates that the phrase "heap/e of data" has dimensions of meaning additional to its logical function. If, for Rosenberg, data has the general *rhetorical* meaning of that which is given or taken for granted in an argumentative context, then, in Hammond's concession of Cheynell's views, what is given or taken for granted are the *principled views or ideas* of one's interlocutor. Data's emergence in a high-stakes disagreement about salvation practices suggests an *ideational* quality of Hammond's use of "data." This ideational quality of the data is constitutive of its usage, even as "heape of" suggests a significant, quantifiable number. Indeed, "heape" is an idea about a large quantity. This aspect of "heap/e of data" points to an additional feature of the meaning of data, too often overlooked by conventional associations between data and quantification, namely that all data, qualitative or quantitative, are *ideas*. Numbers are ideas that quantifiers have about the world. Hammond's usage in 1646 is instructive in the history of "data" beyond its rhetorical function.[108]

POETIC DATAVENTIONS

I have quoted extensively from Hammond's text to illustrate its discursive difference from prior usages, and I do the same with *The Trissotetras* (1645), Urquhart's trigonometry study in which he used "data," "datas," "data qaesitas," and what I will call, in the spirit of his work, other *dataventions*. *The Trissotetras* is one of the most linguistically inventive texts I have ever encountered. Richard Boston, the editor and translator of Urquhart's works, points out that, despite *The Trissotetras*'s "impeccable" treatment of the subject, it "receives no mention in the histories of mathematics."[109] "Urquhart's manifest love of and zest for learning enliven even this unutterably dull subject," but the work's dense use of "unusual words and neologisms" made it "near-unintelligible."[110] Urquhart's Wikipedia entry describes his style as "unique."[111]

Attentive to the intentional literary style of Urquhart's abstruse writing, I suggest it is better characterized as "poetic."

Urquhart was surely aware of the poetic quality of his writing. He concludes one of his later works, *Jewel* (1652), with an awareness that he "could truly have enlarged this discourse with a choicer variety of phrase; and made it overflow the field of the reader's understanding with an inundation of greater eloquence: and that one way, tropologetically, by metynomical, ironical, metaphorical, and synecdochical instruments of elocution, in all their several kinds."[112] Typical of his abounding expression, the statement goes on and on. When it finally reaches an end, Urquhart delivers original poetic verse: "Pity it were to refuse such/As ask but little, and give much."[113] "Giving much" aptly describes Urquhart's relation to the subject matter of *The Trissotetras*—both what he receives and what he teaches from its many datas.

For Urquhart, the science of trigonometry "unlocks" the "mysteries of Mathematicks."[114] The full title of *The Trissotetras*, written on its original cover page and quoted here, inserts the work into the geometric, mathematical, navigational, cartographic, astronomical, and general scientific discursive contexts we have already considered, for which the "lately invented, and perfected" knowledge of trigonometry is required:

The Trissotetras: Or, A Most Exquisite Table For Resolving all Sphericall, Rectangular or Obliquangular, with greater facility, then ever hitherto hath been practiced: Most necessary for all such as would attaine to the exact knowledge of Fortification, Dyaling, Navigation, Surveying, Architecture, the Art of Shadowing, taking of Heights, and Distances, the use of both the Globes, Perspective, the skill of making Maps, the Theory of the Planets, the calculating of their motions, and of all other Astronomical computations whatsoever. Now lately invented, and perfected, explained, commented on, and, with all possible brevity,

and perspicuity, in the hiddest and most re-searched mysteries, from the
very first ground of the Science it selfe, proved, and convincingly dem-
onstrated. By Sir Thomas Urquhart of Cromartie Knight. Published
for the benefit of those that are Mathematically affected.[115]

In Furner's terms, the different usages of "data" gain their meaning within a narrative that is intensely mathematical and geometric.
The early pages of *The Trissotetras* contain drawings and measurements of different triangles explained in the study. The discussions
are replete with numbers, angles, degrees, sines and other technical terms of geometric and mathematical analysis. It is a work that
aspires to what Urquhart terms "the exactnesse of a research."[116]

To describe the meaningfulness of "data" and its related terms
solely in mathematical and geometric terms, however, falls terribly short. Urquhart's use of the word is part of the linguistic
"novelty"—his term—that he displays on nearly every page
of the work.[117] Most illustrative of this novelty are Urquhart's
neologisms. He creates acronyms for geometric theorems using
their different component parts and attributes. Boston explains
Urquhart's method with an example drawn from the following
abbreviated list of symbols:

A	angle
E	side
O	Opposite Angle
PRO	proportion
S	sine
U	hypotenuse
Y	side required.

Thus, the coined word "Eproso" is a succinct statement of the
plain triangle axiom "side proportional to sine of opposite angle."

The theorem names are ingeniously constructed so that the last vowel is the quantity—side or angle—required, and the preceding vowels are the given quantities or data. Thus "Upalem," a theorem for a right-angled triangle, calculates the third vowel *e*, that is side, when the hypotenuse (U) and angle (A) are given. Some theorems relate three quantities, and others relate four—hence the name *Trissotetras*.[118]

Each neologism invokes *quantities given* for mathematical and geometric interpretation. Urquhart views his neologisms, which resist the immediate grasp of their reader, as "inventions" for "learning." They help commit the theorems to memory: "The novelty of these words I know will seeme strange to some, and to the eares of illiterate hearers sound like termes of Conjuration: yet seeing that since the very infancie of learning, such inventions have beene made use of, and new words coyned, that the knowledge of severall things representatively confined within a narrow compasse, might the more easily be retained in a memory susceptible of their impression."[119]

"Datas"—Urquhart's anomalous spelling that appears in the *OED*—occurs first as part of the heading "Datas. Quaesitas" on several tables that describe obscure symbolic abbreviations for the attributes of different triangles, such as "The Planorectangular Table" of "The Trissotetrase," and "The Othogonospherical Table" of "The Sphericall Trissotetras."[120] This usage is clearly informational.

The first use of "datas" in the body of the text occurs *after* these tables, under Urquhart's "Explanation" of the abbreviations for *The Trissotetras*. Two of these abbreviations—A and E—were mentioned in Boston's explanation of Urquhart's method. Urquhart describes them more fully using the language of "the given," which, like several of the other texts revisited here, pervades his text without the use of the word "data."[121] In order to illustrate both the novelty of Urquhart's expression as well the density of the text, I quote from the three symbols that preceded the word's first use.

The explanation of the *Trissotetras*.

A. signifieth an Angle: Ab. in the Resolvers signifieth abstraction, but in the Figures and Datoquaeres the Angle between: Ac. or Ak. the acute Angle. Ad. Addition. AE. the first base: Amb. or Am. an obtuse Angle: As Angles in the plurall number. At. the double verticall, whether externall or internall. Au. the first verti-call Angle: Ay, the Angle adjoyning to the side required.

B. or Ba. the true base: Bis the double of a thing.

Ca. the perpendicular: Cra. the concurse of a given and required side: Cur. the concurse of two given sides.

D. the partiall or little rectangle or rectanglet. Da. the datas. Di. or Dif. the difference: Dir. the directories. D. q. Datoquaeres. Diss. of unlike natures.[122]

The concept "datas" appears several times in the main text. A query of the online digital text reveals forty-eight usages of the word in geometric and informational contexts. Urquhart uses the phrase "datas thus obtained"—the phrase cited in the *OED*—several times, albeit with some unusual turns, as in "happily obtained" and "obtained *by* the datas."[123] In each of its usages, the meaning of "obtained" appears to be "found" or "found out," the phrase Urquhart uses elsewhere.[124]

The only usage of "data" *without an s*, on my reading and search, appears in Urquhart's "lexicidion" to the text, from which Furner quotes. Urquhart supplies that lexicon to familiarize readers with "the most important of those Greek, and Latin termes, which, for the more efficacy of expression, I have made use of in this Treatise."[125] In his entry for "data," he traces its usage to the original Latin:

Data,

> is said of the parts of a Triangle, which are given us, whether they be sides or Angles, or both, of *do, datum, dare.*

His lexical entries include his other dataventions, which he defines in relation to the words "datas" and "data." Without an "s", the word data appears only three times, under "data" itself and in his definitions of "datamista" and "datisterurgetick." *With* an "s" it appears five times and is the form that Urquhart uses most frequently.

Datimista,

> are those Datas, which are neither Angles onely, nor sides onely, but Angles, and sides intermixedly: of *data,* and *mista,* from *misceo.*

Datangulary,

> is said of the Concordances of those Moods, for the obtaining of whose Praenoscendas, we have no other Datas, but Angles, unto the foresaid Moods common.

Datapurall,

> comes from *datapura,* which be those Datas, that are either meerly Angles, or meerly sides.

Datolaterall,

> is said of the Concordances of those Moods, for the obtaining of whose Praenoscendas, the same sides serve for Datas.

Datoquaere,

> is the very Problem it selfe, wherein two or three things are given, and a third or fourth required, as by the composition of the word appears.

Datisterurgetick,
>   is said of those Moods which agree in the Datas of the last
> work: of data, [Greek text], postremum, and [Greek text], opus.[126]

The *OED* contains no listing for any of these terms. As noted above, many of the related usages of data are deeply challenging intellectually and combine data, data quaesitas, and other *dataventions.*

Urquhart's inventive word play with "datas" suggests a literary approach to the word—an understanding of Urquhart's relation to his subject matter that is supported by Boston's detailed analysis of the literary originality of Urquhart's other works, especially *Jewel* and his translations of Rabelais (1653). Both works display Urquhart's love for expansive linguistic wordplay and metaphor.

Jewel contained Urquhart's proposal, "The Grammar and Lexicon of an Universal Language," which aimed to standardize the references and pronunciation of all words, and contained a complete, universal alphabet to make up for any lack in existing ones. It would also have eleven genders. To explain the systematicity of his universal language, Urquhart offered an "allegory" (his term) of cities, streets, lanes, houses, stories, and rooms. Boston says that Urquhart's elaborate scheme "has been too easily dismissed as further evidence of the author's craziness," but Boston demonstrates, to the contrary, its resemblance to Roget's *Thesaurus*, published exactly two hundred years after *Jewel*.[127] Comparable to Urquhart's city metaphor, Roget uses "heads," sections, and numbers to relate word to topic."[128] "As with *The Trissotetras*," writes Boston, "the 'Universal Language' has only to be studied with a little care for it to reveal method in its oddness." Boston is right to insist upon a little *care*. Care *reveals method* where one was not apparent.

Even more exemplary of Urquhart's love for wordplay is his translation of Rabelais's *The Life of Gargantua and Pantagruel.* Urquhart takes Rabelais's already linguistically inventive text and *exceeds it.*

> Urquhart's mastery of obscure language is only equaled by his command of the colloquial and idiomatic, the earthy and the bawdy, with which Rabelais's name is associated. The enormous lists of synonyms that Rabelais piles up present a frightful problem for the translator: for many of the items on the list there will be no exact equivalent in English (or, indeed, in modern French). Urquhart rightly decided to follow the spirit rather than the letter: instead of trying to translate item by item, what he usually does is simply to provide his own list. It would have been remarkable if in doing so Urquhart had been able to match the gusto and exuberance of Rabelais. He does not. Instead he repeatedly outstrips Rabelais, producing lists that are even longer (often considerably longer) than those of the original.[129]

For example, Rabelais gives Gargantua 108 games; Urquhart supplies 238. Urquhart takes Rabelais's thirteen terms for the infant Gargantua's penis (e.g., "my stopper" and "quiverere") and offers twenty-five additional, very colorful descriptions (e.g., "bunguetee," "gallant wimpble," and "futilletie"). The "cakemakers of Lerné, who in Rabelais hurl twenty-eight insults at the shepherds of Gargantua country, in Urquhart's version they have forty-three and each of them a double insult" (e.g., "jobbernol goosecaps," and "grouthead gnat-snappers").[130] "Perhaps the most remarkable of all is Urquhart's rendering of the sounds of animals."[131] Rabelais's nine sounds "become an astonishing seventy-one" in Urquhart's translation (e.g., "bumbling bees," "whicking pigs," and "curkling quails").[132] Urquhart appears to receive the given data as imaginative prompts for more giving.

Each instance, Boston asseverates, is "justifiable both as a creative act itself, and as being entirely in the spirit of Rabelais."[133] He compares these translations to the translations of the Bible, as works of art in and of themselves. The best translations "are not necessarily particularly faithful to the original, but they will endure because they are in their own right *living* works of art" (emphasis added).[134] In other words, the best translations are the *living on* of the original. The 1955 Penguin translation of Rabelais by J. M. Cohen, Boston writes, is "not bad," but it will be superseded by others (and it has, twice), "whereas Urquhart and the Authorised Version will go on being read as long as the English language is spoken."[135]

Boston makes an additional observation to relate Urquhart's translation directly to poetry, a felicitous reference in the context of the current study: "Someone once defined poetry as being the quality that gets lost in translation. The great translations have their own poetry. It may not be the same poetry as the original, but it is still poetry. Successfully to translate a work of art one must produce another work of art. Everything else is just dictionary labor."[136]

Everything else is, as Asya al-Ulama might say, something a machine could do.

Translation is poetry because it is the *living on* of the original as a work of art, as that work intercepts and entrusts itself to the creative and responsible caring and bearing of its other. Urquhart's usages of "data" as "datas," as well as each of his datoventions, must be considered in this context, as *the artful and poetic* living on of data. These usages are literary "works of art." "Data" palpitates with possibilities as "datas," "datimista," "datangulary," and so forth. Each may be understood as something *given* for poetic, imaginative possibility *by* data, indeed, by the givenness of data *as* the given. Data, in Urquhart's various usages, is given to give (or make, *poesis*) other givings: *to yield* more, as the data *gives*. In poetic attunement, Urquhart receives the creative potentiality of *the given*, entrusted to him for his caring and bearing as a mathematician and writer dedicated to learning, for *more giving*. Urquhart's usage of *datas* must be understood, therefore, as a literary and poetic gift—a chance for a poetically attuned relation to a given subject matter. Like Hammond's usage, Urquhart's is instructive in the history of data beyond its empirical and rhetorical function. It was the first poetically attuned intervention in the history of data, a precedent for all that followed.

POETIC ATTUNEMENT AND
THE HISTORY OF DATA

Over the long term, the concept of "data" represents a site of remarkable thought and possibility. The reason for this, I think, lies in the meaningfulness or sense that it maintains from its most original usage in the Latin language as "that which is given." Data is that which is given for thought and expression in a field of open, imaginative possibility. The word comes to English, and all other non-Latin languages, as what the *OED* calls a "borrowing." As such, data is *already* living on in borrowed translation and give-and-take possibility from one meaningful context to another, even as its meaning may be contingently narrowed in the course of this living.

Its meaning cannot be reduced to any *particular* giving because data, as the given, gives much. The "much" that is given is also given in the concept itself: data are the many gifts, things, truths, premises, conditions, and bases given to find other things, truths, premises, conditions, and bases that are heretofore "unknown" or "sought for." They are the givens for various forms of knowing under *varying* conventions of *varying* argumentation and rhetoric. They are things *sent*, as in a letter sent in a particular time and place and received in another. Even in Latin, "data" has never had a single meaning. The Latin word *do*, from which it is derived, may mean to give, dedicate, sell, pay, grant, bestow, impart, offer, lend, devote, allow, make, surrender, give over, ascribe, attribute, give birth, produce, utter, and send to die.[137] Shades of these meanings may be found in the various givens in the history of "data;" there is more in the history of data than meets the empiricalist eye.

Data thus always already resides in a space of palpitating meaning, and, in this regard, embodies poetic potential. Attunement to the poetics of the early history of data requires more than attending to its hermeneutical variety, however. It requires receiving the history as a site of ample poetic expression that entrusts itself to the other—to our responsible bearing care.

Poetic attunement to these foundational texts in the history of data therefore must go beyond the goal of analyzing their various and changing constitutive meanings. Received in poetic attunement, each contribution to the history of data does not simply have meaning. It *moves* others to bear both the effort to give it meaning and the meanings given to it. The desire *to establish something as given* for purposes of knowledge or truth may itself be received as "other." Poetically attuned engagement with the history of data therefore involves receiving both the sign "data" and that which it is said to represent as expression that is *entrusted or given for bearing and caring responsibility*. In this reception, the experience of attuning to data happens as the sign *gives*, and, as it does, one becomes *data affected*. The many epistemic and argumentative contexts of the earliest English language usages of "data" prompt several salient paths of fruitful poetic attunement.

Batten and Halley's texts may be received as entrusted to bear and care for their aspiration to achieve natural and social scientific precision. For Batten, logarithmic calculation, as a way "other" than the compass for knowing one's true and fixed place on Earth, resolves a gap in measurement experienced around the world for centuries. For Halley, the application of scientific analytical methods to extant historical reports is "other" in relation to living with multiple or incomplete historical accounts of key events in national and world history. To bear and care for their shared desire for data-based precision is to receive data as a new mode of communicating technical and scientific certainty.

"Data" was not a new concept, as such. Scientists already had "the given." But data stands as a new signpost, a turning point in the language of scientific research, and Batten and Halley were among the first to *write* this purpose in English. Like a strange word encountered for the first time in poetic verse, their *data* entrusts itself for participation in a new world of "precisely given calculation or information" and a new way of being in the world in which knowledgeable authorities bring that precision to expression by writing *data*. This world esteems the *data* knower, interpreter, and analyst. Receiving the texts of Batten and Halley in a poetically attuned fashion offers a chance, therefore, to bear and care for the once-upon-a-time otherness of a precision-based, logarithmic orientation toward knowledge.

In highlighting the originality of this form of data-based experience, attunement further discloses that the "plaine and easie way" of scientific precision historically emerged as significant only in relation to other ways. It was not the *only* way, and in order to become an only way, it has had to displace other ways of knowing and living—ways that are *other* to this new "plaine, easy, or precise" way. These other ways—like sailing into the horizon according to the loadstone without logarithmic calculation, or studying history with something other than a concern for conclusive certainty—include ways that may have had, or may have, nothing to do with plainness, ease, precision, and certainty as such. Or they may have been constituted by other understandings of plainness, ease, precision, and certainty. "For finding the true Azimuth of the Sunne," Batten wrote, "you are to know *or imagine* your Latitude."[138] Other ways to "know" or "imagine" one's "latitude." As knowing and imagining palpitate, inquiring imaginations vary and one finds a little latitude in Latitude, and oneself open to different Latitudes. These ways other than calculated precision have had to *recede* or *fail* for the otherness of the modern, data-precise subject to become familiar and habitual.

Batten and Halley's texts thus also secretly entrust their subaltern otherness for bearing and caring, ways of living that under the terms of the new data-based scientific precision live on as inaccurate: the ways of the ancient sailor or (hi)story teller, slightly wayward at sea, undetermined by precision, perhaps certain otherwise about other things, perhaps uncertain, in some other way. Perhaps something else. A subaltern hermeneutical attentiveness and receptivity to the teachings of these other ways happens in the silence of their erasure as imprecise in the history of data, where no response happens, where no "them" resides, where the historical record may be seized and poetically rewritten or redrawn otherwise, on behalf of the loadstone and unfixed or pre-fixed consciousness. The clear voice of the modern, data-centric scientific subjectivity in Batten and Halley's texts, memorialized in their *OED* entries, makes possible attunement to other ways of living in space and time.

More precise, as it were, to Batten's subject matter, the heading of his tables of attribute values announces the end of other "truths," and his text entrusts these truths, in their devalued displacement and transcendence, to the other for responsible bearing and caring. The heading "Data" moves us to receive all other truths of human observation, all ways of knowing and imagining one's relation to the sun, the skies, and earth before or contemporaneous with azimuths, amplitudes, zeniths, summes, Doctrines of Triangles, remainders, or logarithms before any and all-gorithms. Ways of locating, moving, and thinking of place other than ways, latitude, and place. Perhaps other plains and easies that are unadded, unsummed by Batten's logarithms, *remaining* as something other. These *other ways*, perhaps false and varying, perhaps not so false and not so varying, are *entrusted or given* by Batten's Data heading as it is received in poetic attunement. His givens give more (how could they not?) than meets the eye. The heading occupies a site of collision between the "true and fixed" and the implied "false and varying." In addition to the "three things to be given in any Triangle" and the *error* that Mercator also observed, there were/are *other* givens and (subaltern) "observations" (in many other senses of observation), that, in their ineffable silence and opacity, come into conversation without response. There, they teach the *contingency* and *relativity* of the truth of the new data heading and of data centrism. They teach that being somewhere, elsewhere, and otherwise in relation to the directions pointed out by the logarithmic episteme are *possible*. How much does "data" arbitrate location, direction, and desire?

To receive Batten's Data for ethical entrusting and subaltern teaching is not to take the side of either the logarithmic or its others. Those outside of power embrace logarithmic demonstration—for survival and justice—as much as those in power. In poetic attunement, bearing and caring occur *for the encounter*, because the site of data is *given* for many poetically attuned possibilities. Neither the way of the logarithmic nor its others is simply plain or easy. Data appears, and is thus entrusted to our responsibility, at the site of difference—where ways of living in relation to the differences between them occur—here, where it had been "known" during the Tang dynasty "that magnetic compasses did not point exactly to geographical north, as defined by the stars." All othernesses at that site of encounter entrust themselves for poetic attunement. Data as a table heading—any table heading, any *dataset*, in any scientific study—is not simply a site for the recording of attribute values. It is the guide for bearing and caring for all ways of knowing and imagining one's place on earth in relation to the cosmos.

Halley's essay may be received in similar poetic fashion, as entrusting both "the curious" and their disfavored (uncurious?) others for ethical bearing and caring. The curious, if they are anything like Halley, favor precisely determined historical awareness when "dealing with the lunar phase at the time of Caesar's invasion, ancient star catalogues, archaeology, or the age of the world."[139] They judge traditional texts as incomplete or unreliable and wish to "fix and ascertain" "the Times of Memorial Actions" through dispassionate scientific-historical research. Their others appear to think, feel, and relate to stories of the past and their gaps or unresolved wonders otherwise, with a desire different from "scientific historical consciousness." When Halley confidently asserts his desire to determine the exact date of Caesar's location from the available data, the study secretly entrusts both desires other than exactness and relations to the past other than calendar-based dating (date-ification) into one's bearing and caring responsibility.

The data of Halley's dramatic narrative of Caesar's expedition also secretly move and entrust others into one's responsible bearing and caring, namely those experiencing the invasion. It was the night of the sudden tempest. Until the invasion, Britain was considered by "inhabitants of the continent" "as a separate world," a "hitherto unknown country" of "barbarians."[140] We may bear and care for the unknown country, for its inhabitants' unknown-ness and unknowability; for their only being known as barbarians; for living in a condition of separateness that at once protected them from colonizing invasion, and also, tragically, invited it; and for the suffering they would endure in its course.

The Roman "invasion," or as historians record it, "crossing over into Britain," involved close to a hundred Roman warships and ten thousand Roman soldiers.[141] It lasted twenty-five days and included several major battles. As the invaders approached the coast, the Britons "endeavoured to prevent" their advance from the Dover cliffs with spears, darts, and javelins.[142] Caesar ordered "the enemy to be beaten off and driven away, with slings, arrows, and engines." The Romans initially struggled to fight from the rough and high waters below. An anonymous but legendary bearer of the Roman standard led the soldiers as they regrouped in a battle that "was maintained vigorously on both sides."[143] Poetically received, the narrative secretly entrusts for bearing care the intense vigor with which each side maintained battle—one side aiming to conquer, the other resisting; each aiming to beat and destroy the other, conqueror and conquered, victor and vanquished, darter and the darted, wounded and the fallen, each enemy to the other.

The Romans gained the upper hand and drove the Britons back. Four days into battle, the Britons sued for peace. Conquest was delayed, however, because the Roman warships, carrying horses and additional cavalry, "had not been able to maintain their course at sea and reach the island."[144] As they approached, they suddenly encountered the tempest. Caesar's description (written in the third person) of the voyage follows:

A peace being established by these proceedings four days after we had come into Britain, the eighteen ships, to which reference has been made above, and which conveyed the cavalry, set sail from the upper port [on the continent] with a gentle gale, when, however, they were approaching Britain and were seen from the camp, so great a storm suddenly arose that none of them could maintain their course at sea; and some were taken back to the same port from which they had started; others, to their great danger, were driven to the lower part of the island, nearer to the west; which, however, after having cast anchor, as they were getting filled with water, put out to sea through necessity in a stormy night, and made for the continent.

It happened that night to be full moon, which usually occasions very high tides in that ocean; and that circumstance was unknown to our men. Thus, at the same time, the tide began to fill the ships of war which Caesar had provided to convey over his army, and which he had drawn up on the strand; and the storm began to dash the ships of burden which were riding at anchor against each other; nor was any means afforded our men of either managing them or of rendering any service. A great many ships having been wrecked, inasmuch as the rest, having lost their cables, anchors, and other tackling, were unfit for sailing, a great confusion, as would necessarily happen, arose throughout the army.[145]

The Britons tried to take advantage of the Roman delay. They attacked soldiers who were searching the country for supplies, but the assault backfired. Caesar's troops employed "every kind of missive weapon to drive the enemy away" and then "pursu[ed] them as far as they could, killed many of them, and burnt all their houses for some distance round."[146] Still lacking the men and resources to complete the conquest, however, Caesar decided to return to Gaul for the winter. He undertook a second invasion the following year. These border crossings were preludes to the full Roman conquest of Britain a decade later.

Halley writes of the great danger faced by the ships caught up in the storm, but his data secretly entrust other othernesses to bear: the experience of conquest, invasion, and resistance. The terror of sudden tumult and loss of control. The scorched earth and ruined homes. The great confusion. The drowning horses and soldiers. In poetic attunement, the bodies scream, corpses stink, ashes rise, circumstances confuse, wreckage floats, and fish feed among the skeletons and rusted javelins and chariots in the watery grave. Halley's data on Caesar's invasion also entrusts to our bearing responsibility the *desire* to conquer, occupy, and order; to accrue power and expand it; to chase, kill, terrorize, burn, and subordinate others; and to be chased, killed, terrorized, expelled, and subdued. Also to plunder, to be plundered, and to become known to new rulers: It is said that "fresh-water pearls seem to have been the lure that prompted his invasion of Britain; [Caesar] would sometimes weigh them in the palm of his hand to judge their value."[147] In Caesar's own account, "he thought it would be of great service to him if he only entered the island, and saw into the character of the people, and got knowledge of their localities, harbours, and landing-places, all which were for the most part unknown to the Gauls."[148] Poetic attunement carries us again into deep thought and feeling of these still pervasive individual and collective, imperial and colonial impulses—to cross and penetrate other societies violently in order to discover, see, know, plunder, subordinate, and assimilate them to the greatness of the conqueror. At the same time, it entrusts the contingency and fragility of such impulses—an even greater service. The unexpected tempest teaches surprise and the limits of human design. The sea burst into itself and momentarily disrupted the Roman colonization of Britain.

Amid all this, Halley's concern to specify the exact date and place of the invasion emerges in its otherness as a shared desire among the scientifically curious. Data give and give; accordingly, his data gave themselves to other inquirers who later challenged his findings. These included a twenty-first-century research team from Texas State University—another place and time—whose conclusions enable us to attune to the contingent and variable character of scientific knowledge. Halley applied concepts of meteorology and astronomy to reports in historical documents. In August 2007, these researchers traveled to the site with a GPS and dropped apples into the sea to observe the flow of the current, as the conditions for the tempest reoccurred. Donald Olsen, the team leader, explained, "We realized we could go out in a boat and observe the current for ourselves. The year 1901 would have been just as good for this experiment, but no one noticed," and no one had apples *and* a GPS.[149] Olsen's team concluded that the invasion occurred four days earlier than previously thought, on August 22–23, not August 25–27. The "the channel was flowing the wrong way" during the storm—southwest toward Dover, not northeast as would be required to suit the historical description.[150] The "revised date . . . gives Caesar the ocean current he needed to maneuver *right*, proceed seven miles" north to the area of Deal where most historians mark the landing. It "reconciles an ancient record of a 'falling tide' with Caesar's own description of the coastline topography as he moved his fleet along the white cliffs of Dover."[151]

Halley's text intercepts us in the wake of the 2007 experiment and entrusts the *contingency* of precise scientific knowledge to our bearing and caring responsibility. Halley's desire to determine the exact date enters the archives as an assertion of scientific certainty that, like all such assertions in the history of science, inexorably faces the possibility of future critique, revision, and rejection. Data give much more and keep on giving. Other determinations are always possible, especially in changing epistemic and technological conditions of experimentation. As a scientific thinker of renowned integrity, Halley should have anticipated that his "exact" determination could be made more exact. He must have known that science ultimately involves conjecture, not absolute certainty, and that, putting aside ways of knowing other than exactness, exact knowledge one day may be inexact on another. All knowledge claims open themselves to review, reconsideration, and reinterpretation by others.

In poetic attunement, one receives the sustained consideration given by many observers—Dion Cassius, Caesar, Halley, Airy, the Texas team—to the event and its significance. Bearing Halley's text involves bearing and caring for these others and their relation to each other. As such, it involves attuning to the inexorable provisional quality of strong knowledge claims and the experience of evaluation, critique, revision, refinement, rejection, and affirmation in the history of scientific inquiry. There is a kind of affirmation in the rejection; the memory of Halley's achievement is recalled and passed along. Its cares are cared for as a prior effort, an "other" effort relative to present examinations. Theory replacement is not simply an abstract relation between claims. It is a weighty relation between others who have engaged the given data under changing research conditions. The history of science is a history of relationships between all observers and, of course, those whose lives are said to be represented in the data (Britons, Romans, horses, and the moon and stars in the sky).

Interestingly, the data at the heart of the studies of Caesar's invasion—the storm that took lives and destroyed ships—provide a connection in memory to William Petty's "Treatise on Naval Philosophy." From a poetically attuned perspective, the treatise may be received as a bearing and caring response to shipwrecks. Petty makes it very clear that his immediate analytical purpose is to contribute to the production of "vessels and their appurtenances" that will survive "injuries of *water, weather, worms* and *weeds*."[152] Material conditions palpitate as an analytical category in the famed political economist's alliteration.[153] However, the treatise, unlike the other texts in the early history of data, mostly entrusts to our bearing responsibility the author's use of objectified data for the sake of his own political ambitions.

By objective, I am speaking to the common, if philosophically uncompelling, convention that scientific data analysis is free from the subjective political or ethical values, interests, opinions, appetites, and passions of the inquirer. (Postempiricist philosophy of science has compellingly shown that all scientific activity is constituted by human interest and value.)[154] The subjective political interest constitutive of the treatise emerges as other in relation to Petty's objectivist reputation. It may be borne less as a contradiction than a disclosure about the relation between subjective intention, knowledge, and power, especially the allure of national and imperial power. Subjective interests need not deviate from the purely scientific aims of scientific inquiry. An inquirer may have a subjective interest in preserving the objective reputation of their work. Or they may have a subjective interest in seeing their work employed for the benefit of others. It appears that Petty wrote the work mainly to serve the interests of those in power and himself, like a salesman pitching a well-researched idea to a potential employer. Here, egoistic subjective intentions effectively undermine any presumed objectivity.

To receive this subjective egoism in its otherness is to bear an awareness that interests, needs, and desires unrelated to any given data may inform data analytics. Apparently neutral expressions of number, weight, or measure are constituted and therefore possibly compromised by motives external to the research. How much do the lives of data analysts constitute their data? Is there other data—in this case, about the data analysts—other than and beyond the reported data that may be equally if not more relevant to the analysis than the data provided? All sorts of purposes inform scientific practice; the intended effect of any invocation of data may not be those explicitly expressed in the study.

Moved to this kind of questioning and wonder, Doctor Cemal's undisclosed purposes for concealing the dirt in Yaşar's lungs come back to mind. Petty's penchant for power makes him unlike the doctor, however. The attention Petty gives to the sturdy construction and preservation of colonial ships eclipses any concern for those on the other end of Britain's power in the "new Countries, new Passages, new Mines of Gold, of Silver." Petty and Doctor Cemal represent others to each other. Doctor Cemal poetically bears the subalternity of the data accurately, in a deeply caring relation to the lives of its many others. Petty is more like an unattuned social scientific manager of the lives of his data's others, as epitomized in his famous "Down Survey" (1656–58). "Lauded then and since as the first scientific mapping of much of Ireland," the study "surveyed Irish lands confiscated from 'rebel' Irish . . . for allocation to troops in Ireland and investors in London."[155] It advocated coercive population transfers and intermarriage (a model Petty suggested for use in the Americas as well). The confident knowledge Petty offers regarding the "strength of the knees, bolts, and nails" corresponds, in poetic attunement, to the weakening of other worlds that, through the injuries of colonization, exploitation, dispossession, and forced assimilation, will be caught in the expanding nets of Great Britain's "world." No shortage of data exists on what must be borne in the disruptions, destructions, subordinations, resistances, and responses to the colonial condition that will follow where the new seaworthy and well-armed ships will anchor.

Power relations across different worlds must be borne in Henry Hammond's usage of "data" as well. He and Francis Cheynell disagree severely about which practices—"ways and forms of serving God publicly"—ought to govern the eternal salvation of the Christian believer in the diverse contexts of official Christianity. Their dispute entrusts to responsible bearing and caring highly contentious debates over preserving or deviating from traditional practice. Salvation and true belief are at stake here. Hammond and Cheynell each have a view that they consider true, and they view the other as a threat to that truth. Cheynell fears Hammond is seeking to abolish forms of prayer that depart from the set forms of the apostles. Hammond claims to support the former but wants an ongoing central role of the latter. Their exchange entrusts promoters and defenders of clashing truths for bearing and caring.

And all others who are threats to all truths: Their focus on set forms of prayer secretly entrusts all prayers of all forms of prayer for bearing and caring—prayers of prayers that are set, not set, and something other than set or non-set, according to a gospel and otherwise, and all those who pray according to all gospels and all things otherwise. All ways: lawful, unlawful, or not constituted in any juridical direction whatsoever; commanded, permitted, and other than emanating from any commanding or permitting authority; prudent or imprudent, pious or impious, serving or not serving God, gods, or any higher power, and all other ways of experiencing life in ways that find some relation to the idea of prayer; the details, textures, relations, and feel of those ways. Things the church, or all churches, think fit and things that don't fit the church, or any church, in England and elsewhere, with or without books; common, particular, or something other than either (uncommonly fleeting, rare, etc.); miraculous, ordinary, miraculous in their ordinariness, or ordinary miracles, ministers for Christ and all ministers "imbued with the spirit of prayer;" true, untrue, and experienced in terms other than true and false; religious, irreligious, antireligious, areligious, and believing or not believing in ways that make no reference to religiosity; faithful, blasphemous, and all other ways of believing or being an infidel, or something other than believer or infidel. All those who argue, do not argue, and make no sense of religious truth through argument; who prove, do not prove, and think the world in other ways than proof or its absence, who may stipulate and concede premises and who live in a realm constituted by terms of communication other than the exchange of premises, for whom heaps of data will make sense or no sense, with or without data of any kind. All others who are otherwise where the contest between truths opens up many other truths, and othernesses to truth, where balances and imbalances between tradition and innovation evolve otherwise—all enter one's bearing care in poetically attuned receptivity to Hammond's heap of data. In poetic attunement, every concession may be made to bear and care for the others entrusted by the data. Everything given by that heap—under, over, or alongside it—may be received, thought, felt, and borne.

Addressed in a space of open indeterminacy and prepared to be moved into an ethical relation with *the givens*, poetic attunement lets the most truth-determining assertion initiate other imaginative associations, near and remote, each affectively borne and cared for. Poetic encounter is indeed modeled in Urquhart's

Trissotetras. The work entrusts the creative teaching of trigonometry to our care, and with it, all creative teachings of all topics. Urquhart "published [*The Trissotetras*] for the benefit of those that are Mathematically *affected.*"¹⁵⁶ In poetic attunement, this benefit redounds to the benefit of all affected and affectable learners—that is, for all who bear and care for their learning as a site of poetic possibility. In its usage of "datas," specifically, *The Trissotetras* entrusts inventive pedagogies to the care of its other, its students. Urquhart coins memorable acronyms (other words) so that they remember the theories he, as teacher-other, teaches. The datas he gives are not only obtained but happily so, allowing one to bear and care for all teaching where every obtainment gives more to obtain, with and beyond the existing obtained data, happily or *otherwise.*

Urquhart's dizzying, erudite, and amplifying translations of Rabelais exemplify this *other* way of writing and teaching, where, for every given data, more is given. This is this teacher's teaching: to make every teaching a chance for more teaching, to ensure that every subsequent given both imaginatively relates to and exceeds all previously imagined and delivered givens. Urquhart's teaching makes the life of the current teaching signate with wonder so as to wonder more. In teaching the givens, moreover, he teaches the experience of giving, so that those affected experience the giving. To take his text into our bearing and caring responsibility involves being *affected* by the ongoing poetic potency of teaching as giving. Giving much *is* teaching. This teaching about teaching signates for the ages, since data, as this poetically attuned response to the history of the concept shows, gifts *giving* for bearing and caring responsibility. The overarching meaning of data since its earliest known Anglophone usages is *not* rhetorical. It is *poetic.*

In its dominant empiricalist discourses, data *affects* by producing a *data-fiable* human subject capable of having something established, demonstrated, determined, or proved through quantitative or qualitative analysis of some kind. In poetic attunement, data affects by producing a data-fiable subjectivity that is capable of receiving the many and varied givens in and of the data for imaginatively open and affectively profound bearing and caring.

A POETICALLY ATTUNED UNDERSTANDING OF DATA

A poetically attuned revisiting of the history of data radically alters our sense and relation to the concept and what it offers, gives, or yields. As *all* Things or Quantities *supposed to be given*, or known, "in Order, from them, to find out other Things or Quantities, which are *unknown, or sought for*," data is anything that gives, and, by necessity, keeps on giving.[157] In whatever form data is posited, in and through whatever established horizons and practices, data *lives on* in its positing as *something, all things*, given for more giving, inexorably migrating from one semiotic context to another, wherein it takes the place as the given of prior analysis, positioned to give more.[158] "The given" palpitates in argumentation and outside of it, for more giving.

Importantly, givenness is constitutive of data *prior* to, or outside of, varying contexts of argumentation. This does not mean that the data are not subject to interpretation, reinterpretation, and contestation. It means that the interpretations of and contestations over data are given in the givenness, or givingness, of data. As the site of intense analysis, debate, and ethically disposed revision, data gives for such contestation without stipulating a final closure of its meaning. This giving is indeed a poetic gifting, an opening offered by data that both precedes and makes philosophical or analytical argumentation happen. That which gives is that which offers, calls upon, or turns the attention of the researching subject, as if to another in the event of attunement, toward it. The researcher who posits data *lets* the data give. Research is the practice of giving (meaning, significance, description, etc. in the analytical engagement with data) from the givenness of data by letting the given give. It is a reciprocal receiving and giving back, to, and with, the given. The continuous and infinite quality of giving that is inherent to data exists and survives beyond the control of the researcher. It is the givenness of data that makes arguments over, for example, its access and transparency part of the history of data, given by data.

In short, "data" not only palpitates in a field of open, indeterminate, and never final meaning. It is poetic verse itself. It intercepts us in a space of open indeterminacy and addresses us with a remoteness of the one nearest to us. The closer we get to the data, the more it gives for additional consideration, like the other entrusting itself to our bearing and caring responsibility. This is because data is the means by which datafied subjects express their foundational *principles*, *truths*, *beliefs*, and *knowledges*—their shared givens—to others. "These are the givens" is commonly said, confirming the inextricable value and poetic quality of data's original etymology in both everyday lived experience and research. They are not given as raw; rather, they are given as received or valued for giving, and this receptivity and valuation are constitutive of data relations. "It is given" is said when people establish things they understand—in both life and research—as *knowable as truth* (meaningful in its contingency). It is said as a full living on of the meaningfulness of the *idea* of *data*, borrowed here and there as that which has been given or sent, imperceptibly in relations between others, for such borrowing. The inescapable irony of the problematic empiricist usage of data as "extractable sense-data" is that it makes possible—it gifts—debate over the foundational truths and meaning of data in social scientific inquiry. This work would not have been possible without that giving. A similar significance resides in the *OED*'s entries under "data" and "datum," where the entries are giftings or givens for more giving. What makes data data is that they always already give more beyond they've always already given.

My analysis here reveals the immense difficulty of fully imagining what is given by any data or any single datum. In the givenness of data, there is always much that remains silent, and silenced, by what has been given. These silences reside not only in constraints of accessibility or completeness. They reside in the inexhaustibility of giving. All data give, and this giving may always be something else, something more and something other than what had been transparent or accessible. This includes personal data in the age of big data. The colonizing use and surveillance of such data is a taking and giving that cannot be enclosed by a regulative purpose. Regulated data already give resistance to their regulation. The subversive, poetic power of data resists absolute transparency, access, and closure.

What I am suggesting is that a poetically attuned relationship to data and data analysis is a relationship to the givenness of the given. This relationship welcomes all data, lets them palpitate openly and imaginatively, and receives them as entrusted for bearing care in a relationship of ethical responsibility. This understanding of data is "other" to the dominant, empiricist, and postempiricist protocols of social science, but it underlies Asya al-Ulama's attunement to (love:anything else<which has roots>) and why pumpkin, cabbage, or any vegetable love is not "so ridiculous." It also provides one way to understand and confirm Asya's, Doctor Cemal's, and Thomas Urquhart's deeper sense that data analysis must involve more than producing machine identifiable code.

By the time Asya used the concept of "dataset" as a meaningful category in her doctoral research, "data" had come to be singularly associated with empiricist data analytics and statistics. The official history of data was being written and lived in exclusively empiricist terms. According to the *OED*, "dataset" was coined in 1958 during data's migration to America. It appeared in an empiricist political science journal, the *Western Political Quarterly*: "Since three data-sets were utilized, guide-lines . . . were defined in terms of the proportion of three cases in which a certain correspondence was observed."[159] Asya's originality in the moment she pauses before her dataset does not lie solely in her resistance to empiricist or even postempiricist understandings of the data analytical relationship. Nor does it reside in her inspiring display that a different relationship to data—another data world—is possible. As our study has shown, by the time she deployed data-set in her account of poetic metaphor, "data" had already had many forgotten meanings beyond its scientific, informational, and computational usages. It still does. Asya's originality lay in her insight that data may be received, in inquiry, as poetic verse. She allows us to receive dataset and the data in her set as poetry, as *settings* for more ways of seeing data, and, therefore, for more ways of relating to the givens of data analysis.

CONCLUSION

Attuned in the Dataverse

Throughout this work, I have suggested that a poetically attuned disposition toward political inquiry *intensifies* already existing forms of explanatory attention to causality, meaning, ideology, structure, affect, and discourse in contemporary social and political science. The form and levels of attunement in the examples presented vary. Some are creative literary and autobiographical characters and their stories, others actual persons and phenomena, and yet others analysts and interpreters of these texts, lives, and phenomena.

A contemporary social scientific example of the palpitating, affective, and ethical deepening that can occur when poetic attunement is purposefully brought to analysis is Christina Sharpe's stellar work *In the Wake: On Being and Blackness.*[1] Sharpe writes as though Black lives "swept up in the wake" of the afterlife of transatlantic slavery have been profoundly entrusted to her, and our, bearing and caring responsibility. Her "wake work" lets "wake" palpitate "in all of its meanings as means of understanding how slavery's violences emerge within contemporary conditions of spatial, legal, psychic, material, and other dimensions of Black non/being as well as in Black modes of resistance."[2] Sharpe affectively receives these dimensions and modes in poetic encounter. "Thinking needs care," she avers, as she responds poetically in each line, and on every page, of her overwhelmingly moving and insightful account.[3] Sharpe's work has been especially helpful to me in teaching the possibilities of poetic attunement in critical social scientific inquiry. Given the prominence of the politics of race in students' lives and studies, they are inspired to design and compose poetically attuned work with the gripping analytical verse of *In the Wake* as a model.

Poetic attunement, however, not only occurs where poetic sensibilities are explicitly mobilized for analysis. Just as qualities of poetic attunement have been unacknowledged aspects of the history of "data," they are unacknowledged aspects of contemporary social science research devoted to de facto modes of empirical social science, including research of empiricist political science carried out according to the new Data Access and Research Transparency (DART) publication requirements of the discipline.

In 2019, I presented an early draft of chapter 2 at the annual convention of the American Political Science Association, where I attended the panel of a former student, on which several empiricist colleagues discussed their data in ways that suggested a poetically attuned disposition. They did not explicitly characterize their approach in these terms, of course. They spoke of their data in quintessentially de facto and objectivist terms. My experience nonetheless prompted me to open the most recent issue of the *American Political Science Review* (the *APSR*), widely recognized at the world's premier journal of empiricist social science, and peruse it in an entirely new way. Espying qualities of poetic attunement in dominant empiricalist work within the discipline offers a chance to underscore the analytical potential and significance of a poetically attuned approach to social scientific explanation.

Proclaiming DART standards to be "timely changes that need to be made to promote research transparency and trust in our scholarship," the *APSR*'s editors rushed in 2015 to codify submission guidelines "consistent with" DART objectives.[4] Central to this effort was the creation of a "dataverse"—an online repository where researchers share the "replication data" upon which their primary claims are based.[5] A dataverse is a peculiarly Urquhartian datavention at the center of the empiricist universe. Formally, it is an immense digital archive where social scientists upload and disseminate the "informational bases" of their knowledge claims. In poetic attunement, dataverse palpitates with the possibility that it is the place where such data become *verse*.

The first article in the *APSR* that caught my eye was "Deliberative Democracy in an Unequal World: A Text-As-Data Study of South India's Village Assemblies," by Ramya Parthasarathy, Vijayendra Rao, and Nethra Palaniswamy.[6] It is the lead research essay in the issue that was published just before the conference. The authors examine a large set of transcripts from India's constitutionally mandated local citizens assemblies, the *gram sabha*s, to evaluate whether they meet standards of "good deliberation," as those standards have been developed by the prominent political scientist Jane Mansbridge.[7] The authors provide 109 files in the *APSR*'s dataverse to demonstrate that, despite impressions to the contrary, deliberation occurs in the *gram sabha*s but that it is unequal according to gender.

> These assemblies are not merely empty spaces where state officials bluster and read banal announcements; rather, they provide meaningful forums for citizens to challenge their elected officials, demand transparency, and provide information about very real local development needs. . . . However . . . gender inequalities meaningfully impact citizens' ability to be heard; across all of our measures of deliberative influence, women are at a considerable disadvantage. They are less likely to be heard, less likely to drive the agenda, and less likely to receive a relevant response from state

officials. Indeed, even when we account for the particular issues raised, women still remain at a disadvantage—often ignored while their male peers receive a direct response.[8]

Each of the authors is involved in large-scale poverty reduction and women's empowerment programs in India—Parthasarathy as a political scientist and Rao and Palaniswamy as economists affiliated with the World Bank's development research center, the Social Observatory.[9] They conducted their study in 2014 in collaboration with the Tamil Nadu Empowerment and Poverty Reduction (*Pudhu Vaazhvu*) Project, "a woman-centered poverty alleviation program funded by the World Bank."[10] "With assistance of local women" and a data research firm, the authors recorded, transcribed, and translated proceedings of the *gram sabha*s of fifty villages on Republic Day, "one of the four mandated days for all villages in the state to hold a *gram sabha*."[11] This research yielded 1,736 documents for analysis.[12]

The authors used a natural language processing (NLP) approach to code patterns of participation, agenda-setting power, and dialogical responsiveness from one speaker to another and between speakers and the local politicians. NLP computer programs treat "text as data." They scan thousands of exchanges to track patterns in the data, in this case patterns that correspond to, or deviate from, standards of good deliberation theorized by Mansbridge. The authors further employed a structural topic model (STM), which offers a software algorithm that identifies precoded words as "topics"—from "water and sanitation issues, to wage payments and government service failures."[13] The authors describe the STM as a "discovery" tool. It "allows us to inductively discover topics, or clusters of words that commonly co-occur within the data."[14] Computers programmed with NLP and STM are exactly the "interpreting" machines that Asya al-Ulama foresaw as she coded poetic metaphor during her doctoral research. STM is central because it "outputs (1) a set of topics, which are defined as mixtures of words, where each word has a probability of belonging to each topic, and (2) for each document analyzed, the proportion of the document associated with each topic."[15]

Parthasarathy, Rao, and Palaniswamy reflect upon the scope and limits of these methods. They acknowledge that "the complexity of language will never be fully captured by an automated method," but they argue that machine-driven data analysis offers advantages over "hand-coded" research techniques:

> NLP analysis can help to overcome meaningful challenges in hand-coded analyses of deliberation—including biases due to the researcher's priors and inconsistencies in coding across various settings. Hand-coding usually begins with a predetermined set of categories into which documents are classified—based on their content, tone, etc. By contrast, the unsupervised approach allows us to learn the underlying features of the text without imposing our own assumptions. Though this is necessarily imperfect and requires *ex post* validation, it can be useful for identifying previously understudied or theoretically new aspects of speech in these settings, as well as scaling up large volumes of textual data.[16]

This view of the data analytical relation corresponds to the empiricist view of data and the data analytical relation, recently reasserted in the DART debate. Data are understood as existing prior to and independent of any predetermined ideas analysts have about them. They may be discovered through the senses or machines used to enhance them, extracted from the social world, and analyzed in neutral ways by independent observers who, in principle, are able to make the same inferences and draw the same conclusions from the same data. This view contrasts with the postempiricist view that data are constituted by the concepts, values, and judgments that analysts bring to their work, including their automated code. For postempiricist social science, these concepts, values, and judgments are themselves shaped by varying methodological, epistemological, technological, etiological, biographical, social, and political commitments and discursive contexts. Data are thus not independent and discovered. They are constituted, relational, and contingent. For postempiricists, this perspective on data is not a problem that hinders analysis—one of the implications of the empiricist concept of *bias*. Rather, it is seen as an inescapable and fruitful *condition* of all analysis.

Postempiricism offers a different reading of the methodological position of Parthasarathy, Rao, and Palaniswamy, who assert that their unsupervised approach helps to overcome or reduce researcher bias. From a postempiricist view, no approach reduces bias; the *idea* of reducing bias is one of the conceptual foundations of any approach that seeks to do so. The authors' approach thus does not reduce bias as much as it reflects their methodological presupposition that unsupervised machine-coded analysis reduces biases of hand-coded analysis. The authors *constitute* their data with this presupposition. It shapes each and every aspect of their data analytical encounter, along with other presuppositions, such as the idea that machine-coded analysis has benefits for knowledge ("identifying previously understudied or theoretically new aspects of speech in these settings, as well as scaling up large volumes of textual data"); their judgment that the *gram sabha*s are sites where deliberative democratic life may be shown to occur; their selection of a particular vision of deliberative democracy (as opposed to other deliberative or democratic models, as well as other practices that may also be occurring in the *gram sabha*s); and the importance of gender-based inquiry therein.

All of these (and other) judgments, concerns, criteria, categories, presuppositions, and values constitute the authors' methodological, theoretical, professional, paradigmatic, and discursive contexts for inquiry. They cannot be bracketed, overcome, or their influence reduced because they make the inquiry what it is, and in turn, make the data what it is. All analysis is constituted in this sense—all of it is *hands on*. The authors' hands are those of the computational and conceptual tools they have judged as analytically superior to other hands. This judgment is *in* the data. The APSR dataverse, therefore, does not contain any raw data. It provides other observers access to what "may be the 'least interpreted'" data of the study, which are always already constituted by—and thus interpreted within—the concerns and cares of each observer.[17] I turn now to the authors' engagement with their data not to continue the postempiricist critique but to illuminate and amplify qualities of poetic attunement in their approach. In poetic attunement, data are also coconstituted. Coconstitution is the condition of attunement within which things given are received in an open, affective, and ethical relationship of bearing and caring responsibility.

The authors illustrate their primary claims with several instances of deliberative practice in the *gram sabha*s. I focus on an archival moment that supports their finding that the "ability to influence the discussion" is greater for men than for women.[18] This pattern runs counter to standards of good deliberative practice requiring citizens to display "mutual respect," "listen attentively" to one another, and "acknowledge what is said by others—not merely push their own agenda forward."[19] Specifically, the authors examine "whether there is a disparity between men and women in their ability to redirect conversation toward their own ends."[20] They use several measures: "whether a speech [made by a female or male citizen] is followed by one on the same topic (nextSame), the share of the following five speeches that are on that same topic (prop5same), and the number of uninterrupted speeches that continue to discuss that topic (lengthTopic)." The NLP/STM observed patterns show that "male citizens are *most* likely to set the agenda," "suggesting that the common man is incredibly powerful within the *gram sabha*."[21] They "have the speech following theirs stay on the same topic."[22] As such, "women are consistently *less* likely than men to drive the agenda."[23]

The setting of the instance provided by the authors is a village in Tamil Nadu where citizens "are complaining about various public goods and infrastructure needs."[24] A female citizen voices a complaint. A male citizen interrupts her and voices another complaint. The male official takes up the male citizen's complaint without acknowledging the female citizen's prior complaint. I reproduce the exchange as it is shared in the main text of the article. The authors use bold type to show that the coded topics the woman raised were not taken up in the conversation.

FEMALE 1: There are many wells in our village, but **the wells are without a pulley wheel.** Moreover, since the water is not used for any purpose, it gets wasted. So if you can **desilt the wells,** we can not only use the water for drinking purposes but for other purposes also . . .

MALE 1: The kitchen has been constructed in the balwadi [preschool] in our village. It is not used. Please arrange for **the construction of a toilet for women.** We also need a playground for games. The canals are muddy. **We have to desilt the canals. We need a library.** All our children are going to school with a dream of becoming IAS and IPS officers. But to get general knowledge, they need books in the library. Our President has not said "no" for any of our requests. With the hope that he will definitely do whatever we have asked, I take leave.

MALE (OFFICIAL): We have a library in our panchayat. We have arranged for five magazines—an English paper, the *Hindu*, and four Tamil magazines. All the elderly persons and children are reading. I am also asking the **officers to improve the library and have passed resolution** in this regard. We have already **desilted the canal** and cleaned it under Mahatma Gandhi Rural Employment guarantee scheme.[25]

The authors write,

> Here, a woman raises a particular issue about well water, but before she is able to get a resolution, a man interrupts to raise a separate set of issues, which then generate a response and resolution from the village official. That a speaker is so obviously ignored by other participants represents a marked departure from good deliberation.
>
> More generally, by examining patterns in the topic of discussion across whole assemblies, we can identify the speakers who are most likely to drive conversation. As the example above highlights, we ought to be particularly concerned about the way in which gender may influence agenda-setting power—a disparity that has been well documented in other contexts and that may be present here as well.[26]

I have several reservations about this account, but I want to suggest that we are witnessing *a kind* of poetic attunement to the voice of "Female 1" and to others like her, in other contexts. Allow me to briefly express my reservations first. They relate to several subaltern dimensions of the study.

The authors' evaluation of the deliberative practices appears to risk simultaneously representing and erasing meanings constitutive of *gram sabha* practices that differ from the authors' presuppositions about "good" (and "bad") deliberation. Both the authors and the participants in the *gram sabha*s may value listening and not being interrupted, for example, but they may have different understandings of what listening and interrupting encompass, within and across genders, and how listening and interrupting relate to practices of deliberation as citizen subjects. These differences may or may not be adequately characterized by categories of "disregard"and practices of immediate continuity of a topic.[27]

In addition, even within the authors' presuppositions about good, continuous deliberation, their NLP/STM coding highlights some issues (e.g., desilted wells, constructing toilets for women, desilted canals, and a library) as topics and not others. If, for example, the topic were seen as "use," then it does not shift as much as the authors suggest. After the female citizen observes the well water may be used (stated twice) for many purposes, including drinking, the male citizen states that the kitchen constructed in the *balwadi* is not being used before he shifts the topic to canal desilting. Female 1's particular concerns about the wells are not picked up, but there is continuity in the discussion of use from her to Male 1. This suggests that she may have "set the agenda" or driven this exchange in some sense, while also being interrupted and disregarded (by both males) in another. Indeed, some of Male 1's concerns resonate with hers, even as he appears to be "pushing his own agenda." They both talk about the wells and their desilting, as well as "use." But that last one is not among the precoded (bolded) topics in the study's computational tools. The STM coding may teach a machine to read for topics that are coded, but that's about it. The mentioning of the unused new kitchen by Male 1 may also be studied in gender-related terms, perhaps as <"woman":"kitchen">. To this point, the authors also show that the gender dynamics change when the officials are female: "Women's voices are more likely to be amplified with female presidents—under whom women are more likely to be heard and more likely to receive a state response."[28]

The authors are not unreflective about the possibility that the linguistic meanings and practices under analysis may be more complicated than their methods discern. They state that unsupervised computation is imperfect. They also implicitly acknowledge concerns about evaluating *gram sabha* practices through potentially colonizing concepts. In their view, the *gram sabha*s are themselves products of multiple precolonial, colonial, anticolonial, and postcolonial dynamics. The relationship between the Western liberal democratic standards and those of the *gram sabha*s are more complicated than simple imposition.

Deliberative democracy has deep historical roots in India, where, for centuries, deliberative bodies were central to systems of local governance, and religious discourse and dialogue. In the period of colonial rule in the nineteenth century, the interplay of ideas between western liberal philosophers and Indian intellectuals led to India becoming a fertile ground for experiments in governance. The idea of self-sustaining village democracy, in particular, appealed greatly to Mahatma Gandhi, who made it a central tenet of his philosophy. In 1993, 45 years after independence, the Gandhian push for deliberative village democracy was given constitutional sanction with the passing of the 73rd amendment to the Indian constitution. The amendment mandated that all Indian villages would be governed by an "executive" elected village council, and a "legislature" formed by the *gram sabha*, to which every citizen of the village would be a member, with meetings held at least two times a year. Lastly, the amendment required that at least 33 percent of seats in village councils would be reserved for women, and a number proportionate to their population in the village reserved for disadvantaged castes. Today, every one of India's eight hundred million rural residents is a member of a *gram sabha*, where important issues such as the allocation of public funds and the selection of beneficiaries for public programs are discussed.[29]

The authors therefore *let* meanings constitutive of Gandhian postcolonial practice, different from those of the model they apply, enter the space of the conversation, even if the entire range of those other meanings is not central to their analysis. I shall return to this issue shortly.

The most striking subaltern quality of their work is the authors' attentiveness to the "voice consciousnesses" of the women in the *gram sabha*s. Relevant here are their robust standards for evaluating gendered power differentials. For the authors, it is not sufficient to know the high percentage of women attending the assemblies or *that* they have opportunities to voice their views—to name two common but minimal indicators of gender-power relations in discourses of political participation. Even speaking about general issues (e.g., those of use) is not enough to gauge the level of access or participation. What *matters* is being listened to, having their specific ideas taken up and considered in demonstrable ways. What matters is their influence in and on concrete topics of deliberation.

To be sure, the study's attentiveness is made possible by its computational tools, at least in the processing of the transcripts. The major claims of the study are derived from machine-coded categories, such that, in the assertion that women "*speak* less, are less likely to *drive conversation*, and are less likely to *get a response* from government officials," the words in italics are *coded* categories.[30] They are operationalized derivations from "measures of deliberative influence—namely, equality of participation, agenda-setting power, and dialogic responsiveness—" that the computers use to discover patterns or relations between other coded categories, such as female, male, and government official.[31]

Resonances between the authors' relation to their data and a fuller relation of poetic attunement appear most significantly in the *authors'* recorded response to the gendered politics of the *gram sabha*s. Parthasarathy, Rao, and Palaniswamy not only point out that Female 1's topics have been ignored and that the moment represents the incredible power of the common man in the *gram sabha*s. They assert that the woman is "*so obviously* ignored" by the male citizen. I read the "so obviously" as an affective response to the fact that the subject the woman wanted to discuss, as the authors read it, was severely disregarded and dropped from consideration. They receive her interruption, feel a frustration in the rupture, and amplify the disrespect that she experiences. The woman raises an issue. One man interrupts her, and then another ignores her. Neither listens attentively, shows respect, or acknowledges her. The authors are *moved* by that disregard.

Moreover, in the authors' discussion of the data, after they point out the statistical evidence showing that women are at a disadvantage in their ability to set the agenda, they write, "To be fair, disparities in agenda-setting power may be inconsequential from a development perspective if men and women tend to discuss the same issues; however, if there are issues that are disproportionately addressed by women, who are also more likely to get ignored, then we may be particularly worried about development outcomes."[32]

We may be particularly worried. Parthasarathy, Rao, and Palaniswamy are *worried* about the outcome of a process that systematically, and disproportionately, disadvantages women.

And *we all* may be. The text thrusts a need to bear and respond to these patterns upon the readers of the *APSR*. It entrusts worry for the women of the *gram sabha*s whose issues and voices are routinely subordinated, ignored, redirected, and silenced. "From the perspective of deliberative equality, for women to influence conversation as democratic equals, they should not have to wait for men to elevate their concerns."[33] They should not have to wait. "These patterns reiterate a need to better design deliberative institutions to elevate the voices of women."[34] And it's not only these women.

> Our results are likely to be relevant for much of rural India, since the 73rd amendment to the Indian constitution mandates that *gram sabha*s be regularly held to serve all 840 million rural Indian residents, and most Indian states have worse measured gendered inequality than Tamil Nadu [the site of this study]. They are also likely to be relevant to most of South Asia, which is home to almost a quarter of the world's population, and where gender inequality is pervasive. Afghanistan, Nepal, Pakistan, and Sri Lanka have all recently enacted legislation to strengthen local governments and increase citizen participation. Our results may also have broader relevance since the gendered nature of participation has been documented in a variety of settings, both in the developed and in the developing world.[35]

"So obviously," "particularly worried," "not wait," "relevant for much," and "reiterate a need" reverberate within and beyond the specific empirical site of the analysis.

"Need" now concerns most women in most of South Asia, "home to a quarter of the world's population."

Homes where gendered inequality is "pervasive."

"Need" for women in Afghanistan, Nepal, Pakistan, and Sri Lanka, where governments are strengthening local participation.

"Need" for women facing the "gendered nature of participation" in "the developed" world.

These women,

all women,

"should not have to wait for men to elevate their concerns."[36]

So obviously, we should be particularly worried about the need that all women face in all these homes where they are not listened to or respected, where they are interrupted and disregarded in deliberations that matter to them.

The patterns show that women are not driving the conversation. "We ought to be particularly concerned," and we ought to be generally concerned. As the authors move analytically from the instance of the *gram sabha* to the general phenomenon of gendered relations of participation, they are affectively moved to worry and concern, and we, others, are invited to be similarly moved. They read the gendered patterns of relation like Asya al-Ulama reads coded poetic metaphors of love. The authors receive and let Female 1 mean all Female 1 citizens, in all deliberative contexts, and when they apply the standards of their lives to the data, they write *the world is unequal*, a sentiment they record in the title of their work—*democracy in an unequal world*—not only intellectual but ethically inspired, affective expression that palpitates in conversation with *war in the eye of the sun* and *Blackness in the wake*. An *unequal world*. They have received the subaltern voice of the other as though it were entrusted to their bearing and caring responsibility, and others can hear, feel, and respond with them.

What might the teachings of that voice be? What might the data *further give* in poetic attunement? The authors offer Female 1 a chance to be received, heard, and made influential. What desires might she *rearrange*?

One teaching may stem from the authors' concern that the woman *should not need to wait* to have her concerns heard and acknowledged. Her intervention about desilting the wells should not function as a segue to recommending use of the newly constructed kitchens and women's toilets. Wells—small and large, rough and rounded brick, granite, or cement walls sunk into the earth—provide water to drink, clean, feed, and use in homes, gardens, fields, toilets, libraries, and sanctuaries. Water is life in an unequal world, and wells and canals are *ways* of life in this world, sacred basins and conduits of immediate and intergenerational sustenance from time immemorial. In their essential function and the artistry of their makeshift or newly engineered construction, they mirror the innate human capacity to associate nature with purpose and livelihood.[37] In times of flooding, drought, erosion, developmental destruction, climate change, and water wars, these ways of life are threatened by contamination and collapse. The topic of desilting the wells is not a transition to issues promoted by male citizens. It is Female 1's contribution to her community's legislative deliberations. *She is not heard but she is most definitely fully involved.* Her not being heard does not diminish her participation.

The authors relate her situation to other women whose voices may never have a chance to be heard. Their voices in their assemblies are unavailable in the archives or the *APSR* dataverse, but they, too, are waiting to be heard—waiting for a response where transparency is supposed to happen and where their needs may be validated and replicated. Waiting without wanting to wait, and waiting for not having to wait. Female 1's intervention in the *gram sabha* exchange *gives* that no woman should have to wait to have their concerns responsibly received by others. The authors' affective emphasis on the obviousness of this disregard and the need to rectify it resembles Gayatri Chakravorty Spivak's passionate lament that the subaltern "cannot speak." Female 1 can speak, has spoken, but has yet to be heard. The wells still need to be desilted. . . . Interrupted, redirected, so obviously ignored/ We may be particularly worried/Likely to be relevant to much, to most/In an unequal world.

As a further teaching, I suggest that the very analysis found in "Deliberative Democracy in an Unequal World" teaches as well that qualities of poetic attunement, as an approach, can always occur in the unlikely site of empiricist political science research today. The authors receive their coded transcripts in a relationship of affective and ethical bearing and caring. The use of bold type to identify coded topics is significant in this context. By bolding very particular concerns in each speaker's expression, the authors **highlight** them and **follow their course**, almost like dwelling upon specific words or images in **poetic** verse. Attuned for repetition and nonrepetition, topics become more than coded word clusters: they are things given with relatable and sensible densities, shapes, and feels that inspire imaginative and affective curiosity and ethical consideration. Bolding is not only "extractive"; it **transforms** the unsupervised raw text-as-data into the **meaningful, palpitating thought** and **articulated feeling** of the citizens. It **entrusts** their speech, whether it is heard or not by the local official, into our **bearing and caring responsibility**.

Wells without a pulley wheel. Desilt the wells. We have to desilt the canals. We need a library. Passed resolution.

And how to receive the difference between the demands of different citizens assembled in the *gram sabha*s? Are we to assume that the people who use the wells and canals do not also care about toilets and a library? Do those who want toilets and a library favor silt in the wells and canals? The verses express the *collective* needs of the citizens of the *gram sabha*. In poetic attunement, an assembly of needs convenes and, with it, relations among wells, wheels, canals, toilets, libraries, and a playground for games. Each bold plea for help enters a space of receptivity where needs circulate in association with each other. Every thing, all together and in their complicated interrelation, *counts*. As the topics flow into an assembly, so, too, do the citizens of the *gram sabha*.

The patriarchal government official refuses this complete and full relation between the missing pulley wheels and silted waters, but, in poetic attunement, it comes to mind to ask this question: How are *we* going to receive this relation? It is all very good that there is a library in the panchayat, that there are five magazines in three languages, that the elderly and children are reading, that the officers will improve the library as required by the passed resolution, and that one canal has been desilted (as the male official says). But the desilting has not gone far enough. The acknowledgment and listening have not gone far enough. Not only one canal. All canals need desilting, and not only the canals but the wells, too, for drinking and other purposes.

Female 1 spoke of these "other purposes," just as she was interrupted: "So if you can **desilt the wells**, we can not only use the water for drinking purposes but for other purposes also." The computer program did not bold these other purposes, but they may be bolded, underscored, and italicized in poetic attunement. *Other purposes* are purposes that clean water may serve for Female 1 or others with those purposes. Those other purposes did not make the list of codable, boldable topics, but they haunt the discussion as silenced, other purposes that provide emphasis for the mentioned purposes. A poetically attuned analyst, male or female, would begin with those other purposes and with topics and readings from the "we" that do not make it into the code or appear on the transcript. "Of what other purposes do you speak, Female 1?"

An answer is suggested upon entry into the dataverse, a space of attuned possibility convened by the DART-ified *APSR* and funded in this case by the World Bank. The dataverse offers a chance to receive more from Female 1.

A review of the longer transcript of this *gram sabha* reveals that her "other purposes" may be continuous with purposes articulated previously by a second male official—the secretary of the *gram sabha*—who spoke just *before* Female 1 voiced her concerns. Female 1 was the third person to speak. She was preceded by two others, identified on the written transcript respectively as "Female (Enumerator)" and "Male (Secretary)." The enumerator offered greetings and informed the gathered citizens that she would be recording the proceedings. The secretary reported on several development issues and invited the citizens to express their views on additional topics, including drought-related projects:

> Protecting water sources, action against drought, irrigation canal, small irrigation, desilting of lakes, land reforms, laying of new roads, works related to cattle, works related to fisheries, works related to drinking water at village side and works related to sanitation. . . . You can convey your views about your panchayat. All your views will be considered. You please tell us how much amount has to be spent for the following works: Protection of water sources, water conservation, setting up of moats, setting up of filled tanks, blocking the canal, setting up of concealed canal, protective wall for tank and lakes, uniform moats and plantation of trees. Action against drought condition: Promotion of nurseries, development of forests, fragile forest, restoring barren lands, road side canals, plantation of trees, setting up of gardens at block level, strengthening of canal banks, using of small and minor canals for irrigation.[38]

The male secretary does not mention wells explicitly. They are Female 1's unique urging. But, in the terms of the study, he has set the agenda for discussing water-related development projects, such that Female 1's other purposes may be said to gesture toward the many collective purposes articulated by the male official.

According to the transcript, the expressed concerns of Female 1 and the secretary converge explicitly in a moment that reveals a difference between the record of the event in the dataverse and the authors' account of the event. Where the authors insert ellipses at the moment of interruption, the dataverse records Female 1 expressing two additional thoughts. After she mentions "other purposes also," there is a full stop, and she then says, "All the lakes were seen dried up without water. Therefore I will convey my thanks if you renovate the wells."[39] Both lakes and drought were first mentioned by the secretary.

I imagine that the authors used their discretion to insert ellipses where there was an audible interruption in the recording of the *gram sabha*. Male 1, the second citizen to speak in the exchange, drove the conversation elsewhere at the very moment Female 1 was acknowledging something that had been said by the secretary.

Entering the dataverse in attunement is not reducible to questioning the validity of the authors' claims, or offering other interpretations, though these responses surely occur in attunement. Entering the dataverse in attunement is fundamentally about the possibility that all observers will be affected differently as they let the data palpitate in ethical bearing and caring responsibility. The narrowness of the debate over the DART requirements should not blind us from seeing the dataverse as a trove of extraordinary poetic possibility.

One male interrupts Female 1 as she acknowledges purposes expressed by another. Continuities in the assemblage of spoken and other purposes among the interlocutors in the *gram sabha* signate to suggest a different relationship among the speakers than the linear order produced by their machine-coded scanning. The authors regard the separate utterances as independent political speech of autonomous citizens. This political-theoretical prejudgment is embedded in theories of good, liberal democratic deliberation that affords each individual speaker—each utterance—the same respect and treatment. This prejudgment shapes the authors' evaluation of who speaks and interrupts, who regards and ignores, and who hears or redirects. In this view, the utterances all have, or ought to have, equal standing and influence and receive equal response. They all share the character of being individual utterances. In poetic attunement, the sequence of utterances matters, but the relation between them may be received on terms other than prior and subsequent speech by independent voices.

Beginning with "other purposes," the utterances may be threaded together differently. The assembly of citizen speakers with assembled needs may be rearranged into what *they refer to* as a "we." The circulating poetic possibility of a possible "we" does not eliminate the separateness of the separable utterances, but it makes their utterances something other than simply autonomous, individual utterances. These utterances may be "individual" utterances in some ways, and "we"-utterances in others. Read in the assembly of a "we," they share in a discussion of topics that stretches continuously back to the other purposes mentioned by Female 1 and the male secretary.

This attention to the "we" and its other purposes returns us to the transcript once more, where it becomes evident that Female 1's "we" has not received the attention it deserves. She says, "So if you can **desilt the wells**, we can not only use the water for drinking purposes but for other purposes also." Compare this statement with her male counterpart's "we" in verses four and five: **We have to desilt the canals. We need a library.** Female 1's "we," like her "other purposes," remains unbolded. The unsupervised machine has bolded only the male's use of "we.". Perhaps more hands-on supervision is needed to overcome this heavy-handed, programmed bias.

Significantly, before she uttered her "we," Female 1 uttered "you," which she repeats in her interrupted expression of gratitude to the officials. Her "you" suggests a quality constitutive of her "we" that distinguishes her speech from the other speakers.[40] Listening again, her **initial** words were, "So if you can **desilt the wells**, we can . . ." Bold, inspiring words spoken to the officials: If you can, we can. Notably, her **you** comes in the same utterance as her **we**. "**If you** . . . **we** . . ." Her "we" invites a "you" into a reciprocal arrangement for collective purposes. There is a subaltern teaching here, one that suggests a lapse in the prior analysis of her speech and position in the deliberations. The lapse is to consider her an "I" like the others in the transcript. Without asking, Female 1 subtly rearranges the meaning, and desire, of "we." In deliberation and gratitude, "you" are invited into a relationship with her "we."

This you/we arrangement slightly contrasts with the explicit and dominant I/we discursive emphasis in the philosophically liberal analytical, political theoretical framework of the study. Female 1 shares in the I/we and offers another possibility. Indeed, from what we hear from her, Female 1 may not view Male 1 as a "1" or an "I." For her, Male 1, Male 2, Female 2, Female 3, Male Government Official, Male Secretary, Female Government Official, etc. may all be *you* (with names and as persons she may know). Her you/we releases other conceptions of the assembly into an analytical space occupied by autonomous Is, 1s, 2s, etc. It offers a chance to think of the citizens of the *gram sabha* as *yous*, where every you, along with their other purposes, *matters* to and for any *we*.

This is not to deny Female 1 an "I." She expresses her gratefulness ("I will convey my thanks."). It suggests there is something other than an 1/I/we in the conception of the citizen subject who has been classified as Female 1. Because of her words, "If you can . . . , we can . . .", we may imagine a you/we assembly. If you can, then we can. Linked abilities, if you will. If you, we. If you cannot, we cannot. If not you, not we. If you, we are a different we. We rely upon each other. There is no we without a you. To imagine this assembly with Female 1 in this way is to begin to imagine any assembly in this way.

Male 1's interruption thus may be *more severe* than we had originally thought. He not only redirects the topic from wheels and wells to kitchens, toilets, canals, playgrounds, and libraries. He drives the exchange away from the potentiality of her deliberatively posed you/we. It may not be a decisive diversion. His constituted subjectivity is also not easily discerned here. His "we" has an "our." He speaks of "our children," "our President," and "our requests." Given the groups whose needs he expresses, he may be seen, like Female 1, as representing other voices and other purposes, too. He values general knowledge that the children need to fulfill their dreams of becoming IAS and IPS officers. Female 1 may as well. He is attentive to the dreams of the children and hopeful that the president, who has not said "'no' for any of our requests . . . will definitely do whatever we have asked." With that, he says, "I take leave." And yet, we may nonetheless wonder how his discourse and performance might have been different had he deliberated with, or heard himself addressed and entrusted by, Female 1's "if you . . . then we." Her "you/we," uninterrupted, may engender more respect, care, and continuity within the assembly, and it may even lend itself to a reduction of the unequal gender power relations between her and Male 1, between uninterrupted women and interrupting men. Of course, a different "you/we" is no guarantee that her " . . ." would have set the agenda. Even if it did, there will be other subaltern " . . ." that will always give beyond the immediate record.

The poetics of bold citizen speech offers us a chance to be touched and reached, as well as to think, feel, bear, and care for things differently and in . . . relations and arrangements. Parthasarathy, Rao, and Palaniswamy carry teachings from the subaltern women in the *gram sabha*s and release them into the space of *APSR* and its dataverse, where others *will* receive the data for what, *as data*, they necessarily *give on* for further bearing and caring, for other purposes and receptions in other conceptual, paradigmatic, relational, and responsive contexts. Others will validate the bold data of the citizens of the *gram sabha* and may bear and care for them otherwise, originally, in replications of their givenness to come.

Poetic attunement combines hermeneutical attentiveness to the silenced meanings and teachings of the subaltern other with open, affective, and ethical bearing and caring to generate original thought about the social and political world. Making such attunement happen as a consistent part of explanatory efforts, I have argued, intensifies the empirical, pragmatic, and normative qualities of existing political analysis. It discloses inklings of deeply cared for causal possibility that reside amid patterns of causality discerned with empiricist insight; it draws out the affective subtleties of meaningfulness within matrices of constitutive meanings perspicaciously surfaced through hermeneutical conversation; it opens up surprising, worthwhile, and profoundly moving transformative avenues for practical and discursive intervention within and around the structures and constituting discourses of power raised for contention by critical theory; and it yields an abundance of poignant subtle teachings within subaltern silences brought to presence in postcolonial, subaltern studies.

At the same time, as seen in the entrusting expressions of "worry" and "need" above, as well as in the authors' attentiveness to the concerns of those most disadvantaged by power, poetic attunement is already happening—transparently and reliably— even in contemporary political science not centrally motivated by such attunement.[41] It is happening in bold moments of critical and original insight, where inquirers *so* obviously cannot but convey the palpitating, affective, and ethical depth of their study and the profound needs it suggests. The qualities of poetic attunement in contemporary political science research should be endorsed, embraced, and elaborated as integral to serious social scientific data analysis. Receiving them as such—as data given for new assemblies of attuned social and political analysis— would constitute receptivity to the teachings of Asya al-Ulama, Emine Sevgi Özdamar, Bhubaneswari Bhaduri, Gayatri Chakravorty Spivak, Doctor Cemal, Ercan Kesal, Henry Hammond, Thomas Urquhart, Ramya Parthasarathy, Vijayendra Rao, Nethra Palaniswamy, and Female 1. If **you** can . . . , **we** can. *And you are.*

NOTES

INTRODUCTION: POETIC ATTUNEMENT

1. Ahdaf Soueif, *In the Eye of the Sun* (New York: Anchor, 1992), 430.
2. Soueif, *In the Eye of the Sun*, 674.
3. Soueif, *In the Eye of the Sun*, 677.
4. Soueif, *In the Eye of the Sun*, 434. The verse is from "A Song," written by Digby Mackworth Dolben (1848–1867); this citation does not appear in the novel.
5. Soueif, *In the Eye of the Sun*, 434.
6. Soueif, *In the Eye of the Sun*, 434. The verse is from "His Coy Mistress," written by Andrew Marvell (1621–1678); this citation does not appear in the novel.
7. Soueif, *In the Eye of the Sun*, 434.
8. Empiricism aims to show that specific phenomena may be explained as instances of general patterns among operationalized and statistically coded variables, and interpretive inquiry studies the constitutive languages of social and political life to identify and analyze patterns of conceptual meaning. For extensive exposition and comparison with other modes of contemporary social scientific inquiry, see Andrew Davison and Mark Hoffman, *Interpreting Politics: Debating the Foundations and Objectives of Political Analysis* (New York: Sloan, 2019).
9. Gerald Bruns is characterizing and discussing Hans-Georg Gadamer's account of poetry, "The Remembrance of Language: An Introduction

to Gadamer's Poetics," in *Gadamer on Celan: "Who Am I and Who Are You?"* (Albany: State University of New York Press, 1997), 26.

10. Bruns, "The Remembrance of Language," 26.

11. Bruns, "The Remembrance of Language," 26.

12. Bruns, "The Remembrance of Language," 24. He emphasizes that poems "turn [speakers] into listeners" (8).

13. Jacques Derrida, "Rams: Uninterrupted Dialogue—Between Two Infinities, the Poem," in *Sovereignties in Question: The Poetics of Paul Celan*, ed. Thomas Dutoit and Outi Pasanen (New York: Fordham University Press, 2005), 159.

14. Soueif, *In the Eye of the Sun*, 436, emphasis in original.

15. Asya goes on to complete the work of her dissertation within the limits and constraints of the methods she applies (Soueif, *In the Eye of the Sun*, 684). She classifies what she needs to classify, counts and calculates what she needs to count and calculate, and shows what she needs to show, but later, she is more dismissive. She describes her comprehensive and nuanced data-based analyses of the factors, levels, and mathematical symbolics and measurements of particular kinds of MMUs as "completely stupid' and "useless" (678). "I can't bear it," she tells her mother at one point. This is not the kind of "radically new" and "important" literary project upon which she had hoped to embark for her doctorate (421).

16. Gayatri Chakravorty Spivak, "In Response: Looking Back, Looking Forward," in *Can the Subaltern Speak? Reflections on the History of an Idea*, ed. Rosalind C. Morris (New York: Columbia University Press, 2010), 230, 235.

17. Jürgen Habermas, *Knowledge and Human Interests* (Boston: Beacon, 1972), 308–314.

18. In 2012, the American Political Science Association formalized these requirements as part of its ethics guide, declaring, "Researchers have an ethical obligation to facilitate the evaluation of their evidence based knowledge claims through data access, production transparency, and analytic transparency so that their work can be tested or replicated." "2012 DART Ethics Guide Changes," https://www.dartstatement.org /2012-apsa-ethics-guide-changes. See also "Appendix A: Guidelines for Data Access and Research Transparency for Qualitative Research in

Political Science, Draft August 7, 2013," *PS: Political Science and Politics* 47, no. 1 (January 2014): 25–37.

19. Arthur Lupia and Colin Elman, "Introduction: Openness in Political Science: Data Access and Transparency," *PS: Political Science and Politics* 47, no. 1 (January 2014): 20. DART's strongest supporters acknowledge the methodological diversity of political science and argue that data transparency standards should be welcome by all, since such standards will facilitate "cross-border understanding" within the discipline (20). They view data transparency standards as "epistemically neutral," applicable to research conducted across "research traditions" and "communities" of political science, including nonquantitative research (20–22). See also Colin Elman and Diana Kapiszewski, "Data Access and Research Transparency in the Qualitative Tradition," *PS: Political Science and Politics* 47, no. 1 (January 2014): 43–47.

20. Timothy Pachirat, "The Tyranny of Light." *Qualitative & Multi-Method Research* 13, no. 1 (Spring 2015): 28; and Andrew Davison, "Hermeneutics and the Question of Transparency," *Qualitative and Multi-Method Research* 13, no. 1 (Spring 2015): 43–47. As Björkman, Wedeen, Williams, and Hawkesworth write, "The current transparency initiative can be seen . . . as an effort to discipline the discipline by making qualitative data more legible to scholars of quantitative political science, thereby riding roughshod over potentially fecund areas of epistemological, methodological, and political discovery and disagreement" (Lisa Björkman, Lisa Wedeen, Juliet Williams, and Mary Hawkesworth, "Interpretive Methods," *American Political Science Association Organized Section for Qualitative and Multi-Method Research, Qualitative Transparency Deliberations, Working Group Final Reports, Report III.2* (January 2019): 6–7, 9, https://ssrn.com/abstract=3333411). Similarly, Luke, Vázquez-Arroyo and Hawkesworth charge that, "under the banner of 'research integrity,'" advocates of DART "invent certainty where certainty is implausible, invent unity where it often has not existed, and create continuity out of discontinuities." See Timothy Luke, Antonio Vázquez-Arroyo, and Mary Hawkesworth, "Epistemological and Ontological Priors: Explicating the Perils of Transparency," *American Political Science Association Organized Section for Qualitative and Multi-Method Research, Qualitative Transparency Deliberations, Working Group*

Final Reports, Report 1.1–2 (December 2018): 8, 18–19, https://ssrn.com /abstract=3332878.) Jeffrey C. Isaac further expresses concern about the absence of political engagement in DART discussions: "The DART initiative is animated by a preoccupation with methodological purity, and an interest in institutionalizing new forms of expectation and evaluation of scholarly work. Behind these commitments is a particular view of social science—that it is not a never-ending contest between perspectives on politics but instead about the veridical understanding of the world as a set of objective processes. Almost a century ago, John Dewey referred to this conception of science as a "quest for certainty." There are many reasons, both epistemological and practical, to be suspicious of this quest." (Jeffrey C. Isaac, "For a More Public Political Science," *PS: Political Science and Politics* 13, no. 2 (June 2015): 275–76).

21. Dvora Yanow and Peregrine Schwartz-Shea, "Introduction," in *Interpretation and Method: Empirical Research Methods and the Interpretive Turn*, ed. Dvora Yanow and Peregrine Schwartz-Shea (New York: Routledge, 2014), xix. See also Mark Bevir and Jason Blakely, *Interpretive Social Science: An Anti-Naturalist Approach* (Oxford: Oxford University Press, 2019). Bevir and Blakely endorse an interpretive understanding of "data collection" as "collecting information . . . about the meanings, beliefs, actions, practices, and so on that comprise social reality" (89–90).

22. For review of classic philosophical statements by Wittgenstein, Kuhn, and Quine, see Davison and Hoffman, *Interpreting Politics*, 33–52.

23. Sabina Leonelli, *Data-Centric Biology: A Philosophical Study* (Chicago: Chicago University Press, 2016), and "What Counts as Scientific Data? A Relational Framework," *Philosophy of Science* 82, no. 5 (December 2015): 810–21. Leonelli emphasizes data's alterability in their portability, as they are disseminated within and across differently located conceptual, interpretative, material, and social settings. "Data are not only modifiable in principle but in fact frequently modified during their travels in ways that profoundly affect their ability to function as evidence" ("What Counts," 820).

24. Yanow and Schwartz-Shea, "Introduction," xix.

25. Katherine Cramer, "Transparent Explanations, Yes. Public Transcripts and Fieldnotes, No: Ethnographic Research on Public Opinion,"

Qualitative & Multi-Method Research 13, no. 1 (Spring 2015): 19. Similarly, in relation to ethnographic field notes, Pachirat observes, "There is no prior non-relational, non-interpretive moment . . . no prior raw 'data' to reference back to" (Pachirat, "The Tyranny," 30).

26. Luke, Vázquez-Arroyo, and Hawkesworth, "Epistemological and Ontological Priors," 9. "Observation is always linguistically and culturally mediated. It involves the creative imposition of expectations, anticipations and conjectures upon external events. . . . The pervasive role of theoretical assumptions upon the practice of science has profound implications for notions such as empirical 'reality' and the 'autonomy' of facts, which posit that facts are 'given' and experience is ontologically distinct from the theoretical constructs that are advanced to explain it. The postpositivist conception of a 'fact' as a theoretically constituted entity calls into question such basic assumptions" (13). The postempiricist approach to data revives the central idea of Wilfrid Sellars's classic essay, "The Myth of the Given," in *Science, Perception and Reality* (London: Routledge & Kegan Paul, 1963), 127–96.

27. For theoretically informed discussions of datafication, algorithmic governance, and big data, see John Cheney-Lippold, *We Are Data: Algorithms and the Making of Our Digital Selves* (New York: New York University Press, 2017); and Rob Kitchin, *The Data Revolution: Big Data, Open Data, Data Infrastructures & Their Consequences* (Los Angeles: Sage, 2014).

28. Leonelli, *Data-Centric Biology*; and Sabina Leonelli, "Learning from Data Journeys," in *Data Journeys in the Sciences*, ed. Sabina Leonelli and Nicollò Tempini (Cham, Switzerland: Springer, 2020), i, 5–9.

29. On issues of presence and absences, see Sabina Leonelli, Brian Rappert, and Gail Davies, "Data Shadows: Knowledge, Openness, and Absence," *Science, Technology, & Human Values* 42, no. 2 (2017): 194. The authors consider "absence" an "umbrella term" for these words: missing, incomplete, unreliable, ignored, unwanted, untagged, "not there," "not useable toward proving claims or fostering discoveries," invisible, tacit, denied, expected, forbidden, private, inaccessible, unknown, or unexplored (192–93).

30. On antidemocratic practices of data governance, see Cheney-Lippold, *We Are Data*; Shoshana Zuboff, *The Age of Surveillance Capitalism: The*

Fight for a Human Future at the New Frontier of Power (New York: Public Affairs, 2019); Virginia Eubanks, *Automated Inequality: How High-Tech Tools Profile, Police and Punish the Poor* (New York: St. Martin's, 2018); Safiya Umoja Noble, *Algorithms of Oppression: How Search Engines Reinforce Oppression* (New York: New York University Press, 2018); Ruha Benjamin, *Race After Technology* (Cambridge: Polity, 2019); Byung-Chul Han, *Infocracy: Digitalization and the Crisis of Democracy* (Cambridge: Polity, 2022), and *Psychopolitics: Neoliberalism and New Technologies* (New York: Verso, 2017); and Cathy O'Neil, *Weapons of Math Destruction: How Big Data Increases Inequality and Threatens Democracy* (New York: Crown, 2016).

31. Sabina Leonelli, "Locating Ethics in Data Science: Responsibility and Accountability in Global and Distributed Knowledge Production Systems," *Philosophical Transactions: Mathematical, Physical and Engineering Sciences* 374, no. 2083 (December 2016): 6.

32. Rob Kitchin, *Data Lives: How Data Are Made and Shape Our World* (Bristol: Bristol University Press, 2021), 222. See also Kitchin and Alistair Fraser's discussion in *Slow Computing: Why We Need Balanced Digital Lives* (Bristol: Bristol University Press, 2020), 135–39. On the empiricist flaws of technocratic governance, see Jeffrey Friedman, *Power Without Knowledge: A Critique of Technocracy* (Oxford: Oxford University Press, 2020), 139, 237, 329.

33. Cheney-Lippold, for example, finds "reflexive" possibility and a "sliver of agency" in what he calls "the else," which he describes as a kind of "wiggle room" between "the patterns shaped by algorithmic governmentality and life" or "the subjective surplus that maintains" "gaps . . . between datafied and non-datafied life" (Cheney-Lippold, *We Are Data*, 18, 194, 179). Zuboff draws on Hannah Arendt and George Orwell and argues that the "smooth flows of coercive confluence" of surveillance capitalism can be interrupted with a concept of freedom as "being the friction" (Zuboff, *Surveillance Capitalism*, 524).

34. Sabina Leonelli, "Scientific Research and Big Data," *Stanford Encyclopedia of Philosophy*, 2020, https://plato.stanford.edu/entries/science-big-data.

35. Leonelli, Rappert, and Davies, "Data Shadows," 192.

36. Leonelli, "Learning from Data Journeys," 6; Leonelli, "What Counts as Scientific Data," 818; and Leonelli, *Data-Centric Biology*, 71–75.

I. LIVING ON AT THE BORDER

1. Emine Sevgi Özdamar, *Mother Tongue*, trans. Craig Thomas (Toronto: Coach House, 1994), 12. The spelling of *gecirmek*, here and below, is a vernacular usage, accurate to the original German and English translation.
2. Reece Jones, *Violent Borders: Refugees and the Right to Move* (New York: Verso, 2016), 3–4.
3. Andrew Davison, *Border Thinking on the Edges of the West: Crossing Over the Hellespont* (New York: Routledge, 2014).
4. "They are not immigrants. They are not immigrants. They're . . . they're invaders. They are not immigrants. They are not immigrants, they are invaders. . . . There is no other word to describe it. . . . If you do not have permission to be in our country and you cross our border, by definition, you are an invader."—Steve Cortes, *CNN*, June 19, 2018, https://www.cnn.com/videos/politics/2018/06/19/invaders-steve-cortes-maria-cardona-family-separations-ebof.cnn.
5. "They could be murderers and thieves and so much else." Donald Trump, quoted in Katie Rogers and Sheryl Gay Stolberg, "Trump Resisting a Growing Wrath for Separating Migrant Families," *New York Times*, June 18, 2018, https://www.nytimes.com/2018/06/18/us/politics/trump-immigration-germany-merkel.html; and Donald Trump, "Former President Trump's 2024 Campaign Announcement," accessed April 27, 2023, https://www.c-span.org/video/?524197-1/president-trumps-2024-campaign-announcement.
6. Joseph R. Biden, press conference, March 25, 2021, accessed March 26, 2021, https://www.whitehouse.gov/briefing-room/speeches-remarks/2021/03/25/remarks-by-president-biden-in-press-conference/.
7. Reece Jones, *Violent Borders*, 4, 10, 179–80.
8. Geoffrey Lewis, *The Turkish Language Reform: A Catastrophic Success* (Oxford: Oxford University Press, 2002).
9. Özdamar, *Mother Tongue*, 34.
10. Özdamar, *Mother Tongue*, 15.
11. Özdamar, *Mother Tongue*, 33–34.
12. Özdamar, *Mother Tongue*, 24.
13. Özdamar, *Mother Tongue*, 29.
14. Özdamar, *Mother Tongue*, 35.
15. Özdamar, *Mother Tongue*, 34.

16. Özdamar, *Mother Tongue*, 46. Both words for patience appear as in the original.
17. He says, "I will lose my work. You don't know, there is an Orientalist woman, she asks me very precise questions about the accusative, the dative" (Özdamar, *Mother Tongue*, 50).
18. Özdamar, *Mother Tongue*, 46.
19. Özdamar, *Mother Tongue*, 50–51.
20. Özdamar, *Mother Tongue*, 52.
21. Özdamar, *Mother Tongue*, 54.
22. Özdamar, *Mother Tongue*, 54.
23. Özdamar, *Mother Tongue*, 55.
24. Özdamar, *Mother Tongue*, 55–57.
25. Özdamar, *Mother Tongue*, 57.
26. Hans-Georg Gadamer, *Truth and Method* (New York: Continuum, 1989), 297. For an adaptation of Gadamer's philosophical hermeneutics to the goals of political inquiry, see my *Secularism and Revivalism in Turkey: A Hermeneutic Reconsideration* (New Haven, CT: Yale University Press, 1998); and "Hermeneutics and the Politics of Secularism," in *Secularism and Politics in a Global Age*, ed. Linell Cady and Elizabeth Shakman Hurd (New York: Palgrave, 2010), 25–39.
27. Gayatri Chakravorty Spivak, "In Response: Looking Back, Looking Forward," in *Can the Subaltern Speak? Reflections on the History of an Idea*, ed. Rosalind C. Morris (New York: Columbia University Press, 2010), 230.
28. Spivak, *Can the Subaltern Speak*, 63.
29. Spivak, *Can the Subaltern Speak*, 62.
30. Spivak, *Can the Subaltern Speak*, 62.
31. "This is widow sacrifice. (The conventional transcription of the Sanskrit word for the widow would be *sati*. The early colonial British transcribed it as *suttee*.)" In her archival research on the practice, Spivak found it impossible to encounter what she called "the voice consciousness" of the widows. Their subject position, Spivak observed, was simultaneously represented and erased in both British colonial and Indian patriarchal discourse. One could search and search the archives and "never encounter [their] voice consciousness" (Spivak, *Can the Subaltern Speak*, 49–50).
32. Spivak, *Can the Subaltern Speak*, 62.

33. Spivak, "In Response," 235.
34. Spivak, "In Response," 235.
35. Özdamar, *Mother Tongue*, 47.
36. Compare Hélène Cixous's characterization of "the chanciness, the accidence" of such happenings. See "My Algeriance, in Other Words: To Depart Not to Arrive from Algeria," *TriQuarterly* 100 (1997): 259.
37. Walter Benjamin, "The Task of the Translator," in *Walter Benjamin: Selected Writings, Volume 1, 1913–1926*, ed. Marcus Bullock and Michael W. Jennings (Cambridge, MA: Harvard University Press, 1996): 253–63.
38. Jacques Derrida, "The Last Interview," special issue of *SV*, accessed August 2, 2024, https://xdoc.mx/preview/jacques-derrida-the-last -interview-5ee3ef135e5a3.
39. Derrida, "The Last Interview."
40. Jacques Derrida, *Parages*, ed. John P. Leavey (Palo Alto, CA: Stanford University Press, 2010), 106.
41. Derrida finds "what is proper to an act or instance of living on" in a passage from Maurice Blanchot's *Death Sentence*, where the narrator writes, "She was gay, and I was gay too." Derrida underscores "the levity of its affirmation, of the *yes, yes, yes* to *yes*" in relation to the receptivity displayed by the narrator toward the other, a receptivity or hospitality that, for Derrida, happens "without self-recollection" (Jacques Derrida, *Parages*, 153–54).
42. "It is unusual to find the verb *fortleben* (or noun *Fortleben*) in any but the largest German dictionaries, and almost impossible to find it in dictionaries predating the composition of *Die Aufgabe* (1921). This suggests that *fortleben* was not at all common currency at the time that Benjamin wrote his essay. Nor, for that matter, was the English word 'afterlife,' which is also seldom to be found in older dictionaries. More recent, large, bilingual dictionaries such as the *Oxford-Duden* do sometimes include *fortleben* (1991, *s.v.*). An English equivalent is not provided; the entry is simply followed by 's. *weiterleben*' (where s. = *siehe*, 'see'). The English equivalents for *weiterleben* are: 1. continue or carry on one's life; 2. (*am Leben bleiben*) go on living; 3. (*fig.*) live on." Caroline Disler, "Benjamin's "Afterlife": A Productive (?) Mistranslation in Memoriam Daniel Simeoni," *Érudit: TTR: traduction, terminologie, redaction* 24, no. 1 (2011): 186.
43. On accident tied to trauma, compare Cathy Caruth, *Unclaimed Experience: Trauma, Narrative, and History* (Baltimore, MD: Johns Hopkins

University Press, 1996). For accidents' relation to poetic experience, see "Words and Wounds: A Conversation with Geoffrey Hartman," in Cathy Caruth, *Listening to Trauma: Conversations with Leaders in the Theory and Treatment of Catastrophic Experience* (Baltimore, MD: Johns Hopkins University Press, 2014), 212–35.

44. Derrida, *Parages*, 107.

45. *Rive* also means "shore" or "bank."

46. Derrida, *Parages*, 107.

47. Many other words have survived as well. This recalls the debate within the nationalist movement at the time of the language reforms, with the purificationists endorsing a thorough formal purging and others arguing that words from Arabic and Persian that have become part of the living language of the Turks should be retained. They should remain, survive, and live on, and, indeed, some have.

48. Derrida, *Parages*, 110.

49. Derrida, *Parages*, 107.

50. Özdamar, *Mother Tongue*, 9.

51. "My mother and I sometimes spoke in my mother tongue. My mother said, 'You know what? You just keep on talking, you think you're saying everything, but suddenly you jump over unspoken words, and you just keep talking" (Özdamar, *Mother Tongue*, 9).

52. Özdamar, *Mother Tongue*, 15.

53. Walter Brogan, "Basic Concepts of Hermeneutics: Understanding Gadamer's Sense of Tradition and Community," *Duquesne Studies in Philosophy* 1, no. 1 (2020): 3.

54. Özdamar, *Mother Tongue*, 12.

55. For compatible criticism of the colonizing potential of dominant categories of migration, see the "autonomy of migration" literature in critical border studies. This literature emphasizes the fullness of migrant politics, subjectivities, and socialities that are independent from, or at least not reducible to or exhausted by, the politics and discourses of state immigration and border management, regulation, and control. See Dimitris Papadopoulos and Vassilis S. Tsianos, "After Citizenship: Autonomy of Migration, Organizational Ontology and Mobile Commons," *Citizenship Studies* 17, no. 2 (2013): 178–96; and Sandro Mezzadra, "The Gaze of Autonomy: Capitalism, Migration, and Social

Struggles," in *The Contested Politics of Mobility: Borderzones and Irregularity*, ed. Vickie Squire (London: Routledge, 2010): 121–42. Mezzadra suggests that the "autonomy" concept reaches back to early "mainstream" migration studies. See Stephen Castles and Mark J. Miller, *The Age of Migration: International Population Movements in the Modern World* (New York: Guilford, 2003). The discourse analytical emphasis of the autonomy of migration literature on (potentially emancipatory) struggles, strategies, tactics, and resistances undertaken by migrants contrasts with the emphasis I am placing, in conversation with Özdamar and Derrida, on the constitutive qualities of survival as living on.

56. For the presentation of an early version of this chapter at Sabanci University on October 24, 2018, I included the following comments: "I want to pause and connect this subaltern teaching to what is happening at that moment south of the U.S. border. Perhaps you have heard of the so-called 'caravan' of migrants whose march to the United States the U.S. President has characterized as an 'invasion' of 'criminals' and many 'bad people.' He often says 'bad *hombres*'; so much for 'his' 'wall.' If you listen to those walking north, they constitute their movement in terms very closely related to surviving as living on, not in relation to the violent matrix of meanings associated with the idea of crossing over a border that is projected onto them in today's dominant discourse of immigration. Reading the news and listening to the radio these past few days, I have collected a few of the words they have shared with reporters: One person described their movement as looking for a future that was unavailable back home. No work back home, 'no future' (*CNN*), so this person is living on as *living for a future*; another says, 'We won't be broken' (*Time*)—this person is living on as *not being broken*; another: 'I just want to be able to provide for my children. I can't do that at home'—living on as *providing for one's children*; another: 'We just want to move ahead with our lives'—living on *as living ahead*; another: 'I'm going anywhere I can find a job'—living on as *living anywhere there is work*; another, asked by a reporter to give a message to Donald Trump, says, 'All we want is to be able to give our children a better life' (*MSNBC*)—living on as *giving a better life to one's children*. These are not *crossers*, as projected in the discourse of border crossing. The dominant border imagination does not speak to and with the primary constitutive

terms of their experience." "No future" from Dakin Andone, Patrick Oppmann, and Natalie Gallón, "Migrant Caravan Resumes March North from Mexico-Guatemala Border," *CNN*, October 22, 2018, https://www.cnn.com/2018/10/21/americas/migrant-caravan-mexico /index.html; "We won't be" from Ioan Grillo, "'We Won't Be Broken.' Caravan of Migrants Sets Sights on U.S., Defying President Trump's Threats," *Time*, October 21, 2018, https://time.com/5430436/migrant -caravan-mexico-guatemala-border/. The others are notes I took while watching and listening to various news reports in the days preceding the talk. Such testimony exists in abundance.

57. "If you take a look at the number of people who are coming, the vast majority, the overwhelming majority of people coming to the border and *crossing* [emphasis added] are being sent back—are being sent back. Thousands—tens of thousands of people who are—who are over eighteen years of age and single—people, one at a time coming, have been sent back, sent home. We're sending back the vast majority of the families that are coming."—Joseph R. Biden, press conference, March 25, 2021, https://www.whitehouse.gov/briefing-room/speeches-remarks /2021/03/25/remarks-by-president-biden-in-press-conference/. Also, "if you come to our border ['illegally'], you will be turned back"—Kamala Harris, quoted in Felicia Sonmez, Colby Itkowitz, Eugene Scott, and John Wagner, "Harris Warns Guatemalans They Will Be Turned Back If They Come to the US Border," *Washington Post*, June 7, 2021, https:// www.washingtonpost.com/politics/2021/06/07/joe-biden-live-updates/.

2. POETIC POSSIBILITY

1. Plato, *The Republic*, trans. G. M. A. Grube, revised by C. D. C. Reeve (Indianapolis, IN: Hackett, 1992), 279.

2. Gayatri Chakravorty Spivak, *Can the Subaltern Speak? Reflections on the History of an Idea*, ed. Rosalind C. Morris (New York: Columbia University Press, 2010), 230.

3. For "the care of the other," see Jacques Derrida, *Sovereignties in Question: The Poetics of Paul Celan*, ed. Thomas Dutoit and Outi Pasanen (New York: Fordham University Press, 2005), 159. For the element of control, see Gerald Bruns, characterizing and discussing Hans-Georg

Gadamer's account of poetry, in "The Remembrance of Language: An Introduction to Gadamer's Poetics," in Hans-Georg Gadamer, *Gadamer on Celan: "Who Am I and Who Are You?"* (Albany: State University of New York Press, 1997), 26.

4. Scholars in many social science disciplines are calling for more literary and poetic forms of writing. A classic is Deirdre N. McCloskey's *The Rhetoric of Economics* (Madison: University of Wisconsin Press, 1985). McCloskey argues that the social scientific discourse of economics, which uses metaphors as "instruments of thought," is already highly "literary" and could "improve" with more purposeful "rhetorical thinking" (*The Rhetoric*, 68, 65, 74, 175). Similarly, Andrew Abbott draws on literary theory and classical poetry to endorse a form of sociological analysis that he calls "lyrical sociology." Lyrical sociology offers "an emotional sense of social reality" by conveying "a particular author's emotional relation to a particular social moment" (Andrew Abbott, "Against Narrative: A Preface to Lyrical Sociology," *Sociological Theory* 25, no. 1 (March 2007): 73, 77). See also Tim Cresswell, "Geographies of Poetry/Poetries of Geography," *Cultural Geographies* 21, no. 1 (2014): 141–46; and Sarah de Leeuw, "Writing as Righting: Truth and Reconciliation, Poetics, and New Geo-graphing in Colonial Canada," *Canadian Geographies* 61, no. 3 (Fall 2017): 306-18.

5. For a recent scholarly demonstration and analysis, see Walt Hunter, *Forms of a World: Contemporary Poetry and the Making of Globalization* (New York: Fordham University Press, 2019).

6. Terry Eagleton, *How to Read a Poem* (Oxford: Blackwell, 2007), 25.

7. Gerald Bruns, "The Remembrance," 18.

8. Naomi Shihab Nye, "Before I Was a Gazan," in *Voices in the Air* (New York: Harper Collins, 2018), 138.

9. Nye, "Before I Was a Gazan."

10. Nye, "Before I Was a Gazan."

11. Jeffrey Wainwright, *Poetry: The Basics* (New York: Routledge, 2004), xxi.

12. Hamid Dabashi, *The World Is My Home*, ed. Andrew Davison and Himadeep Muppidi (New Brunswick, NJ: Transaction, 2011), 237–48.

13. Compare discussion of Gadamer on poetry in Bruns, "The Remembrance," 6. Gadamer writes of the poetic word as "withdrawing from its

function as a sign." For Dabashi, a sign with no meaning makes sense. For Gadamer it does not; the poetic word ceases to be a sign.

14. In that space, it is as if the reader, in wonderment, sees their "own language staring [them] back in the face" (Bruns, "The Remembrances," 7). The reader sees what philosophers, following Martin Heidegger, have called the "bareness" or "materiality" of the word, the word before all meaning occurs (Eagleton, *How to Read a Poem*, 47). Of course, thinking hermeneutically, the language is not "bare," which is the response to the unfamiliar difference of signs that have lost familiar meaning, and there appears to be only the word palpitating with possibility. See also Gerald Bruns, "Almost as If," *The Iowa Review* 37, no. 2 (2007): 170.

15. Dabashi, *The World Is My Home*, 240 ("rebel"); Bruns, "The Remembrance," 1, 10.

16. Bruns, "The Remembrance," 7.

17. Bruns, "The Remembrance," 44.

18. Elizabeth Bishop, "One Art," in *Poems* (New York: Farrar, Straus, and Giroux, 2011), 198.

19. Bruns, "The Remembrance," 18.

20. Rukmini Bhaya Nair, "Genderrole," in *Language for a New Century: Contemporary Poetry from the Middle East, Asia, and Beyond*, ed. Tina Chang, Nathalie Handal, and Ravi Shankar (New York: Norton, 2008) 126. The editor notes that the "poem is written in the run on graphemic style of Sanskrit" (127).

21. Eagleton, *How to Read a Poem*, 21.

22. On "affect" in the social sciences, see Gregory J. Seigworth and Melissa Gregg, eds., *The Affect Theory Reader* (Durham, NC: Duke University Press, 2000). In characterizing affect, Seigworth and Gregg emphasize preconscious "forces and passages of intensity" in "intimately impersonal," "prepersonal," and "sub-personal" "folds of belonging (and not belonging) to a world" (3).

23. This thought is in conversation with Mary Kinzie, *A Poet's Guide to Poetry*, 2nd ed. (Chicago: University of Chicago Press, 2013), 2–11.

24. Gadamer follows Paul Celan, who described the poem as "an instance of language, hence essentially dialogue" (Celan, quoted and discussed in Bruns, "The Remembrance," 16).

25. Quoted and discussed in Bruns, "The Remembrance," 28.

26. Bruns, "The Remembrance," 26.

27. Gadamer, *Gadamer on Celan*, 96. See also discussion in Derrida, *Sovereignties*, 145.

28. Rainer Maria Rilke, "Initiation," in *An Invitation to Poetry*, ed. Robert Pinksy and Maggie Dietz (New York: Norton, 2004), 197.

29. Bruns on Heidegger, in Bruns, "The Remembrance," 23.

30. Helen Vendler, *The Ocean, the Bird, and the Scholar: Essays on Poets & Poetry* (Cambridge, MA: Harvard University Press, 2015), 12.

31. Behçet Necatigil, "Nilüfer," in *Şiirler* (Istanbul: Yapı Kredi Yayınları, 2002), 209.

32. Steven Burt, *the poem is you* (Cambridge, MA: Harvard University Press, 2016), 21.

33. John Ashbery, "Paradoxes and Oxymorons," quoted in Burt, *the poem*, 17.

34. Burt, *the poem*, 18.

35. Burt, *the poem*, 18.

36. Jorie Graham, "Prayer," in *Never* (New York: Ecco, 2002), 3.

37. Khadija El Alaoui and Maura Pilotti, "Walking with Lips Raining Fire and Love! Arab Poets' Testimony to the World," *Interventions* 21, no. 5 (2019): 714.

38. Bruns, "The Remembrance," 21.

39. Bruns, "The Remembrance," 24, 26. He emphases that poems "turn [speakers] into listeners" (8).

40. Mong-Lan, "Overhearing Water," in Chang, Handal, and Shankar, *Language for a New Century*, 23.

41. Derrida, *Sovereignties*, 141.

42. Paul Celan, "The Meridian [1960]," quoted in Derrida, *Sovereignties*, 159.

43. Emphasis in original, quoted in Derrida, *Sovereignties*, 9.

44. Gerald Bruns, *What Are Poets For? An Anthropology of Contemporary Poetry and Poets* (Iowa City: University of Iowa Press, 2012), 24. In "Remembrance," Bruns suggests that the "wholly other" points to a "pure [poetic] exteriority," one liberated from all hermeneutic or ethical status: "an otherness more Blanchovian than Levinasian, not just that which is otherwise than being, the ethical [Levinas], but that which is neither one nor the other, outside even the ethical relation in which an I is turned inside out before the *Autrui*. A pure exteriority: a freedom for which we have no words. . . . For Celan, as for Maurice Blanchot, freedom is the outside,

the region of the other, of *others near and far*, of foreignness itself. The movement of poetry is toward this region" ("The Remembrance," 23, emphasis added). See also discussion in Catherine Homan's philosophical account of a poetically attuned—conversationally playful, responsible, vulnerable, transformative, liberating—model of education in *The Hermeneutics of Poetic Education: The Play of the In-Between* (Lanham, MD: Lexington, 2020), 7–8, 64–67, 175.

45. The reader's recognition of this otherness raises questions about the "wholly otherness" of the wholly other; some have described this wholly other as the other that is within the self, the other that is constitutive of the self but of which the self is consciously unaware.

46. Kevin Young, "Brown," in *Brown: Poems* (New York: Knopf, 2018), 67.

47. Bringing the content of one's attuned response to expression requires thoughtful reflection, but the experience of bearing and caring that makes the attunement and its expression possible occurs prior to that reflection. I follow Emmanuel Levinas and Andrew Bush here. See Levinas, *Totality and Infinity* (Pittsburgh, PA: Duquesne University Press, 1969); and Bush, *Jewish Studies* (New Brunswick, NJ: Rutgers University Press, 2013). For discussion, see Bruns, "Should Poetry Be Ethical or Otherwise?" in *What Are Poets For? An Anthropology of Contemporary Poetry and Poets* (Iowa City: University of Iowa Press, 2012), 19.

48. Theorists of "care ethics" similarly recognize care to comprise a wide range of complex practices, including "responsibility for the other." See Daniel Engster and Maurice Harrington, "Introduction," in Engster and Harrington, eds., *Care Ethics and Political Theory* (Oxford: Oxford University Press, 2015), 3. See also Joan Tronto, "Theories of Care as a Challenge to Weberian Paradigms in Social Science" in the same volume. Tronto writes that care "is a complex set of practices . . . require[ing] caring about, caring for, caregiving, care receiving, and caring with. They also require the refinement of many moral qualities, including attentiveness, deep reflection on responsibility, competence in caregiving, and responsiveness both to care receivers and to the process and effectiveness of care itself. Finally, caring with requires the qualities of solidary and trust" (Tronto, "Theories of Care," 162).

49. Vendler, *The Ocean*, 3.

50. Kinzie, *A Poet's Guide to Poetry*, 16.

51. Rishma Dunlop, "Saccade," in Chang, Handal, and Shankar, *Language for a New Century*, 579.

52. Eagleton sees the poet's decision to end a line as one of the central, distinguishing characteristics of poetry. Line breaks can signify and "even act as a kind of image" (Eagleton, *How to Read a Poem*, 25–26). James Longenbach quotes George Oppen: "The meaning of a poem is in the cadences and the shape of the lines and in the pulse of the thought that is given in those lines" (James Longenbach, *The Art of the Poetic Line* (Saint Paul, MN: Graywolf, 2008), vii). Longenbach writes, "Poetry is the sound of language organized in lines. More than meter, more than rhyme, more than images or alliteration or figurative language, line is what distinguishes our experience of poetry as poetry, rather than some other kind of writing. Great prose might be filled with metaphors. The rhythmic vitality of prose might be so intense that it rises to moments of regularity we can scan. Its diction may be more sensuous more evocative than that of many poems. We wouldn't be attracted to the notion of prose poetry if it didn't feel exciting to abandon the decorum of lines" (xi).

53. Arvind Krishna Mehrotra, "The World's a Printing House," in Chang, Handal, and Shankar, *Language for a New Century*, 157.

54. Walter Benjamin, "Thesis V," in Michael Löwy, *Fire Alarm: Reading Walter Benjamin's "On the Concept of History"* (New York: Verso, 2005), 40.

55. Bruns, *What Are Poets For?*, 4, 20.

56. I am grateful to Justin Saret for this formulation, in conversation, February 28, 2020.

57. In conversation about Eagleton's discussion of empiricism and "the largely pragmatic uses to which we put our speech" (Eagleton, *How to Read a Poem*, 11–12, 21).

58. Ahdaf Soueif, *In the Eye of the Sun* (New York: Anchor, 1992), 59.

59. Soueif, *In the Eye of the Sun*, 511–12.

60. Soueif, *In the Eye of the Sun*, 579.

61. Soueif, *In the Eye of the Sun*, 231–32. All quotes from this scene are from these pages.

62. Soueif, *In the Eye of the Sun*, 232.

63. Soueif, *In the Eye of the Sun*, 233–34.

64. Soueif, *In the Eye of the Sun*, 234.

65. Matthew Arnold, "Dover Beach," accessed October 29, 2018, https://www.poetryfoundation.org/poems/43588/dover-beach.

66. Soueif, *In the Eye of the Sun*, 37–38.

67. Soueif, *In the Eye the Sun*, 234.

68. W. H. Auden, "Musée des Beaux Arts," in *The Complete Works of W. H. Auden: Poems, Volume I: 1927–1939*, ed. Edward Mendelson (Princeton, NJ: Princeton University Press, 2022), 338.

69. Soueif, *In the Eye the Sun*, 234–35.

70. Matthew 19:14; see also Luke 18:16–17.

71. Édouard Glissant, *Poetics of Relation* (Ann Arbor: University of Michigan Press, 2010), 32.

72. Soueif, *In the Eye of the Sun*, 272.

73. "With the most distant" is from the final line of Nâzım Hikmet's "Angina Pectoris," accessed September 16, 2018, https://www.lyrikline.org/en/poems/angina-pektoris-7536; and "for Fuad as well" is from Soueif, *In the Eye of the Sun*, 439.

74. Soueif, *In the Eye of the Sun*, 334.

75. Latife Tekin, *Dear Shameless Death* (London: Marion Boyers, 1983), 180.

76. Soueif, *In the Eye of the Sun*, 451–52.

77. See classic statements in Steven Lukes, ed., *Power* (New York: New York University Press, 1986), especially essays by Dahl, Max Weber, Hannah Arendt, Jürgen Habermas, and Michel Foucault. Power as behavioral control relates to a range of contemporary views of power, from conservative claims to authority (to compel, preserve, impose tradition, etc.) to radical views of social transformation (to alter, break down, improve structures, etc.). Across the spectrum, power is equated with the capacity of those who possess power, alone or collectively, to affect change in the lives of others, sometimes consistent with the will of the latter, sometimes against it.

78. Bruns, "Almost as If."

79. Conventionally understood. There are other discursive aspects of power at work, of course, in establishing a relationship between discursively occluded others and othernesses.

80. See Dabashi, *The World Is My Home*, 239–49. For other, other-oriented Abrahamic views of "Christian republics" and "Jewish states" see John Howard Yoder, *The Politics of Jesus* (Grand Rapids, MI: Eerdmans,

1994); and Judith Butler, *Parting Ways: Jewishness and the Critique of Zionism* (New York: Columbia University Press, 2013).

81. On poetic republics, see also Martín Espada's "The Republic of Poetry" (for Chile) in *The Republic of Poetry* (New York: Norton, 2006), 3–4.

82. Compare Aristotle, for whom the excellence of the citizen in a "good" state is defined as one who knows ruling from the points of view of both the rulers and the ruled, such that, when in power, citizens can rule in a way that is just for those outside of power (because the citizens know their position as well), and when out of power, the citizens can hold those in power accountable (because the citizens know their positions as well). This view is organized around empowerment through ruling (practices of sharing in the administration of justice and holding office). See Aristotle, *The Politics*, especially Book III.

83. Rob Sears, *The Beautiful Poetry of Donald Trump: Strictly Unauthorized* (Edinburgh: Canongate, 2017), 59.

84. Sears, *The Beautiful Poetry*, 77.

85. Sears, *The Beautiful Poetry*, ix ("remarkable poet"); Sears's second quotation is from Sian Cain, "He Gets Verse: The Poetry of Donald Trump," *Guardian*, September 1, 2017, accessed September 17, 2018, https://www.theguardian.com/books/booksblog/2017/sep/01/he-gets-verse-the-poetry-of-donald-trump.

86. Sears, quoted in Sian Cain, "He Gets Verse."

87. Rob Sears, "I Discovered the Secret Poetry of Donald Trump—and It's Tremendous," *New Statesman America*, September 17, 2017, accessed September 17, 2018, https://www.newstatesman.com/world/north-america/2017/09/i-discovered-secret-poetry-donald-trump-and-its-tremendous. Sears uses the phrase "allowing us to listen" in his opening remarks to the volume as well, where he comments on less "bracingly braggadocious" dimensions of the poems: "If we allow ourselves to listen, we can also hear the counterpoint of a quieter, less self-assured Trump, as when he breaks off his list of boasts in 'I am the Best,' to worry about the size of his appendages" (*The Beautiful Poetry*, x).

88. Sears, "I Discovered."

89. The point here is not to ignore the different constitutive purposes with which a poet writes and a politician speaks, or different perspectives on poetics. I am, however, offering a "nonessentialist" view of what

constitutes a literary text, suggesting that we may treat texts written with purposes other than literary ones as readable in literary terms. We may experience poetic qualities in political speech (assertions, slogans, etc.) and, even if those qualities appear absent, still bring a poetical attuned disposition to our analysis of them. All political expression may be received as poetic expression and, thus, as a subject of poetic attunement.

90. The line in the poem is from a tweet Donald Trump sent in September 2012, promoting his appearance in a video of Miss America contestants mouthing the lyrics of "Call Me Maybe." In between scenes of happily singing and dancing pageant contestants, the camera cuts twice to Trump, once near the beginning of the video and once at the very end, sitting at a desk in his suit and tie, where he mouths the two famous lines from the song's chorus. In their study, *Switched to Pop*, musicologists Nate Sloan and Charlie Harding consider the lyrics and music of the song "perfect" in poetically attuned terms: "How perfect are those lines? They feel as old as the earth, like something archaeologists would discover carved in stone at an ancient Druid burial ground." See Harding and Sloan, *Switched on Pop: How Popular Music Works and Why It Matters* (Oxford: Oxford University Press, 2019), 1. For the Miss America Pageant video, see Carly Rae Jepsen, "Call Me Maybe" (2012), accessed September 18, 2018, https://www.youtube.com /watch?v=ooyKww_BQ2I.

91. Alan Seeger, "The Torture of Cuauhtémoc," accessed September 21, 2018, https://quod.lib.umich.edu/a/amverse/BAD7802.0001.001/1:4.3?rgn =div2;view=fulltext,.

92. Woodie Guthrie, "I Don't Like the Way This World's A-Treatin' Me," accessed September 23, 2018, Woody Guthrie Publications, Inc. & TRO- Ludlow Music, https://www.woodyguthrie.org/Lyrics/I_Dont_Like_The _Way_This_Worlds_A_Treatin_Me.htm.

93. Helene Cixous, *Stigmata: Escaping Texts* (New York: Routledge, 1998), 134.

94. Sandra McPherson, "Secrets: Beginning to Write Them Out: Revelation, Confession, and Ethics; Discretion and Diplomacy; Health and Art," in *A Field Guide to Poetics and Poetry*, rev. ed., ed. Stuart Friebert, David Walker, and David Young (Oberlin, OH: Oberlin College Press, 1997), 317.

95. Richard Born, "Split-Ticket Voters, Divided Government, and Fiorina's Policy-Balancing Model," *Legislative Studies Quarterly* 19, no. 1 (February 1994): 95–115; and "Congressional Incumbency and the Rise of Split-Ticket Voting," *Legislative Studies Quarterly* 25, no. 3 (August 2000): 365–87.

96. In recent years, ticket splitting has decreased. This appears to be the result of ideological consistency within the dominant parties: "There is no doubt that, over all, the era of polarization and hyper-partisanship above and beyond idiosyncratic factors—that has to lead to a drop in ticket splitting. . . . Democrats and Republicans alike, as part of the polarization phenomenon, are more consistently liberal or conservative across issues, as are the candidates themselves, meaning less likelihood of ticket splitting." Richard Born quoted in Jennifer Steinhauer, "Wary of Trump Effect, Republicans Hope for Split Tickets," *New York Times*, April 28, 2016. See also Ethan Chen, "The Splitting of the Split Ticket: What Happened to the House Incumbency Edge?" *Sabato's Crystal Ball* (UVA Center for Politics), May 13, 2021, accessed May 14, 2021, https://centerforpolitics.org/crystalball/articles/the-splitting-of-the-ticket-split/.

97. For the received view, see Morris P. Fiorina, "The Reagan Years: Turning to the Right or Groping Toward the Middle?" in *The Resurgence of Conservatism in Anglo-American Democracies*, ed. Barry Cooper, Allan Korberg, and William Mishler (Durham, NC: Duke University Press, 1988).

98. "In districts with campaigning incumbents of the winning presidential party, [ticket splitting] made for only about the level of ticket-splitting that could be expected in open seats" (Born, "Congressional Incumbency," 365).

99. Born, "Congressional Incumbency," 381.

100. Born, "Congressional Incumbency," 365.

101. Latoya Hill, Samantha Artiga, and Nambi Ndugga, "COVID-19 Cases, Deaths, and Vaccinations by Race/Ethnicity as of Winter 2022," KFF, March 7, 2023, accessed April 30, 2023, https://www.kff.org/coronavirus-covid-19/issue-brief/covid-19-cases-deaths-and-vaccinations-by-race-ethnicity-as-of-winter-2022/:~:text=Following%20that%20surge,%20disparities%20narrowed,3.2%20per%20100,000%20for%20Asian.

102. "What Does COVID-19 Do to Your Lungs?" accessed May 28, 2020, *WebMD*, https://www.webmd.com/lung/what-does-covid-do-to-your -lungs#2.

103. Meredith Wadman, Jennifer Couzin-Frankel, Jocelyn Kaiser, and Cath- erine Matacic, "How Does Coronavirus Kill? Clinicians Trace a Fero- cious Rampage through the Body, from Brain to Toes," *Science Magazine*, April 17, 2020, accessed May 13, 2021, https://www.sciencemag.org/news /2020/04/how-does-coronavirus-kill-clinicians-trace-ferocious-rampage -through-body-brain-toes.

104. Quoted in Marc Fisher, "The US Death Toll Has Reached 100,000," *Washington Post*, May 27, 2020, accessed May 27, 2020, https://www .washingtonpost.com/graphics/2020/national/100000-deaths-american -coronavirus/. See also a fuller account of Horgus Whitt's experience in David Erickson, "Three Missoula Residents Describe Coronavirus," *Missoulian*, April 25, 2020, accessed May 28, 2020, https://missoulian .com/news/local/three-missoula-residents-describe-coronavirus-infection /article_7a279509-adbe-59ca-840f-012d94e36fb5.html.

105. "'Coughing Like I Was Going to Die.' Here's What It's Like to Survive Coronavirus in Wuhan," *Time*, February 13, 2020, accessed May 28, 2020, https://time.com/5783838/coronavirus-symptoms-wuhan-survivor/.

106. "We Meet COVID-19 Survivors to Hear Their Stories," *Al Jazeera*, May 24, 2020, accessed May 28, 2020, https://www.aljazeera.com /program/the-stream/2020/5/24/we-meet-covid-19-survivors-to-hear -their-stories.

107. Alicia P. Q. Wittmeyer, "1 Million Deaths, 13 Last Messages," *New York Times*, May 5, 2022, accessed May 21, 2022, https://www.nytimes.com /interactive/2022/05/20/opinion/one-million-covid-deaths-texts.html.

108. Fisher, "The US Death Toll."

109. Fisher, "The US Death Toll."

110. Emerson Roberto "Tromps" da Costa, "Coronavirus in Belém: A Sur- vivor's Story," *Brasil Wire*, May 8, 2020, accessed May 28, 2020, https:// www.brasilwire.com/coronavirus-in-belem-a-survivors-story/.

111. See Kate Linthicum and Patrick J. McDonnell, "In Tijuana, Paramedics Uncover a Hidden Death Toll Not Captured in COVID-19 Statistics," *Los Angeles Times*, May 21, 2020, accessed May 28, 2020, https://www .latimes.com/world-nation/story/2020-05-21/in-tijuana-paramedics

-reveal-hidden-death-toll-not-captured-in-official-covid-19-statistics. For a comparative, critical data studies discussion of this underestimation, see Rob Kitchen, *Data Lives: How Data Are Made and Shape Our World* (Bristol: Bristol University Press, 2021), 208–12.

112. John Revill and Emma Farge, "Real COVID-19 Death Toll Could Be 'Two to Three' Times Above Official Stats: WHO," *Reuters*, May 21, 2021, accessed May 21, 2021, https://www.reuters.com/world/covid-19-death -tolls-are-likely-significant-undercount-who-says-2021-05-21/.

113. "Global Excess Deaths Associated with COVID-19, January 2020- December 2021," World Health Organization, May 2022, accessed April 27, 2023, https://www.who.int/data/stories/global-excess-deaths -associated-with-covid-19-january-2020-december-2021.

114. Ian Richardson, "Is US Coronavirus Death Toll Inflated? Experts Agree It's Likely the Opposite," *USA Today*, April 17, 2020, accessed May 10, 2021, https://www.usatoday.com/story/news/factcheck/2020/04/17/fact -check-covid-19-death-toll-likely-undercounted-not-overcounted /2973481001/.

115. See James Glanz and Campbell Robertson, "Lockdown Delays Cost at Least 36,000 Lives, Data Show," *New York Times*, May 20, 2020, accessed May 20, 2020, https://www.nytimes.com/2020/05/20/us/coronavirus -distancing-deaths.html; and Amanda Holpuch, "US Could Have Averted 40 Percent of Covid Deaths, Says Panel Examining Trump's Policies" *Guardian*, February 11, 2021, accessed May 14, 2021, https://www .theguardian.com/us-news/2021/feb/10/us-coronavirus-response-donald -trump-health-policy; and Zeynep Tufekci, "How Millions of Lives Might Have Been Saved from COVID-19," *New York Times*, March 11, 2022, accessed March 11, 2022, https://www.nytimes.com/2022/03/11 /opinion/covid-health-pandemic.html.

3. DOCTORING THE DATA

1. Della Pollock, "The Performative 'I,'" *Cultural Studies—Critical Methodologies* 7, no. 3 (August 2007): 246.

2. Jürgen Habermas, *Knowledge and Human Interests* (Boston: Beacon, 1972), 308–14.

3. Ahdaf Soueif, *In the Eye of the Sun* (New York: Anchor, 1992), 59–60.

4. Soueif, *In the Eye of the Sun*, 59.

5. *Bir Zamanlar Anadolu'da*, directed by Nuri Bilge Ceylan, was released in 2011. The film tied for the Grand Prix award at the 2011 Cannes Film Festival, the festival's runner-up prize to the Palme d'Or, its best picture award.

6. Bülent Diken, Graeme Gilloch, and Craig Hammond, *The Cinema of Nuri Bilge Ceylan: The Global Vision of a Turkish Filmmaker* (New York: I. B. Tauris, 2018), 148.

7. Ercan Kesal, *Aslında* . . . (Istanbul: İletişim, 2017), 152.

8. Ercan Kesal, *Evvel Zaman* (Istanbul: İletişim, 2014), 90.

9. Nuri Bilge Ceylan, quoted in Rob White, "Nuri Bilge Ceylan: An Introduction and Interview," *Film Quarterly* 65, no. 2 (2011): 66.

10. "Most key scene of the film" is quoted in White, "Nuri Bilge Ceylan," 185. *Suça ortak* literally means "partner to the crime" (Kesal, *Evvel*, 135).

11. This story is taken, often verbatim, from Anton Chekhov's story "The Examining Magistrate."

12. In Turkish, the last sentence is *"Olabilir mi öyle bir şey, huh?"* which may be translated more literally as "Is such a thing possible, huh?"

13. Ceylan, quoted in White, "Nuri Bilge Ceylan," 71–72; See also, Kesal, *Evvel*, 135.

14. Kesal, *Evvel*, 76.

15. Diken, Gilloch, and Hammond, *The Cinema*, 105–6, 115.

16. Diken, Gilloch, and Hammond, *The Cinema*, 106.

17. "Arap" is the Turkish word for Arab. It is used as a name for Turkish people of Arabic or African descent and, sometimes, for persons who appear to be of such descent because of the color of their skin.

18. Ceylan, quoted in White, "Nuri Bilge Ceylan," 69.

19. Kesal, *Evvel*, 34.

20. The original Turkish is *"Gene yıllar gececek ve geride benden bir iz kalmayacack . . . Yorgun ruhumu karanlık ve soğuk kuşataca."*

21. Its meaning in English, "I don't know," is untranslated in the subtitles.

22. Zak Bronson and Gözde Kılıç, "The Ghosts of Modernization: Landscape, Time, and the West in *Once Upon a Time in Anatolia*," in *International Westerns: Re-Locating the Frontier*, ed. Cynthia J. Miller and A. Bowdoin Van Ripe (Lanham, MD: Scarecrow, 2014), 16–17. They assert that the exchange with Arap Ali "brings to light the nihilism of the doctor" (13).

23. Bronson and Kılıç, "The Ghosts of Modernization," 13.
24. Ceylan, quoted in White, "Nuri Bilge Ceylan," 71.
25. Ceylan, quoted in White, "Nuri Bilge Ceylan," 72.
26. Ceylan, quoted in White, "Nuri Bilge Ceylan," 71.
27. *Abi* is the abbreviated, colloquial form of *ağabey*, a common informal word for "older brother" used by younger males when they speak to other males who look like they might be the age of an older brother.
28. "*Sana bir soru soruyorum evladım.*" *Evladım* here means "son," or "sonny boy"—untranslated in the subtitles.
29. "*Ne yapacak canım. İçecek işte.*"
30. "My boy," untranslated in the subtitles.
31. "*Maymun ettin.*"
32. "*Saf gördü.*"
33. Ceylan, quoted in White, "Nuri Bilge Ceylan," 72.
34. Ceylan, quoted in White, "Nuri Bilge Ceylan," 72. See also Nuri Bilge Ceylan, *Söyleyişler* (Istanbul: Norgunk, 2012), 188.
35. Ceylan, quoted in White, "Nuri Bilge Ceylan," 72.
36. Ceylan, quoted in White, "Nuri Bilge Ceylan," 72. See also Kesal, *Evvel*, 31.
37. Ahmet Hamdi Tanpınar, *The Time Regulation Institute* (Saatleri Ayarlama Enstitüsü) (New York: Penguin, 2014 [1954]).
38. The Turkish expression translated as "revel" is *halay başı*, literally leader of the *halay. Halay* is the name of the Turkish folk dance in which people join hands and dance in rhythm.
39. "Friend," untranslated in subtitles.
40. "My boy," untranslated in subtitles.
41. "Sir," untranslated in subtitles.
42. "*Çok eksiğimiz var, Doktor Bey.*"
43. "For the love of God," untranslated in subtitles.
44. "*Hayatta en hakiki mürşit ilimdir*"; for critical analysis, see Taha Parla and Andrew Davison, *Corporatist Ideology in Kemalist Turkey: Progress or Order* (Syracuse, NY: Syracuse University Press, 1996).
45. For another important cinematic depiction, see *Gelecek Uzun Sürer* (Future Lasts Forever), dir. Özcan Alper, 2011.
46. Şükrü Argın, "*Bir Zamanlar Anadolu'da*: Asimetrik Şikayet Toplumu," *Birikim* 272 (December 2011): 19, 22.
47. Argın, "*Bir Zamanlar Anadolu'da*," 25. See also Rober Koptaş, "Saf Hayranlık," *Agos Gazetesi*, September 2011; Semir Aslanyürek, "Bir

Ülkenin Otopsi veya NBC'nin Anatomi Dersi," *Sol Gazetesi*, September 1, 2011; and Vildan Şimşek, "Bir Zamanlar Anadolu'da," *İdeal Hukuk Dergisi*, June 26, 2012, all quoted in Nuri Bilge Ceylan, *Bir Zamanlar Anadolu'da*, ed. Aslı Güneş (Istanbul: Doğan Kitap, 2019), 181, 183, and 210. Koptaş writes that the film is a "masterpiece" that reveals Türkey's "*ruh*." Alsanyürek sees Ceylan as carrying out an autopsy on the country, and Şimşek suggests it underscores the need for one.

48. See Alev Fatoş Parsa and Zuhal Akmeşe, "*Nuri Bilge Ceylan Sinemasında Anlatı Kodları ve Arketipler Bir Zamanlar Anadolu'da*" (presented at the 6. Oturum, Sinemamızda Toplumsal Arketipler, Türk XIII. Film Araştırmalarında Yeni Yönelimler Konferansı: Sinema ve Bellek, Kadir Has Üniversitesi İletişim Fakültesi Uluslararası Konferans, May 2012), 8, 12, accessed October 2, 2018, academia.edu.

49. "Tamamlanmamış bir erkek," *ekşisözlük* (January 28, 2018), accessed August 20, 2018, https://eksisozluk.com/entry/73808154; see also Şimşek, "Bir Zamanlar Anadolu'da."

50. Ercan Kesal, "*Biri konuşunca aydınlık oluyor*," accessed November 2018, http://www.ercankesal.com/biri-konusunca-aydinlik-oluyor/.

51. Kesal, *Evvel*, 14.

52. Kesal, *Evvel*, 132.

53. "*Doktorun omzu ve bacakları sucluya değer (sucluya sempati), kelepçeleri gösterme!*" (Kesal, *Evvel*, 30).

54. Kesal, *Evvel*, 109.

55. Kesal, *Evvel*, 109.

56. Kesal, *Evvel*, 184.

57. Kesal, *Evvel*, 25, 38, 184. To describe what it was like to return to the events of his past and make and see them come alive in *Once Upon a Time in Anatolia*, Kesal recalls the legend of a peasant who works so hard one day that he enters a river to cool off. A storm suddenly blows him into a different life, first as a slave, then as the shah's favorite slave, and then, through inheritance, as the shah himself, until on another hot day he jumps into the same river, and another storm takes him back to his youth and his original, sweaty and hot state. That's how it felt, Kesal says. See Kesal, *Aslında*, 36–37.

58. Kesal, *Evvel*, 90.

59. Kesal, *Evvel*, 5, 22–23, 90; *Aslında*, 103, 162.

60. Kesal, *Evvel*, 85. Nuri Bilge Ceylan agrees: "The truth lies in what's hidden, in what's not told. Reality lies in the unspoken part of our lives. If you try to talk about your problems, it's not that convincing. People try to protect themselves; everybody has something they want to hide" (quoted in White, "Nuri Bilge Ceylan," 66).

61. Kesal, *Evvel*, 5, 23, 94.

62. Kesal, *Evvel*, 138.

63. Hans-Georg Gadamer, *The Enigma of Health* (Stanford, CA: Stanford University Press, 1996), 81.

64. Gadamer, *The Enigma*, viii.

65. For discussion of historical shifts in the doctor-patient relation, see Georges Canguilhem, *Writings on Medicine* (New York: Fordham University Press, 2012), especially chapters 1–3; and Ivan Illich, *Medical Nemesis: The Expropriation of Health* (New York: Marion Boyars, 1976), and "Health," in David Cayley, *The Rivers North of the Future: The Testament of Ivan Illich as Told to David Cayley* (Toronto: Anansi, 2005).

66. Gadamer, *The Enigma*, 39.

67. Gadamer, *The Enigma*, ix, 21–23, 31–32, 47–48, 138. "When Aristotle, in the sixth book of the *Nicomachean Ethics*, distinguishes the manner of 'practical knowledge' [*phronesis*] . . . from theoretical and technical knowledge, he expresses, in my opinion, one of the greatest truths by which the Greeks throw light upon the 'scientific' mystification of modern society of specialization" (Hans-Georg Gadamer, "The Problem of Historical Consciousness," in *Interpretive Social Science: A Second Look*, ed. Paul Rabinow and William Sullivan [Berkeley: University of California Press, 1981], 107).

68. Gadamer, *The Enigma*, 81.

69. Gadamer, *The Enigma*, 138.

70. Gadamer, *The Enigma*, 99.

71. Gadamer, *The Enigma*, 42–43.

72. Gadamer, *The Enigma*, 37.

73. Canguilhem prefers "a new state of equilibrium" (Canguilhem, *Writings*, 65). For him, words such as "restore," "reconstruct," "reestablish," "reconstitute," "recuperate," and "recover" overstate possibilities (55). "The restitution or reestablishment of the anterior organic state may prove illusory" (56). Still, he acknowledges the constitutive role of some concept of

equilibrium in the "intersubjective" relation between doctor and patient (54). The practicing of doctoring has produced "the specialist physician" for whom "consultation now consists of a combination between a computer search through semiological and etiological databanks and a formulation of a probability diagnostic supported by the evaluation of statistical information," but doctoring has "retained a few elements of the popular jargon devalorized by [the] scientist's language. Doctors may therefore consent to understand that their client's request could be aimed at reassuring themselves that they will *conserve a certain quality in their state of life*, or that they can *regain an equivalent state*, without worrying whether the objective tests of a cure are positive and in agreement" (39, 59, emphasis added).

74. Gadamer, *The Enigma*, 37, 39.

75. Gadamer, *The Enigma*, 42.

76. Gadamer, *The Enigma*, 43.

77. Gadamer, *The Enigma*, 127, 137.

78. Gadamer, *The Enigma*, 42.

79. Gadamer, *The Enigma*, 63.

80. Ceylan, quoted in White, "Nuri Bilge Ceylan," 71.

81. See also Ceylan, *Söyleyişler*, 209–10.

82. Kesal, *Aslında*, 159.

83. Gadamer, *The Enigma*, 127.

84. Georges Canguilhem, *The Normal and the Pathological* (New York: Zone, 1991), 279.

85. Pollock, "The Performative 'I,' " 246.

86. Pollock, "The Performative 'I,' " 246.

87. Pollock, "The Performative 'I,' " 246.

88. "Live like a rat, die like a rat"—Arap Ali, during the car ride.

89. "*Öfke ve kin*" (Kesal, *Evvel*, 85).

90. The subtitled translation is "Got a cigarette?"

91. He says that he has been eager to talk with the prosecutor about securing funds for a new cemetery wall and morgue—the one to prevent animals from dirtying the gravesites, the other so that the village has a place to wash, clean, and store the dead so that their children who have migrated to Europe can return and kiss them goodbye before they bury them.

92. A more literal translation of the Turkish might be "but his is different, yours are different."

93. "Whatever," which is untranslated in the subtitles.

94. That "Doctor" not in the subtitles.

95. For a discussion of *ciddilik*, seriousness, see my "Modernity in Turkey: Myth and Reality, Storm and Substance," translated into Spanish and published as *"La Modernidad: Mito y Realidad, Tormenta y Verdad,"* in *Vanguardia Dossier* 32 (July/September 2009): 18–23.

96. *"Iyi ya işte. Demek ki kadın ta o zaman kafasına koymuş kendisini öldürmeyi. Ama karnındaki bebeği zarar vermemek için doğuma kadar beklemeye karar vermiş."*

97. A Turkish expression that literally means "may it come with ease." It is said to people while they are working.

98. "I don't know how he died. *Neden öldüğünü bilmiyorum."*

99. The original storyline, described by Ercan Kesal in *Evvel Zaman*, consistently conceived of Kenan as the father. Gülnaz really wanted to get married and so accepted Yaşar's proposal (Kesal, *Evvel*, 75).

100. It is a possible limit to his attunement that the doctor cares more for the autopsy than he does for joking around, which he goes along with in the car ride during the search.

101. *"Bakın, burada soluk borusunda toprak var. Toz toprak. Hatta bu akciğere de girmiş."*

102. *"Bir dakika."*

103. *"Hocam, akciğere . . ."*

104. *"Tamam, bir dakika."*

105. *"Hocam, bunu diri diri gömmüş olmasınlar ya."*

106. *"Adami diyorum, canlı canlı gömmüş olmasınlar?"*

107. *"Evet, Cemal Bey. Ne yazıyoruz?"* literally means "What are we writing?'

108. *"Şöyle yazalım onu."* Literally, it means "Let's write it like this."

109. *"Trakea, ozofagus, ve boyun yumuşak dokularında herhangi bir anormalliğe rastlanmadı."*

110. The blood inspires symbolic speculation. Is it deserved punishment for failing to report the facts? A sacrificial blessing from Yaşar, from the *mavera*, in gratitude to the doctor for his courage and care? Haden Guest suggests that, although Yaşar "cannot speak, he somehow finds a voice in the sounds and unalloyed and almost frightening carnality" of the

vivid sounds of flesh being cut and organs removed. See Haden Guest, "Physical Evidence," *Film Comment* 48, no. 1 (January/February 2012): 59.

111. *"Hocam, siz biraz geri çikin isterseniz, size de bulaşmasın."*

112. Gadamer, *The Enigma*, 42.

113. Gadamer, *The Enigma*, 21.

114. Gadamer, *The Enigma*, 108.

115. See discussion in the introduction.

116. Specifically Ebru Ceylan. See Kesal, *Evvel*, 51. He notes that the sounds of the children are very important, as is hope (22, 59). See also Kesal, *Aslında*, 153.

117. Sahara Pradhan's formulation, in extensive conversation on these issues, November 5, 2018.

118. See also Kesal, *Evvel*, 148.

119. *Rıza olmadan.*

120. *"Bu da patolojik bir iyilik peşinde!"*

4. THINGS GIVEN

1. Terence Ball, James Farr, and Russell L. Hanson, "Introduction," in *Political Innovation and Conceptual Change*, ed. Terence Ball, James Farr, and Russell L. Hanson (Cambridge: Cambridge University Press, 1989), 5.

2. Daniel Rosenberg, "Data Before the Fact," in *Raw Data Is an Oxymoron*, ed. Lisa Gitelman (Cambridge, MA: MIT Press, 2013), 15.

3. Rosenberg, "Data Before the Fact," 15–16.

4. Rosenberg, "Data Before the Fact," 15–16.

5. Rosenberg, "Data Before the Fact," 15–16.

6. Jonathan Furner, "'Data': the Data," in *Information Cultures in the Digital Age: A Festschrift in Honor of Rafael Capurro*, ed. Matthew Kelly and Jared Bielby (New York: Springer, 2016), 289.

7. Furner, "'Data': the Data," 290. Furner explains data's place in Latin grammar: "In classical Latin . . . the present active infinitive of a first-conjugation verb has the suffix -*are*; examples are *amore* ('to love'), and *dare* ('to give')—otherwise commonly denoted by the first person singular of the verb's present active indicative, i.e., *amō* ('I love'), and *dō* ('I give'). The nominative masculine singular form of the perfect participle of *dō* is *datus* ('given'); *datum* is this participle's nominative neuter

singular form, while *data* is both the nominative neuter plural and the nominative feminine singular" (290).

8. Furner, "'Data': the Data," 290.

9. Furner, "'Data': the Data," 292.

10. *Oxford English Dictionary* entry for "date, n.²,", https://oed.com /dictionary/date_n2?tl=true, accessed June 2019. To Furner's analysis, and to see the robust usage of data in this sense, we add the full *OED* entry for *date*: "the date of a letter was expressed by a phrase such as *data xiiii K. Maias de Tarentino* '(letter) sent from Tarentum on 18th April' (Cicero, *Letters to Atticus* 3. 6. 1), *litteras datas a litoribus Britanniae proximis a. d. vi Kal. Octobr.* 'letter sent from the nearest shores of Britain on 26th September' (Cicero, *Letters to Atticus* 4. 18. 5), *litterarum datarum dies prid. Kal. Ian.* 'the day of a letter sent on 31st December' (Cicero, *Letters to Atticus* 6. 1. 2). Hence *data*, the first word of the formula, came to be used as a term for the time and place stated therein. Compare Catalan *data* (fourteenth century), Spanish †*data* (mid thirteenth century), Portuguese *data* (thirteenth century), Italian *data* (a1556). Compare also (after similar dating formulae in postclassical Latin using the neuter singular *datum* [thirteenth century]), Middle Low German *dātum, dāte*, Middle Dutch, Dutch *datum*, Middle High German *dātum* (German *Datum*, in early modern German also *date*)."

11. Furner, "'Data': the Data," 292.

12. Furner, "'Data': the Data," 292. Ellipses in Furner. The quote is from Tuke's (ca. 1590–1657) *Nevv Essayes* (1614).

13. Furner, "'Data': the Data," 292.

14. Furner, "'Data': the Data," 293.

15. Furner, "'Data': the Data," 293.

16. Rosenberg, "Data Before the Fact," 20.

17. Furner, "'Data': the Data," 293.

18. Furner, "'Data': the Data," 293. *Elements* is "an unrivalled candidate for the title of the most influential mathematical work of all time," which "was first translated from its original Greek into Arabic in the eight century and then from Arabic into Latin in the twelfth and into English in 1482" (293).

19. Furner, "'Data': the Data," 293.

20. Furner quotes Ephraim Chambers, *Cyclopaedia: or, An Universal Dictionary of Arts and Sciences*, 1728 ("'Data': the Data," 293); and Furner,

"'Data': the Data," 294–95. For the link to "truth," see Joseph Worcester's *Dictionary* (1860): "Truths or premises given or admitted, from which to deduce conclusions; the facts from which an inference is drawn" (quoted in Furner, "'Data': the Data," 295).

21. Rosenberg, "Data Before the Fact," 20.

22. Rosenberg, "Data Before the Fact," 36. On data's "irreducibility," Rosenberg writes: "If facts can be deconstructed—if they can be shown to be theory—surely data can be too. But it is not clear that such a move would be useful from either a conceptual or a practical point of view. The existing historiography of the fact is strong in its own terms, and no special harm is done by an unmarked, undeconstructed deployment of the term 'data.' What is more, there is a practical consideration: one has to have some language left to work with, and after thrilling conceptual histories of truth, facts, evidence, and other such terms, it is helpful to retain one or two irreducibles" (17–18).

23. Rosenberg, "Data Before the Fact," 20. In this way, the concept differs from what Rosenberg calls "its sister terms": "fact" and "evidence." See Rosenberg's examination of their respective etymologies in "Data Before the Fact," 19, 37.

24. Furner, "'Data': the Data," 295.

25. Furner, "'Data': the Data," 295.

26. Furner, "'Data': the Data," 295, 298.

27. Furner, "'Data': the Data," 296. In a reiteration of the interpretivist critique of the givenness of data, Furner engages the work of Johanna Drucker and Peter Checkland, who propose using the concept *capta* (from the Latin *capere*, "to take") as an alternative to data. Adopting *capta* corrects for positivist-empiricism's naïve "realist ontological assumption that phenomena exist independently of any observers." "Knowledge," Drucker underscores, is "taken, not simply given as a natural representation of pre-existing fact." *Capta* are "the taken," not (simply) the given; they are "those items of data which we focus on, have a concern about, define, and select" (all quotations from Furner, "'Data': the Data," 298n21). Rob Kitchin, who adopts Rosenberg's account of the meaning of data (Kitchin, *The Data Revolution: Big Data, Open Data, Data Infrastructures & Their Consequences* [Los Angeles: Sage, 2014], 4; and *Data Lives: How Data Are Made and Shape Our World* [Bristol:

Bristol University Press, 2021], 25), observes that, "in general use" in the sciences, "data refers to those elements that are taken. Technically, what are understood to be data are actually *capta* . . . those units of data that have been selected and harvested from the sum of all potential data" (Kitchin, *Data Lives*, 25–26, and *The Data Revolution*, 2–5). Favoring *capta* over *data*, Kitchin suggests that more "appropriate" titles for his works would be *The Capta Revolution* and *Capta Lives*, respectively, but "trying to get everyone on the planet to switch terms when 'data' is so thoroughly embedded in our lexicon is not a battle worth fighting" (Kitchin, *Data Lives*, 26).

28. Furner, "'Data': the Data," 296, 299.

29. Furner, "'Data': the Data," 298.

30. First *OED* entry for *datum* ("datum, n."), accessed September 4, 2019, https://www-oed-com.libproxy.vassar.edu/view/Entry/47434?redirecte dFrom=datum.

31. First *OED* entry for *data* ("data, n."), accessed September 4, 2019, https://www-oed-com.libproxy.vassar.edu/view/Entry/296948?isAdvanced =false&result=1&rskey=MCHScb&. There are no other seventeenth -century usages of data (or "datas") as a count noun. The next entry under this meaning of data is 1764.

32. First *OED* entry under 2a of *datum* ("datum, n."), accessed September 4, 2019, https://www-oed-com.libproxy.vassar.edu/view/Entry/47434?re directedFrom=datum.

33. Second *OED* entry under 2a for *datum*, accessed September 4, 2019, https://www-oed-com.libproxy.vassar.edu/view/Entry/47434?redirecte dFrom=datum. The next entry listed is also from the eighteenth cen- tury: "1737 H. Fielding Hist. Reg. 1736 Ded. f. 6ᵛ All . . will grant me this Datum, that the said . . Person is a Man of an ordinary Capacity."

34. "datum, n.", accessed September 4, 2019, https://www-oed-com.libproxy .vassar.edu/view/Entry/47434?redirectedFrom=datum. The next entry is from the eighteenth century: "1792 R. Price Observ. Reversionary Pay- ments (ed. 5) I. 281 Data for computing accurately the values of all life- annuities and reversions."

35. "Contribute to the OED," *Oxford English Dictionary*, accessed January 20, 2020, https://public.oed.com/contribute-to-the-oed/.

36. Cited in Furner, "'Data': the Data," 295.

37. "datum, n.", accessed September 4, 2019, https://www-oed-com.libproxy .vassar.edu/view/Entry/47434?redirectedFrom=datum.

38. Entry 2a under datum.

39. "data, n.", accessed September 4, 2019, https://www-oed-com.libproxy .vassar.edu/view/Entry/296948?rskey=AGswjj&result=1.

40. Including the *OED*: "Etymology: classical Latin *data*, plural of *datum*."

41. William Batten, *A Most Plaine and Easie Way for the Finding of the Sunnes Amplitude and Azimuth, and Thereby the Variation of the Compasse, by Logarithm* (London: Eliz. Allde for J. Tapp, 1630; Ann Arbor, MI: Early English Books Online Text Creation Partnership, 2011), accessed May 2019, https://quod.lib.umich.edu/e/eebo/a05734.0001.001?rgn=main;view =fulltext. All citations are from this page.

42. Furner, "'Data': the Data," 295.

43. "loadstone | lodestone, n.", accessed September 4, 2019, https://www-oed -com.libproxy.vassar.edu/view/Entry/109422?redirectedFrom=loadst one.

44. Batten, *A Most Plaine and Easie Way*.

45. For example, adding ("adde"), halfing (halfe), summing (somme), subtracting, remainders, doubling, quantities, differentials, complements, and many numbers and calculations.

46. Furner, "'Data': the Data," 295n18.

47. William Lowrie, *Fundamentals of Geophysics*, 2nd ed. (Cambridge: Cambridge University Press, 2007), 281–82.

48. Ted McCormick, *William Petty and the Ambitions of Political Arithmetic* (Oxford: Oxford University Press, 2009), 268. Its publicly circulated form twenty years later appears as a separate text, appended to an appeal to Charles II by one Thomas Hale, an employee of a lead-sheathing company and coholder of the lead-sheathing patent, urging the royal family to protect the British Navy's ships with "mill'd lead." (See T. Hale, *An Account of Several New Inventions and Improvements Now Necessary for England* (London: James Astwood, 1691; Ann Arbor, MI: Early English Books Online Text Creation Partnership, 2011), accessed June 22, 2019, https://quod.lib.umich.edu/e/eebo/A44350.0001.001?rgn =main;view=fulltext.

    Charles II had adopted milled sheathing for the royal fleet in 1673, but it was abandoned shortly thereafter when lead was observed to cause structural problems. Hale, an employee of Watson and Howard's Patent Milled Lead Company, sought to persuade the Crown anew based on cost, adaptability, and maintenance (see Andrew Wallace Marr, *A Comprehensive Investigation of Lead Sheathing from the Emanuel Point Shipwrecks in Pensacola Bay, Florida* [MA thesis, Colorado State University, 2006], 18–19). Petty's 1671 "Treatise" mentions sheathing and lead but is not centrally concerned with them.

A shorter, apparent summary of Petty's "Treatise" was published posthumously, in 1693: "What a Compleat Treatise of Navigation Should Contain: Drawn up in the Year 1685," *Philosophical Transactions of the Royal Society* 17, no. 198 (December 1693): 657–58. The author is given as "Sir William Petty, late Fellow of the Royal Society." It is a list of twenty-eight summary points, more concise than the points of the "Treatise."

49. McCormick, *William Petty*, 268.

50. Frances Harris, the contemporary archivist of Petty's papers, quoted in McCormick, *William Petty*, 270. The practice of "'publication' was not yet synonymous with print." "Petty printed comparatively little, but he circulated a very great deal" (McCormick, *William Petty*, 6). See Francis Harris, "Ireland as a Laboratory: The Archive of Sir William Petty," in *Archives of the Scientific Revolution: The Formation and Exchange of Ideas in Seventeenth-Century Europe*, ed. Michael Hunter (Woodbridge: Boydell, 1998), 73–90.

51. McCormick, *William Petty*, 269.

52. William Petty, "A Treatise on Naval Philosophy" (London: James Astwood 1671), 117–32, accessed May 2019, http://name.umdl.umich.edu/A44350.0001.001.

53. For example, chapter 1 contains what Petty calls "experiments," nearly twenty of them, replete with computations and quantifications of physics (e.g., weights, strengths, and resistances; issues pertaining to the motion, strength, course of winds and seas; matters of pumps, leaks, and the "spinning, twisting and wearing [of] *Sail-Cloth, Cables*, and other sorts of *Cordage*" (Petty, "A Treatise," 118). Petty mentions sheathing in this context, asserting the importance of "experiments upon *Pitch, Tarr, Rosin, Oyl, Brimstone, Tallow, Ocum-Leather,* &c. relating to the *Sheathing, Caulking*, and preserving of Vessels, and their appurtenances from

the injuries of *water, weather, worms* and *weeds*, and of their *weight, Extention, Duration, &c.*" (118). Additional topics raised prior to the mentioning of data include "the power of *Oars, Wheels, Poles, draught of men*, and *Horses*," anchors, and nautical instruments; nautical geography, astronomy, statistics, and mechanics; gun powder and effects of "guns and shots"; and "several Observations upon loading of a Ship with Lead, Wood, Cotton, Liquor in Cask, Corn, Salt, Frail and Timber: And the Accidents which usually fall out in each of the said sorts of loading, with reference to the safety and well sailing of a Vessel" (119).

54. McCormick, *William Petty*, 13.

55. Petty, "A Treatise," 129.

56. Petty, "A Treatise," 129.

57. Petty, "A Treatise," 129.

58. Petty, "A Treatise," 130–2.

59. Petty, "A Treatise," 130–1.

60. Karl Marx, *A Contribution to the Critique of Political Economy*, ed. Maurice Dobb (New York: International, 1970), 53fn, 55fn.

61. McCormick, *William Petty*, 10.

62. William Petty, *Political Arithmetick: Or, A Discourse Concerning, the Extent and Value of Lands, People, Buildings . . . &c., as the Same Relates to Every Country in General, But More Particularly to the Territories of His Majesty of Great Britain, and His Neighbours of Holland, Zealand, and France* (London: Printed for Robert Clavel at the Peacock, and Hen. Mortlock at the Phoenix, 1690), 3. Also quoted in McCormick, *William Petty*, 177.

63. McCormick, *William Petty*, 10–11, 209. See also Michael Hunter, "Review of McCormick," *American Historical Review* 115, no. 5 (December 2010): 1524.

64. McCormick, *William Petty*, 178.

65. McCormick, *William Petty*, 178.

66. McCormick, *William Petty*, 177, 178–79.

67. McCormick, *William Petty*, 7, 268.

68. McCormick, *William Petty*, 269. "Petty produced vast numbers of heads, few of which bear much resemblance to the small number of recognizable books he wrote. His *tractiuncli* [heads, short tracts] vary between skeletal lists [or 'heads'] and concise summaries, hardly ever longer than

five or six pages, and more often half that. It would be slightly perverse to see them as no more than heads—unlike the naval 'Treatise,' which did at least purport to be a plan of a larger work, they are often essentially self-contained, and complete as they stand, however terse. But among their primary functions was one that they shared with sets of heads like the 'Treatise,' namely, impressing upon the relevant authorities a sense of Petty's ability, both conceptual and, potentially, administrative. . . . Petty was not engaged in an academic exercise; he wanted a job. . . . Petty did not want to be known as the author of a great book on naval administration (or economic policy, or political demography), but to be a great administrator" (270).

69. McCormick, *William Petty*, 268.

70. Robert Wood, December 1671, quoted in McCormick, *William Petty*, 269. The date puzzles McCormick, since Petty was in Ireland at the time.

71. McCormick, *William Petty*, 269. The position involved the intricacies of law, which were apparently not to Petty's liking. "It gives me no such work as I expected," he wrote, quoted in Harris, "Ireland as a Laboratory," 76; and Lord Edmond Fitzmaurice, *The Life of Sir William Petty* (London: John Murray, 1895), 250.

72. "Edmond Halley," Wikipedia, accessed June 24, 2019, https://en .wikipedia.org/wiki/Edmond_Halley.

73. For more on the role of the Royal Society in the history of the concept of "data," see Chris Meyns, "'Data' in the Royal Society's *Philosophical Transactions*, 1665–1886," *Notes and Records of the Royal Society* 74, no. 3 (October 2020), accessed June 15, 2019, https://royalsocietypublishing .org/doi/10.1098/rsnr.2019.0024.

74. Edmond Halley, "An Estimate of the Degrees of Mortality of Mankind, Drawn from Curious Tables of the Births and Funerals at the City of Breslow; with an Attempt to Ascertain the Price of Annuities on Lives," *Philosophical Transactions of the Royal Society* 17, no. 196 (December 1693): 597.

75. McCormick, *William Petty*, 265.

76. Allan Chapman, "Edmond Halley's Use of Historical Evidence in the Advancement of Science." *Notes and Records of the Royal Society of London* 48, no. 2 (July 1994): 179.

77. Halley later "diagnosed methodological errors of Petty and Graunt who had pioneered analytical demography in the 1660s" (Chapman, "Edmond Halley," 174).

78. Edmond Halley, "A Discourse Tending to Prove at What Time and Place Julius Caesar Made His First Descent upon Britain," *Philosophical Transactions of the Royal Society of Great Britain* 16 (1691): 495.

79. He hypothesizes that "the story" might have been found in one of Titius Livy's lost books (Halley, *A Discourse*, 495).

80. Halley, *A Discourse*, 495.

81. Halley, *A Discourse*, 496.

82. Halley, *A Discourse*, 496–7.

83. Halley, *A Discourse*, 498.

84. Furner quoting *Cyclopaedia* ("'Data': the Data," 294).

85. Chapman, "Edmond Halley's Use," 179.

86. Chapman, "Edmond Halley's Use," 167.

87. Chapman, "Edmond Halley's Use," 185.

88. Halley, *A Discourse*, 501.

89. Halley, *An Estimate*, 596.

90. Neil Lettinga, "Covenant Theology Turned Upside Down: Henry Hammond and Caroline Anglican Moralism: 1643–1660," *Sixteenth Century Journal* 24, no. 3 (Autumn 1993): 654.

91. See John William Packer, *The Transformation of Anglicanism, 1643–1660: With Special Reference to Henry Hammond* (Manchester: Manchester University Press, 1969), 52.

92. Lettinga, "Covenant Theology," 662.

93. Mark Jones, "John Calvin's Reception at the Westminster Assembly (1643–1649)," *CHRC* 91, no. 1–2 (2011): 220; and C. F. Allison, *The Rise of Moralism* (Vancouver: Regent College, 2003), 106. It recalls Furner's observation of the early-seventeenth-century usage of *gratia gratis data* ("grace freely given").

94. Lettinga, "Covenant Theology," 666.

95. Henry Hammond, *A Copy of Some Papers Past at Oxford, Betwixt the Author of the Practicall Catechisme, and Mr. Ch.* (London: Ja. Flesher, 1650; Ann Arbor, MI: Early English Books Online Text Creation Partnership, 2011), 3, 6, accessed May 2019, http://name.umdl.umich.edu/A45407.0001.001.

96. Hammond, *Copy*, 4.

97. Hammond, *Copy*, 56–58, 83–87.

98. Hammond, *Copy*, 12. This is the passage from *Practical Catechism*: "In settling a ministry to pray and intercede for their several congregations, (and enabling them in the very Apostles' time to form a liturgy, of which several passages remain unto us at this day, to continue in the Church to that end,) and thereby helping our infirmities, and teaching us to pray as we ought" (12). See *A Practical Catechism* (Oxford: John Henry Parker, 1645; Internet Archive, 2015), 328, https://archive.org/stream/practicalcatechioohamm/practicalcatechioohamm_djvu.txt, accessed May 2019. The key concept is "to continue."

99. It is "very unreasonable," Hammond asserts, that lawful things (the set forms) "should by being commanded by lawful authority become unlawful" (Hammond, *Practical*, 226).

100. Hammond, *Practical*, 226.

101. "Yes, doubtless: for the Church being obeyed in the observation of the prescribed liturgy in public, permits sometimes, and upon special incidental occasions prescribes, other forms in the public congregation, so it be done prudently, and piously, and reverently, and to edification" (Hammond, *Practical*, 227).

102. Hammond, *Copy*, 25, 26.

103. "Some set Forms may, by some persons, at least for some time, be lawfully used" (Hammond, *Copy*, 25). See also "Sir, is there no ordinary gift of Prayer vouchsafed to the Ministers of Christ? . . . How doe you prove that a man that hath no ordinary wisdom to pray as hee ought, is called by Christ to bee a Minister of the Gospel? Surely Sir, I thinke a Minister should study to pray seasonably, as well as preach seasonably, and if the Primitive method and manner of prayer bee to bee observed, it doth not follow that the Liturgies, which goe under the name of St. James and Marke, and have constantly been suspected by Learned men, *should be rigorously imposed upon the Ministers of the New Testament*, who have an ordinary gift of prayer, nay, are indued with the spirit of prayer" (58–59, emphasis added).

104. "The Church next after the Apostles times may have leave to alter somewhat, (as occasions might alter,) and to adde somewhat (as they thought fit) to the constant Formes used by the Apostles" (Hammond, *A Copy*, 84).

105. The latter ("becoming unlawful") is "much more than to relaxate or forbid a rigorous imposing; and the former [their relaxation, which Cheynell wants and Hammond permits] of these had been possible to have been done, without the latter [imposition]" (Hammond, *Copy*, 83).

106. Hammond, *Copy*, 85–86.

107. Hammond, *Copy*, 10, 77.

108. Hammond's strongly held views won over many, and he became "one of the most influential theologians in the history of the Church of England" (Lettinga, "Covenant Theology," 660).

109. Richard Boston, "Introduction," in *The Admirable Urquhart: Selected Writings* (Cambridge: Gordon Fraser, 1975), 23. Denton Fox agrees with this assessment: "Urquhart's biographer, Willcock, says that 'no one is known to have read it or to have been able to read it,' and [as a result] it 'dropped at once into the depths of oblivion,'" from which the *OED* appears to have saved it. See Denton Fox, "The Admirable Urquhart," *London Review of Books* 6, no. 17 (September 1984): 13–14.

110. Boston, "Introduction," 20, 24.

111. "At its best it can be rich, rapid and vivid, with arresting and original imagery. . . . At its worst, it can descend into almost unintelligible pretension and pedantry" (Thomas Urquhart, Wikipedia, accessed June 25, 2019, https://en.wikipedia.org/wiki/Thomas_Urquhart).

112. Boston, "Introduction," 45.

113. Boston, "Introduction," 49.

114. Thomas Urquhart, *The Trissotetras* (London: James Young, 1645; Ann Arbor, MI: Early English Books Online Text Creation Partnership, 2011), accessed May 2019, https://quod.lib.umich.edu/e/eebo/A95751 .0001.001?rgn=main;view=fulltext.

115. Urquhart, "Introduction," in *Trissoteras*, 19.

116. Urquhart, *Trissotetras*, 1.

117. Urquhart, *Trissotetras*, 12.

118. Boston, "Introduction," 23.

119. Urquhart, *Trissotetras*, 12.

120. Urquhart, *Trissotetras*, 8, 9.

121. For example, in defining his abbreviations for parts of *The Trissotetras*, he writes, "Ca. the perpendicular: Cra. the concurse of a given and required side: Cur. the concurse of two given sides" (Urquhart, *Trissotetras*, 13).

122. Urquhart, *Trissotetras*, 13.

123. Here is the one cited by the *OED*: "The praenoscendas of the Mood, or the verticall Angle, according to the nature of the Case, being by the foresaid Datas thus obtained, must needs concurre with each its correspondent first subtendent, determined by the figuratives of τ. δ. θ for finding out of the Perpendicular, of which work, Ubamen being the subservient, by whose Resolver Nag—Mu—☞Torp☞Myr, the sub-problems of Utatca, Udaudca, and Uthauthca, are made known; if I utter any more of this purpose, I must intrench upon what I spoke before in the second operation of Allaemebne, it being the onely Mood which, with this of Erelomab, hath a verticall, and subtendentine Catheteuretick identity" (Urquhart, *The Trissotetras*, 73). For "datas happily obtained" and "obtained by the Datas," see Urquhart, *Trissotetras*, 25–26; compare 57, 65.

124. E.g., "The Praenoscendas, or the verticall Angles, according to the nature of the Case, being by the foresaid Datas thus found out, must needs joyne with each its correspondent opposite." (Urquhart, *Trissotetras*, 57).

125. Urquhart, *Trissotetras*, 88.

126. Urquhart, *Trissotetras*, 94.

127. Boston, "Introduction," 36.

128. Boston describes the analogy between these works in detail (Boston, "Introduction," 37–38).

129. Boston, "Introduction," 55.

130. Boston, "Introduction," 56.

131. Boston, "Introduction," 56.

132. Boston, "Introduction," 57.

133. Boston, "Introduction," 57.

134. Boston, "Introduction," 57.

135. Boston, "Introduction," 55, 58, 60. Boston admits that Urquhart makes mistakes in his translation, "but they are rarely serious ones; more often he is able to make intelligible passages of Rabelais that are bafflingly obscure in the original" (Boston, "Introduction," 58).

136. Boston, "Introduction," 58.

137. See Latdict, http://www.latin-dictionary.net/search/latin/do, accessed January 2018.

138. Batten, *A Most Plaine and Easie Way.*

139. Chapman, "Edmond Halley," 171–72.

140. Edward Hasted, *The History of Topographical Survey of the County of Kent*, vol. 1 (Canterbury: W. Bristow, 1800), 13. I learned of this work from its reference on the following website dedicated to the invasion: "The Landing-Place in Britain of Gaius Julius Cæsar IV," accessed July 2019, http://www.dealpier.uk/caesar.html#T19; Suetonius, *The Lives of the Twelve Caesars* (New York: Penguin Classics, 2003 [1957],), 19; and Julius Caesar, *De Bello Gallico and Other Commentaries* (New York: Everyman's Library Classics, 1915, Project Gutenberg, 2004), book IV, paragraph 24, accessed July 2019, https://www.gutenberg.org/ebooks/10657.

141. Suetonius, *The Lives*, 35. For the violent qualities of this particular idiom and its political theoretical significance, see Andrew Davison, *Border Thinking on the Edges of the West: Crossing Over the Hellespont* (New York: Routledge, 2014).

142. Suetonius, *The Lives*, 35.

143. Caesar, *De Bello Gallico*, book IV, paragraph 26.

144. Caesar, *De Bello Gallico*, book IV, paragraph 26.

145. Caesar, *De Bello Gallico*, book IV, paragraph 28–29.

146. Hasted, *History of Topographical Survey*, 16, 20.

147. Suetonius, *The Lives*, 30.

148. Caesar, *De Bello Gallico*, book III, paragraph 9.

149. "Doubt over Date for Brit invasion," July 1, 2008, http://news.bbc.co.uk/2/hi/science/nature/7483566.stm. See also Roger W. Sinnott, "Astronomers Re-Date Caesar's Invasion of Britain," *Sky and Telescope*, June 30, 2008, https://www.skyandtelescope.com/press-releases/astronomers-re-date-caesars-invasion-of-britain/; and Mark Waghorn, "First Evidence of Julius Caesar's Invasion of Britain Discovered in Kent," November 29, 2017, https://www.independent.co.uk/news/uk/home-news/julius-caesar-invasion-britain-uk-site-evidence-first-discovered-kent-a8081056.html. Both accessed June 24, 2019.

150. "Doubt over Date."

151. "Doubt over Date."

152. Petty, "A Treatise," 118.

153. See also footnote 59.

154. See also discussion in the introduction: Jürgen Habermas, *Knowledge and Human Interests*; Charles Taylor, *Philosophical Papers*, vol. 2 (Cambridge: Cambridge University Press, 1985); Helen Longino, *Science as Social Knowledge: Values and Objectivity in Scientific Inquiry* (Princeton, NJ: Princeton University Press, 1990); and Heather Douglas, *Science, Policy, and the Value-Free Ideal* (Pittsburgh, PA: Pittsburgh University Press, 2009).

155. McCormick, *William Petty*, 3.

156. From the book's cover page.

157. Chambers's *Cyclopoedia, or an Universal Dictionary of Arts and Sciences*, quoted in Furner, "'Data': the Data," 294.

158. "Posited" is a postempiricist term for characterizing the "constituted"—not "given"—quality of all data. Data are viewed as *posited* by theories that take shape and situate interpreters within particular contexts, as discussed in the introduction.

159. "dataset, n.", accessed September 8, 2019, https://www-oed-om.libproxy .vassar.edu/view/Entry/261122?redirectedFrom=data+set.

CONCLUSION: ATTUNED IN THE DATAVERSE

1. Christina Sharpe, *In the Wake: On Being and Blackness* (Durham, NC: Duke University Press, 2018).

2. Sharpe, *In the Wake*, 13ff.

3. Sharpe, *In the Wake*, 5.

4. "Notes from the Editors." *American Political Science Review* 109, no. 3 (2015): iii–viii.

5. See American Political Science Dataverse, accessed August 13, 2024, https://dataverse.harvard.edu/dataverse/the_review.

6. Ramya Parthasarathy, Vijayendra Rao, and Nethra Palaniswamy, "Deliberative Democracy in an Unequal World: A Text-as-Data Study of South India's Village Assemblies," *American Political Science Review* 113, no. 3 (August 2019): 623–40.

7. They cite Mansbridge's essay "Minimalist Definition of Deliberation," in *Deliberation and Development: Rethinking the Role of Voice and Collective Action in Unequal Societies*, ed. Vijayendra Rao and Patrick Heller (Washington, DC: World Bank Publications, 2015), 27–50. Good

deliberation is "that which (1) gives all participants an equal opportunity to influence the outcome by promoting 'an inclusive and egalitarian political process'; (2) embodies the ideal of mutual respect, whereby citizens listen attentively to one another; and (3) allows citizens to be agents who participate in the governance of their society" (Mansbridge, cited in Parthasarathy, Rao, and Palaniswamy, "Deliberative Democracy," 626).

8. Parthasarathy, Rao, and Palaniswamy, "Deliberative Democracy," 637–38.
9. Parthasarathy, Rao, and Palaniswamy, "Deliberative Democracy," 623.
10. Parthasarathy, Rao, and Palaniswamy, "Deliberative Democracy," 623. Palaniswamy studied the Pudhu Vaazhvu Project with Madhulika Khanna and NIshtha Kochhar in their, "A Retrospective Impact Evaluation of the Tamil Nadu Empowerment and Poverty Alleviation (Pudhu Vaazhvu) Project.pdf," *Pudhu Vaazhvu Project Phase 1 "Retrospective" Evaluation—Household Survey Data from Tamil Nadu*, 2011, 2013. They "find significant effects of PVP on reducing the incidence of high cost debt and diversifying livelihoods. We also find evidence of women's empowerment, and increased political participation" (1). http://pubdocs .worldbank.org/en/623561459872407029/A-Retrospective-Impact -Evaluation-of-the-Tamil-Nadu-Empowerment-and-Poverty-Alleviation -Pudhu-Vaazhvu-Project.pdf, accessed August 9, 2020.
11. Parthasarathy, Rao, and Palaniswamy, "Deliberative Democracy," 623, 628.
12. Parthasarathy, Rao, and Palaniswamy, "Deliberative Democracy," 629.
13. Parthasarathy, Rao, and Palaniswamy, "Deliberative Democracy," 629.
14. Parthasarathy, Rao, and Palaniswamy, "Deliberative Democracy," 629.
15. Parthasarathy, Rao, and Palaniswamy, "Deliberative Democracy," 629–30.
16. Parthasarathy, Rao, and Palaniswamy, "Deliberative Democracy," 629.
17. In postempiricist, interpretive social science, "what is accessed are sources of data; the data themselves are generated, whether by the researcher interacting with visual/tactile/spatial sources or coproduced in conversational and/or participatory interactions. This understanding of 'data' as constituted by human researchers' observations renders problematic the creation of databases of interpretive data for other researchers to use. So-called raw data may be the 'least interpreted' form (in contrast to succeeding stages in the research process), but the 'interpretive moment' cannot be escaped: It colors all stages of the research

process, such that human science data are never really 'raw' and 'unprocessed.' Other researchers would be getting processed, not 'raw,' data—'cooked' and filtered through someone else's interpretive schema" (Dvora Yanow and Peregrine Schwartz-Shea, "Introduction," in *Interpretation and Method: Empirical Research Methods and the Interpretive Turn*, ed. Yanow and Schwartz-Shea [New York: Routledge, 2014], xxi). Thus, Yanow and Schwartz-Shea argue that databases of the kind envisioned by DART could never, in their view, contain any data. They could only provide the "sources of the data"—the texts, images, or numbers that researchers use in their analysis, and that may be used as what Leonelli calls "prospective data" for later analysis (Sabina Leonelli, *Data-Centric Biology: A Philosophical Study* (Chicago: University of Chicago Press, 2016), 77).

18. Parthasarathy, Rao, and Palaniswamy, "Deliberative Democracy," 633.

19. Parthasarathy, Rao, and Palaniswamy, "Deliberative Democracy," 627–28.

20. Parthasarathy, Rao, and Palaniswamy, "Deliberative Democracy," 633.

21. Parthasarathy, Rao, and Palaniswamy, "Deliberative Democracy," 635. Emphasis in the original.

22. Parthasarathy, Rao, and Palaniswamy, "Deliberative Democracy," 635.

23. Parthasarathy, Rao, and Palaniswamy, "Deliberative Democracy," 635. Emphasis in the original.

24. Neganur Village, Viluppuram District, Vallam Block, Neganur Panchayat. Parthasarathy, Rao, and Palaniswamy, "Deliberative Democracy," 627.

25. Parthasarathy, Rao, and Palaniswamy, "Deliberative Democracy," 627.

26. Parthasarathy, Rao, and Palaniswamy, "Deliberative Democracy," 627.

27. This difference is not dependent on the fact that the study is carried out in rural India. The difference may be assumed to exist if the study were carried out next door. The possibility of paradoxically representing and simultaneously erasing the constitutive meanings of others permeates all analysis, including this analysis.

28. Parthasarathy, Rao, and Palaniswamy, "Deliberative Democracy," 638.

29. Parthasarathy, Rao, and Palaniswamy, "Deliberative Democracy," 625. They cite work by two of the authors: Ramya Parthasarathy and Vijayendra Rao, "Deliberative Democracy in India," *The Oxford Handbook of Deliberative Democracy*, ed. Andre Bachtinger, John Dryzek, Jane Mansbridge, and Mark Warren (Oxford: Oxford University Press, 2018).

30. Parthasarathy, Rao, and Palaniswamy, "Deliberative Democracy," 636.
31. Parthasarathy, Rao, and Palaniswamy, "Deliberative Democracy," 637.
32. Parthasarathy, Rao, and Palaniswamy, "Deliberative Democracy," 635.
33. Parthasarathy, Rao, and Palaniswamy, "Deliberative Democracy," 638.
34. Parthasarathy, Rao, and Palaniswamy, "Deliberative Democracy," 638.
35. Parthasarathy, Rao, and Palaniswamy, "Deliberative Democracy," 639. The passage continues, "This is undoubtedly driven by a combination of factors, from information and resource constraints to cultural biases against women. But it also underscores a deeper challenge in deliberation—namely, that using one's voice can be a costly exercise and that imposes a larger burden on those who are least-advantaged" (639).
36. Parthasarathy, Rao, and Palaniswamy, "Deliberative Democracy," 638.
37. The writer Victor Mallet conversed with residents in one village in the heart of India where the men have had a hard time attracting brides because the village lacks enough good water. "Nobody wants their daughter to get married to someone from here because they think their daughters will die carrying water on their heads all their lives." The people of the village have appealed to successive governments for tubewells or canals. . . . The main problem with the groundwater is that at about 160–170 feet, the ground is rocky and we do not have the equipment to dig deeper." **We need equipment to dig deeper.** "Farmers are on the verge of starvation, forced to commit suicide." See Victor Mallet, *River of Life, River of Death: The Ganges and India's Future* (Oxford: Oxford University Press, 2017), 150–51.
38. Parthasarathy, Rao, and Palaniswamy, "Replication for: Deliberative Democracy in an Unequal World: A Text-As-Data Study of South India's Village Assemblies," accessed August 7, 2020, https://dataverse.harvard.edu/file.xhtml?persistentId=doi:10.7910/DVN/NFZLI3/LQXLX1&version=1.0, Harvard Dataverse, V1.
39. Parthasarathy, Rao, and Palaniswamy, "Replication."
40. This difference may result from issues of translation. Her words as transcribed in English may differ from those she spoke, in a number of hermeneutically significant ways. I receive the transcript and its bold print as I do, and, in attunement, the thoughts I record here may happen differently with a differently translated text.
41. Parthasarathy, Rao, and Palaniswamy, "Deliberative Democracy," 639.

SELECT BIBLIOGRAPHY

Abbott, Andrew. "Against Narrative: A Preface to Lyrical Sociology." *Sociological Theory* 25, no. 1 (March 2007): 77–99.

Argın, Şükrü. *"Bir Zamanlar Anadolu'da:* Asimetrik Şikayet Toplumu." *Birikim* 272 (December 2011): 18–25.

Auden, W. H. "Musée des Beaux Arts." In *The Complete Works of W. H. Auden: Poems, Volume I: 1927–1939*, ed. Edward Mendelson, 338–39. Princeton, NJ: Princeton University Press, 2022.

Ball, Terence, James Farr, and Russell L. Hanson, eds. *Political Innovation and Conceptual Change*. Cambridge: Cambridge University Press, 1989.

Batten, William. *A Most Plaine and Easie Way for the Finding of the Sunnes Amplitude and Azimuth, and Thereby the Variation of the Compasse, by Logarithm*. London: Eliz. Allde, 1630. https://quod.lib.umich.edu/e/eebo/a05734.0001 .001?rgn=main.

Benjamin, Ruha. *Race After Technology*. Cambridge: Polity, 2019.

Benjamin, Walter. "The Task of the Translator." In *Walter Benjamin: Selected Writings, Volume 1, 1913–1926*, ed. Marcus Bullock and Michael W. Jennings, 253–63. Cambridge, MA: Harvard University Press, 1996.

Bevir, Mark, and Jason Blakely. *Interpretive Social Science: An Anti-Naturalist Approach*. Oxford: Oxford University Press, 2019.

Björkman, Lisa, Lisa Wedeen, Juliet Williams, and Mary Hawkesworth. "Interpretive Methods." *American Political Science Association Organized Section for Qualitative and Multi-Method Research, Qualitative Transparency Deliberations, Working Group Final Reports, Report III.2*, January 2019. https://ssrn.com/abstract=3333411.

Blakely, Jason. *We Built Reality: How Social Science Infiltrated Culture, Politics, and Power.* Oxford: Oxford University Press, 2020.

Born, Richard. "Split-Ticket Voters, Divided Government, and Fiorina's Policy-Balancing Model." *Legislative Studies Quarterly* 19, no. 1 (February 1994): 95–115.

——. "Congressional Incumbency and the Rise of Split-Ticket Voting." *Legislative Studies Quarterly* 25, no. 3 (August 2000): 365–87.

Boston, Richard, ed. *The Admirable Urquhart: Selected Writings.* Cambridge: Gordon Fraser, 1975.

Brogan, Walter. "Basic Concepts of Hermeneutics: Understanding Gadamer's Sense of Tradition and Community." *Duquesne Studies in Philosophy* 1, no. 1 (2020): 3.

Bronson, Zak, and Gözde Kılıç, "The Ghosts of Modernization: Landscape, Time, and the West in *Once Upon a Time in Anatolia*." In *International Westerns: Re-Locating the Frontier*, ed. Cynthia J. Miller and A. Bowdoin Van Ripe, 3–19. Lanham, MD: Scarecrow, 2014.

Bruns, Gerald. "The Remembrance of Language: An Introduction to Gadamer's Poetics." In *Gadamer on Celan: "Who Am I and Who Are You?"* Albany: State University of New York Press, 1997.

——. "Almost as If." *The Iowa Review* 37, no. 2 (2007): 170–71.

——. *What Are Poets For? An Anthropology of Contemporary Poetry and Poets.* Iowa City: University of Iowa Press, 2012.

Burt, Steven. *the poem is you.* Cambridge, MA: Harvard University Press, 2016.

Canguilhem, Georges. *The Normal and the Pathological.* New York: Zone, 1991.

——. *Writings on Medicine.* New York: Fordham University Press, 2012.

Caruth, Cathy. *Unclaimed Experience: Trauma, Narrative, and History.* Baltimore, MD: Johns Hopkins University Press, 1996.

Cayley, David. *The Rivers North of the Future: The Testament of Ivan Illich as Told to David Cayley.* Toronto: Anansi, 2005.

Chang, Tina, Nathalie Handal, and Ravi Shankar, eds. *Language for a New Century: Contemporary Poetry from the Middle East, Asia, and Beyond.* New York: Norton, 2008.

Chapman, Allan. "Edmond Halley's Use of Historical Evidence in the Advancement of Science." *Notes and Records of the Royal Society of London* 48, no. 2 (July 1994): 167–91.

Cheney-Lippold, John. *We Are Data: Algorithms and the Making of Our Digital Selves.* New York: New York University Press, 2017.

Ceylan, Nuri Bilge, dir. *Bir Zamanlar Anadolu'da.* Turkey, 2011.

——. *Söyleyişler.* Istanbul: Norgunk, 2012.

——. *Bir Zamanlar Anadolu'da,* ed. Aslı Güneş. Istanbul: Doğan Kitap, 2019.

Cixous, Helene. *Stigmata: Escaping Texts.* New York: Routledge, 1998.

da Costa, Emerson Roberto. "Coronovirus in Belém: A Survivor's Story." *Brasil Wire,* May 8, 2020. https://www.brasilwire.com/coronavirus-in-belem-a-survivors-story/.

Cramer, Katherine. "Transparent Explanations, Yes. Public Transcripts and Fieldnotes, No: Ethnographic Research on Public Opinion." *Qualitative and Multi-Method Research* 13, no. 1 (Spring 2015): 17–20.

Cresswell, Tim. "Geographies of Poetry/Poetries of Geography." *Cultural Geographies* 21, no. 1 (2014): 141–46.

Dabashi, Hamid. *The World Is My Home,* ed. Andrew Davison and Himadeep Muppidi. New Brunswick, NJ: Transaction, 2011.

Davison, Andrew. *Secularism and Revivalism in Turkey: A Hermeneutic Reconsideration.* New Haven, CT: Yale University Press, 1998.

——. *Border Thinking on the Edges of the West: Crossing Over the Hellespont.* New York: Routledge, 2014.

——. "Hermeneutics and the Question of Transparency." *Qualitative and Multi-Method Research* 13, no. 1 (Spring 2015): 43–47.

Davison, Andrew, and Mark Hoffman. *Interpreting Politics: Debating the Foundations and Objectives of Political Analysis.* New York: Sloan, 2019.

De Leeuw, Sarah. "Writing as Righting: Truth and Reconciliation, Poetics, and New Geo-graphing in Colonial Canada." *Canadian Geographies* 61, no. 3 (Fall 2017): 306–18.

Derrida, Jacques. "Rams: Uninterrupted Dialogue—Between Two Infinities, the Poem." In *Sovereignties in Question: The Poetics of Paul Celan,* ed. Thomas Dutoit and Outi Pasanen. New York: Fordham University Press, 2005.

——. *Parages,* ed. John P. Leavey. Palo Alto, CA: Stanford University Press, 2010.

Dietz, Maggie, and Robert Pinsky, eds. *An Invitation to Poetry.* New York: Norton, 2004.

Diken, Bülent, Graeme Gilloch, and Craig Hammond. *The Cinema of Nuri Bilge Ceylan: The Global Vision of a Turkish Filmmaker.* New York: I. B. Tauris, 2018.

Douglas, Heather. *Science, Policy, and the Value-Free Ideal.* Pittsburgh, PA: Pittsburgh University Press, 2009.

Eagleton, Terry. *How to Read a Poem*. Oxford: Blackwell, 2007.

Elman, Colin, and Diana Kapiszewski. "Data Access and Research Transparency in the Qualitative Tradition." *PS: Political Science and Politics* 47, no. 1 (2014): 43–47.

Engster, Daniel, and Maurice Harrington, eds. *Care Ethics and Political Theory*. Oxford: Oxford University Press, 2015.

Espada, Martín. *The Republic of Poetry*. New York: Norton, 2006.

Eubanks, Virginia. *Automated Inequality: How High-Tech Tools Profile, Police and Punish the Poor*. New York: St. Martin's, 2018.

Fisher, Marc. "The US Death Toll Has Reached 100,000." *The Washington Post*, May 27, 2020.

Friedman, Jeffrey. *Power Without Knowledge: A Critique of Technocracy*. Oxford: Oxford University Press, 2020.

Furner, Jonathan. "'Data': the Data." In *Information Cultures in the Digital Age: A Festschrift in Honor of Rafael Capurro*, ed. Matthew Kelly and Jared Bielby, 287–306. New York: Springer, 2016.

Gadamer, Hans-Georg. *Truth and Method*. New York: Continuum, 1989.

——. *The Enigma of Health*. Stanford, CA: Stanford University Press, 1996.

——. *Gadamer on Celan: 'Who Am I and Who Are You?'* Albany: State University of New York Press, 1997.

Glissant, Édouard. *Poetics of Relation*. Ann Arbor: University of Michigan Press, 2010.

Graham, Jorie. *Never*. New York: Ecco, 2002.

Guest, Haden. "Physical Evidence." *Film Comment* 48, no. 1 (January/February 2012): 56–59.

Guthrie, Woodie. "Audio of Woody Guthrie Singing about Fred Trump," 1950, https://www.youtube.com/watch?v=jANuVKeYezs&list=PLRw6O ZZufk59Xy7qXNCZ4kVD19H7wNsVS&index=1.

Homan, Catherine. *The Hermeneutics of Poetic Education: The Play of the In-Between*. Lanham, MD: Lexington, 2020.

Halley, Edmond. "A Discourse Tending to Prove at What Time and Place Julius Caesar Made His First Descent upon Britain." *Philosophical Transactions of the Royal Society of Great Britain* 16 (1691): 495–501.

Hammond, Henry. *A Copy of Some Papers Past at Oxford, Betwixt the Author of the Practicall Catechisme, and Mr. Ch.* London: Ja. Flesher, 1650. http://name.umdl.umich.edu/A45407.0001.001.

Han, Byung-Chul. *Infocracy: Digitalization and the Crisis of Democracy.* Cambridge: Polity, 2022.

Harding, Charlie, and Nate Sloan. *Switched on Pop: How Popular Music Works and Why it Matters.* Oxford: Oxford University Press, 2019.

Hikmet, Nâzım. *Bütün Şiirleri.* Istanbul: Yapı Kredi Yayınları, 2016.

Hunter, Walt. *Forms of a World: Contemporary Poetry and the Making of Globalization.* New York: Fordham University Press, 2019.

Illich, Ivan. *Medical Nemesis: The Expropriation of Health.* New York: Marion Boyars, 1976.

Ingersoll, David, Richard K. Matthews, and Andrew Davison. *The Philosophic Roots of Modern Ideology: Liberalism, Conservatism, Marxism, Fascism, Nazism, Islamism, Feminism,* 5th ed. New York: Sloan, 2017.

Isaac, Jeffrey. "For a More Public Political Science." *PS: Political Science and Politics* 13, no. 2 (2015): 269–83.

Jarmusch, Jim, dir. *Paterson,* 2016.

Jones, Reece. *Violent Borders: Refugees and the Right to Move.* New York: Verso, 2016.

Kesal, Ercan. *Evvel Zaman.* Istanbul: İletişim, 2014.

——. *Aslında . . .* Istanbul: İletişim, 2017.

Kinzie, Mary. *A Poet's Guide to Poetry,* 2nd ed. Chicago: University of Chicago Press, 2013.

Kitchin, Rob. *The Data Revolution: Big Data, Open Data, Data Infrastructures & Their Consequences.* Los Angeles: Sage, 2014.

——. *Data Lives: How Data Are Made and Shape Our World.* Bristol: Bristol University Press, 2021.

Kitchin, Rob, and Alistair Fraser. *Slow Computing: Why We Need Balanced Digital Lives.* Bristol: Bristol University Press, 2020.

Kuhn, Thomas. *The Structure of Scientific Revolutions,* 2nd ed. Chicago: University of Chicago Press, 1962.

Leonelli, Sabina. "What Counts as Scientific Data? A Relational Framework." *Philosophy of Science* 82, no. 5 (December 2015): 810–21.

——. *Data-Centric Biology: A Philosophical Study.* Chicago: University of Chicago Press, 2016.

——. "Locating Ethics in Data Science: Responsibility and Accountability in Global and Distributed Knowledge Production Systems." *Philosophical Transactions: Mathematical, Physical and Engineering Sciences* 374, no. 2083 (December 2016): 1–12.

——. "Scientific Research and Big Data." *Stanford Encyclopedia of Philosophy*, 2020. https://plato.stanford.edu/entries/science-big-data/.

Leonelli, Sabina, Brian Rappert, and Gail Davies. "Data Shadows: Knowledge, Openness, and Absence." *Science, Technology, & Human Values* 42, no. 2 (2017): 191–202.

Leonelli, Sabina, and Nicollò Tempini, eds. *Data Journeys in the Sciences*. Cham, Switzerland: Springer, 2020.

Lettinga, Neil. "Covenant Theology Turned Upside Down: Henry Hammond and Caroline Anglican Moralism: 1643–1660." *Sixteenth Century Journal* 24, no. 3 (1993): 653–69.

Lewis, Geoffrey. *The Turkish Language Reform: A Catastrophic Success*. Oxford: Oxford University Press, 2002.

Longino, Helen. *Science as Social Knowledge: Values and Objectivity in Scientific Inquiry*. Princeton, NJ: Princeton, 1990.

Löwy, Michael. *Fire Alarm: Reading Walter Benjamin's "On the Concept of History."* New York: Verso, 2006.

Luke, Timothy, Antonio Vázquez-Arroyo, and Mary Hawkesworth. "Epistemological and Ontological Priors: Explicating the Perils of Transparency." *American Political Science Association Organized Section for Qualitative and Multi-Method Research, Qualitative Transparency Deliberations, Working Group Final Reports, Report 1.1–2*, December 2018. https://ssrn.com/abstract =3332878.

Lukes, Steven, ed. *Power*. New York: New York University Press, 1986.

Lupia, Arthur, and Colin Elman. "Introduction: Openness in Political Science: Data Access and Transparency." *PS: Political Science and Politics* 47, no. 1 (2014): 107–13.

Makhmalbaf, Samira, dir. *At Five in the Afternoon*, 2003.

McCloskey, Deirdre N. *The Rhetoric of Economics*. Madison: University of Wisconsin Press, 1985.

McCormick, Ted. *William Petty and the Ambitions of Political Arithmetic*. Oxford: Oxford University Press, 2009.

McKittrick, Katherine. *Dear Science and Other Stories*. Durham, NC: Duke University Press, 2021.

McPherson, Sandra. "Secrets: Beginning to Write Them Out: Revelation, Confession, and Ethics; Discretion and Diplomacy; Health and Art." In *A Field Guide to Poetics and Poetry*, rev. ed., ed. Stuart Friebert, David

Walker, and David Young, 306–19. Oberlin, Ohio: Oberlin College Press, 1997.

Neimanis, Astrida. *Bodies of Water: Posthuman Feminist Phenomenology*. New York: Bloomsbury, 2017.

Necatigil, Behçet. *Şiirler*. Istanbul: Yapı Kredi Yayınları, 2002.

Noble, Safiya Umoja. *Algorithms of Oppression: How Search Engines Reinforce Oppression*. New York: New York University Press, 2018.

O'Neil, Cathy. *Weapons of Math Destruction: How Big Data Increases Inequality and Threatens Democracy*. New York: Crown, 2016.

Özdamar, Emine Sevgi. *Mother Tongue*. Trans. Craig Thomas. Toronto: Coach House, 1994.

Pachirat, Timothy. "The Tyranny of Light." *Qualitative & Multi-Method Research* 13, no. 1 (2015): 27–32.

Parla, Taha, and Andrew Davison, *Corporatist Ideology in Kemalist Turkey: Progress or Order*. Syracuse, NY: Syracuse University Press, 1996.

Parthasarathy, Ramya, Vijayendra Rao, and Nethra Palaniswamy. "Deliberative Democracy in an Unequal World: A Text-As-Data Study of South India's Village Assemblies." *American Political Science Review* 113, no. 3 (August 2019): 623–40.

Petty, William. "A Treatise on Naval Philosophy." London: James Astwood, 1671. http://name.umdl.umich.edu/A44350.0001.001.

Plato. *The Republic*, trans. G. M. A. Grube, revised by C. D. C. Reeve. Indianapolis, IN: Hackett, 1992.

Pollock, Della. "The Performative 'I.'" *Cultural Studies—Critical Methodologies* 7, no. 3 (August 2007): 239–55.

Rich, Adrienne. *Midnight Salvage: Poems 1995–1998*. New York: Norton, 1999.

Rosenberg, Daniel. "Data Before the Fact." In *Raw Data Is an Oxymoron*, ed. Lisa Gitelman, 14–40. Cambridge: MIT Press, 2013.

Sandoval, Chela. *Methodology of the Oppressed*. Minneapolis: University of Minnesota Press, 2000.

Schaffer, Frederic. *Elucidating Social Science Concepts: An Interpretivist Guide*. New York: Routledge, 2015.

Sears, Rob. *The Beautiful Poetry of Donald Trump: Strictly Unauthorized*. Edinburgh: Canongate, 2017.

Seigworth, Gregory J., and Melissa Gregg, eds. *The Affect Theory Reader*. Durham, NC: Duke University Press, 2000.

Sellars, Wilfrid. *Empiricism and the Philosophy of Mind*. Cambridge: Harvard University Press, 1997.

Sharpe, Christina. *In the Wake: On Being and Blackness*. Durham, NC: Duke University Press, 2018.

Shihab Nye, Naomi. "Before I Was a Gazan." In *Voices in the Air*. New York: Harper Collins, 2018.

Soueif, Ahdaf. *In the Eye of the Sun*. New York: Anchor, 1992.

Spivak, Gayatri Chakraborty. "In Response: Looking Back, Looking Forward." In *Can the Subaltern Speak? Reflections on the History of an Idea*, ed. Rosalind C. Morris. New York: Columbia University Press, 2010.

Tanpinar, Ahmet Hamdi. *The Time Regulation Institute*. New York: Penguin, 2014.

Tekin, Latife. *Dear Shameless Death*. London: Marion Boyers, 1983.

Urquhart, Thomas. *The Trissotetras*. London: James Young, 1645. https:// quod.lib.umich.edu/e/eebo/A95751.0001.001?rgn.

Vendler, Helen. *The Ocean, the Bird, and the Scholar: Essays on Poets & Poetry*. Cambridge, MA: Harvard University Press, 2015.

Wainwright, Jeffrey. *Poetry: The Basics*. New York: Routledge, 2004.

Walker, R. B. J. *Out of Line: Essays on the Politics of Boundaries and the Limits of Modern*. New York: Routledge, 2016.

Wright, Charles. *Chickamauga*. New York: Farrar, Straus, and Giroux, 1995.

Yanow, Dvora, and Peregrine Schwartz-Shea, eds. *Interpretation and Method: Empirical Research Methods and the Interpretive Turn*. New York: Routledge, 2014.

Young, Kevin. *Brown: Poems*. New York: Knopf, 2018.

Zuboff, Shoshana. *The Age of Surveillance Capitalism: The Fight for a Human Future at the New Frontier of Power*. New York: Public Affairs, 2019.

INDEX

GPSR Authorized Representative: Easy Access System Europe, Mustamäe tee
50, 10621 Tallinn, Estonia, gpsr.requests@easproject.com

www.ingramcontent.com/pod-product-compliance
Lightning Source LLC
Chambersburg PA
CBHW032118020426
42334CB00016B/994